BUILDING MENTAL MUSCLE

REVISED AND UPDATED EDITION

BUILDING MENTAL MUSCLE

CONDITIONING EXERCISES FOR THE SIX INTELLIGENCE ZONES

ALLEN D. BRAGDON &
DAVID G. GAMON, PH.D.

FALL RIVER PRESS

*This work is dedicated to
all people who keep their
minds active,
especially those who
have used theirs to explore
that fascinating instrument
of survival and delight
—the human brain.*

ACKNOWLEDGMENTS

The authors drew inspiration and information from many sources. Among the general works we found most useful were Robert Ornstein's books, some written with David Sobel, especially *Evolution of Consciousness*, and William H. Calvin and George A. Ojemann's book *Conversations with Neil's Brain*. Among those who helped acquire and organize the primary source research were Suzanne Corkin, Ph.D., Donna McGovern, and Jane Perkins. Graphic artists and designers who have contrived some of the engaging exercises and layouts include Wally Exman, Leonard Fellows, Peter Osterowski, Cindy Wood, Bill Young, and Carolyn Zellers. The index was compiled by Michael Loo.

© 1998, 1999, 2003 by Allen D. Bragdon Publishers, Inc.

This 2010 edition published by Fall River Press,
by arrangement with Allen D. Bragdon Publishers, Inc.

Cover art © Franck Boston / iStockphoto.com (front foreground);
© Digital Vision / Getty Images (front/back background)
Cover design by Igor Satanovsky

Fall River Press
122 Fifth Avenue
New York, NY 10011

ISBN: 978-1-4351-1965-9

Printed and bound in the United States of America

1 3 5 7 9 10 8 6 4 2

PREFACE
To the 2nd Edition

The considerable success of the first edition surprised and grati-fied us. Its sale of more than 120,000 copies since publication in mid-1998 shows that Americans are beginning to become con-vinced of something the rest of the world already knows: Humans can strengthen and maintain their cognitive skills just as they can the rest of their body. In the last four years even more robust research has reinforced the finding that both men-tal and physical exercise help maintain mental alertness.

We have updated this edition in three major ways:

We added new research results that bear on important human needs. For example: Causes and cures for memory loss due to chronic stress • A new way to help dyslexic children improve language skills • Why cell-phone use reduces reac-tion-time while driving • New evidence that humans also respond unconsciously to airborne chemicals, called *pheromones*, that have a major influence on mating choices in all other mammals • How newly-discovered receptors in the eyes set the body's internal clock • Stem cell research that will soon provide a new treatment for Alzheimer's • Specific lifestyle changes that allow the brain to increase the growth rate of neurons to keep memory sharp, even in old age • Sex-related cognitive strategies.

We created new diagrams and have refined the quality of the art and page design throughout. We also devised new exercises and tests to entertain and stimulate crucial skills.

We made room for an index to allow readers to find informa-tion in areas of their most personal concerns.

Your cortex, the thinking part of the human brain, is endlessly fascinating and loves its job of maintaining the "You" of you. When it emerged 2.4 million years ago, the big issues were dodging dangers, locating mates, finding and killing food. Among the most recent changes in cortical design are the abili-ty to perceive patterns among events, social skills like altruism and emotional control, planning ahead and writing language. Such cortical skills are the last to develop in infancy, the first to decline with age. They see trends for your future and recall pre-cious memories. Their neurons grow with exercise.

In this updated edition we introduce you to their wondrous ways and offer entertaining exercises to rattle their cages.

— The Authors, Cape Cod & San Francisco
January 2003

CONTENTS

INTRODUCTION

Why you need this book

This is a self-help book. It gives you access to recent discoveries about the way your six zones of practical intelligence operate. Your new awareness will give you an edge in using your brain effectively. The exercises are designed to stimulate the cells in different brain zones, some of which you may not use regularly in your personal or professional life. Keeping those cells active prevents their deterioration from disuse caused by ignorance of how your brain functions, by failure to maintain cellular vitality, or because of apathy, laziness or age.

All your cognitive zones must be kept sharp. Most real-world, real-time events are best handled by putting a variety of skills into play, not just one. (For example, to calculate tax and tip on a dinner check, you need both math skills and short-term working memory

EXECUTIVE/SOCIAL ZONE *The front part of the cortex (the wrinkled outer covering of the brain) allows you to foresee goals in the future and take the steps necessary to execute your plans. It also is involved in relating with other people in productive ways—including picking up signals about their attitudes and choosing the most effective responses.*

strength, to keep all the numbers accessible as you perform your mental calculations.) Maintaining your cognitive tools gives you an edge by keeping you "in the zone" in another way. A skill used in one domain can cross over into another to enrich the savor of your life and its other incomes. (For example, when you learn the pattern of number intervals in math you may perceive a pattern of musical intervals for the first time and enjoy the music more. Or vice versa.)

Your brain is there to keep you alive. It is your best weapon. Human evolution has equipped you with such an effective toolbox that your brain can find its best tool, adjust it and apply it. The human brain evolved to keep the organism beneath it alive to hunt in groups, to track and to kill stronger, faster, more agile prey—then find its way home again across ancient plains to a cave in a cliff. It has equipped humans to survive ice ages and dry months when deserts crept across their gardens. But these amazing tools can rust.

The brain cells of your cortex carry the messages that built the life you live in but the human brain is an energy hog in charge of itself. It accounts for only 3% of your total body weight but it burns 19% of the fuel in your bloodstream. It is such a fierce fuel manager

MEMORY ZONE *It is a component of all cognitive skills. The brain codes data it considers useful and stores it in the cortex, often near the sensory area related to each component part of the memory. Before storage, incoming data passes through the brain's interior, more primitive area to take whatever action is required for survival.*

it will shut off its own higher functions if there is no demand for them. Though more primitive systems still operate, the cortex withdraws the dendrites that operate circuits which, for example, allow memories to be formed and retrieved at will. At that moment each idled cell cuts you off from some order of a billionth of your capacity to perceive the significance of what's happening around you or to succeed in your goals.

We hope that some of the information in this book may inspire you to sharpen your mental tools and enrich your life now and as you grow old. (What's more, it is so fascinating in itself that you could suddenly find yourself the center of attention at social gatherings.).

Every year, more published research supports the concept of "Use it or lose it," a phrase that the whisky-voiced actress Tallulah Bankhead once made famous, perhaps in another context. Either way, the idea appears to be a rule of nature.

How this material is organized

This book includes short reports on results of academic research into how the human brain functions, plus tests and mental exercises related to each short report. The editors selected only topics that can be put to practical use in everyday life and that can be understood without scientific background. They clustered the reports into six ways you use your brain: Executive/Social, Memory, Emotional, Language, Math and Spatial. Linked with each text report is a self-test of brain function you can administer to yourself, or an entertaining exercise of the brain function related to what you learned from the report.

The exercises are intriguing challenges, often formatted as puzzles. They are designed to help develop mental skills in two ways. First,

EMOTIONAL ZONE *Our emotional responses, which we are often not consciously able to cause or control voluntarily, tend to be processed in the older, central part of the brain rather than the outer cortex. The brain is primarily a tool to ensure survival, not speculation, so response is often required on a subconscious level.*

LANGUAGE & MATH ZONES *Detailed data that make up the "trees" of the "forest" are mainly processed on the left side of the cortex near the temple. Also nearby the temporal lobe are the parts of the brain that control speech and language—both abstract understanding and motor movements involved in speech.*

they will help you to build mental stamina for sustained concentration, much as aerobics builds physical stamina for sustained exertion. The ability to focus attention is an essential first step for conscious memory. Second, the exercises introduce, in an entertaining format, so many different kinds of data—math, verbal, spatial, logic, etc.—that some of it is bound to be new to you. That new data—and more important, the experience you gain in how to organize data so you can locate a solution—will build links among your brain cells that, later, can help you learn new data and spot the most effective pattern to cope with it.

Use the Hints (printed upside down beneath the exercises) when you need a boost to get started solving the task. These exercises are there to stimulate neural activity, not to frustrate it.

Self-tests allow you to investigate a function or phenomenon related to the adjacent article. They do not rely on any prior knowledge. They allow you to observe your own facility in performing tasks similar to those used under scientifically structured, experimental conditions. The evidence from those experiments produced norms against which you can roughly measure your own score. Also, the very process of taking such a self-test, including the need to follow instructions, challenges your powers of concentration and other memory functions, thereby helping to strengthen them, just as the exercises do.

The graphic icons next to the title of an exercise or self-test indicate which of the six practical, cognitive zones will be stimulated.

When answers to exercises or self-tests are necessary they appear in the Solutions section in the back of the book. ("The Lurch" is no place to be left; we've been there often.)

— Allen Bragdon and David Gamo

SPATIAL ZONE *The brain processes incoming sensory data about size, proportion, shape, relative volume and other spatial values mostly with neurons on the right side. The colored area in the back of the cortex (right) shows the occipital area, where visual data is first processed, then sent elsewhere to be interpreted.*

executive & social function

EXECUTIVE *&* SOCIAL

This is the most recently evolved zone of intelligence in the human brain. It works out plans designed to reach consciously-contrived future goals. It selects the paths of social interaction that will bring the greatest long-term benefit. It retrieves data from long-term memory and uses it to construct images of similar data as it might become active in future time. It is the seat of human "character"—that galaxy of consistent responses that involve social reliability and responsibility.

If the textured layer of gray matter known as the cortex is the source of our uniqueness as humans, it's the parts of the cortex behind the forehead—the frontal lobes—that are most responsible for the differences between us and our closest animal relatives. This region of the brain, apparently, is most responsible for self-awareness—the ability to introspect, to ponder, to not only act, but to be aware of the fact that we're acting, to weigh other conceivable actions, to choose not to act, to imagine how the world might be different if we didn't act or if we weren't alive to act. With this comes freedom from materialistic determination, a philosophical preoccupation with the mysteries of life and with death, a sense of beauty, religion—in short, all those interests related to the past, the future, and the self that we think of as distinguishing us from other animals.

As the most recently-evolved part of the brain, the frontal lobes also house the most fragile parts of our identity—the faculties that require the most conscious effort and practice such as logic, planning, monitoring our own behavior, and achieving desired goals. In the process of becoming responsible social beings, we spend much of the early part of life learning how to modify the impulses that come pulsing upward from the lower parts of the brain. For much of the rest of our life, the conflicts between these different systems—between emotion and rationality, libido and intellect, spontaneity and self-control—ensure our financial contribution to the self-help movement and the psychotherapy business.

Conscious, planned, goal-oriented behavior and emotion are not necessarily in conflict, however. After all, in order to move towards a goal, it certainly helps to desire it. Brain scans show that your left frontal lobe is activated when you feel positive emotions, and the right frontal lobe when you feel negative emotions. Already as babies, some of us have less-than-average activity in one region or the other. If your "positive" frontal region has naturally low activation, you may not have much success in intellectual goal-directed tasks. Some people with frontal-lobe injury lose both their emotions and their decision-making ability; others may become violent criminals. It even seems that "hunches" and "intuitions"—impulses occupying the shadow-world in between rational consciousness and emotion—may have a frontal-lobe locus.

The flip side of the fragility of executive functions is that they are also the most malleable and improvable with practice. The best way to be an expert at organizing information and using it to your advantage is to work at it. Because your frontal-lobe functions are so consciously accessible, this is an easier matter—as long as you're willing to make the effort—than, say, learning to adjust your brain-stem-governed body rhythms.

What part of your brain causes you to respond as a unique individual?

One of the more difficult tasks neuroscience is currently faced with is that of identifying the part or parts of the brain responsible for defining an individual's personality as a unique and stable entity. Lots of progress has been made in associating certain regions of the brain with specific abilities and functions: the hippocampus with the mediation of memory formation, the amygdala with the processing of emotion, areas along the sylvian fissure with various aspects of language. But where is the locus of conscious self-awareness, the site that makes one person have a different identity from another, the region that unites the experiences of an individual human organism into a stable sense of self, despite the fluctuations of mood, affect, drive, and emotion? As Calvin and Ojemann's epilepsy patient asks in *Conversations with Neil's Brain*, "Where is the real me?"

Is identity an illusion?

A point that Calvin and Ojemann make is that this stable sense of self may be less real than we sometimes imagine. There seem to be many different parts of the brain competing for dominance, with any one part winning out at any given moment. Our sense of our unity of consciousness may result from the fact that there's only one winner at any one time.

But if any region of the brain were to be implicated as the seat of identity, it would probably be included in the front third of the brain called the frontal lobe. That area is the most recently evolved. It allows humans to imagine goals for themselves in the future and select appropriate behavior—an ability that suffers when part of the frontal lobe is knocked out of commission by disease or injury, such as a tumor or a stroke.

What happens when you're no longer you?

The most famous and dramatic case of frontal lobe injury is that of Phineas Gage, a promising young railroad construction crew supervisor who, in 1848, had an iron tamping bar shot into his upper jaw and through the midfrontal regions of his brain. Although he survived and, in some respects, recovered amazingly well, he changed from a soft-spoken, responsible man into a foul-mouthed, erratic, inconsiderate boor. His friends complained that he had changed into a different person—that he was "no longer Gage."

In general, personality-related symptoms of frontal-lobe damage may include changes in drive or motivation, mood, and affect (emotional expression), and in the ability to plan or make decisions. Diminished reliability or foresight, socially inappropriate behavior, depression, euphoria, and lethargy are some of the many complaints that have been reported.

We may understand this wide range of symptoms as due to the other parts of the brain for which the frontal regions serve as association areas. The dorsal frontal system connects to parts of the brain involved in the sequential organization and processing of information. The ventral system connects to emotional regions,

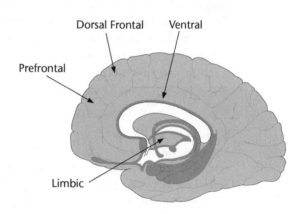

including three different limbic systems. The pre-frontal cortex also has strong connections to all sensory regions, as well as to motor regions. This has inspired the identification of the pre-frontal cortex as the "final common pathway," integrating information from a variety of brain regions for the proper motor response.

Awareness is a relationship, not a thing or place

According to some researchers, many kinds of frontal-lobe pathology may be grouped under the umbrella of self-reflective awareness, or the ability to be aware of oneself and one's relation to others and the environment. Based on studies of children, "meta-awareness"—the awareness that one is aware—depends on the relatively late infant development of subparts of the frontal region. The frontal lobe, then, seems to house integration or association regions which are crucial to our stable identity. As is true for so many aspects of cognition, those vexing questions of the source of consciousness and identity may be answered in the associations between many parts of the brain, rather than in one self-contained locus or "module." But, to the extent that we have one, the "driver" of the whole cognitive apparatus—the particular associations that make you different from me—may well be seated, appropriately enough, right up front.

WHAT HAPPENED TO PHINEAS GAGE

This illustration is a computer reconstructions of the skull of Phineas Gage, who lived for 14 years after a crowbar-sized tamping rod entered his cheek, passed through his prefrontal cortex, and exited his forehead. As foreman of a railroad-building gang, he was tamping down explosive charges when a spark set one off. The rod took with it the portion of his brain that nobody knew the function of until then—the part that allows humans to make mental images of what has not yet happened. It is known as an "executive" function.

This is the skill that allows chess masters to foresee the results of a move. Business executives use it to plan for expansion. We all use it to plan the route to do a string of chores and to get along with other people.

After he recovered from his accident, young Phineas changed from a kind man and responsible foreman into a foul-mouthed, unreliable social outcast.

EXERCISE: Mixed-up toons

Your frontal lobes plan the best sequence of events to achieve goals. Try to rearrange each of the five sets of mixed-up cartoon panels on pages 18–22 into the most amusing sequences. Replace the incorrect numbers with correct ones.

A

(cont'd on next page)

(cont'd on next page)

(cont'd on next page)

(cont'd on next page)

E

Your right frontal lobe registers negative emotions: how that fact can be useful to you

We sometimes think of our emotional selves—our fears, delights, and outbursts of anger—as diametrically opposed to the cool reason, planning, and logic required for identifying and reaching goals. This is only partly true. Here's why.

Emotions are processed in the frontal lobe

The frontal lobe is a crossroads of the emotional centers of the brain. Negative emotions—disgust, fear, and anger—are registered in the right frontal lobe, and happiness is registered in the left. How do we know? For one thing, these are the regions that electroencephalograph (EEG) readings show to be activated when people are exposed to stimuli that evoke one of these emotional responses—a picture of a dog eating its own vomit, for example.

Emotion and reason are linked

The frontal lobe also controls executive functions such as intention, conscious self-regulation, and planning. People with damage to the left frontal lobe may have difficulty planning a simple sequence of actions and even in initiating voluntary actions, and they may be listless, apathetic, and depressed. Approach-related behavior—movement towards literal or metaphorical goals—requires not only planning a strategy for getting there, but the desire to get moving in the first place.

Low activity in your left frontal lobe correlates with depression

Some people have *low* baseline readings of *left* frontal lobe activity. They may often be labeled as inhibited or shy. Their left frontal lobe also shows low response to positive stimuli— happy scenes in films, for example. People who have an unusually *high* level of *right* frontal lobe activity tend to be anxious and leery of danger. Depression and sadness are usually categorized by most people as negative emotions, along with fear, anger, and disgust. Even so, it seems that depression is better understood, neurally speaking, as a *low* level of activity in the *left* frontal lobe—the "happy" region. It does not show as unusually high activity in the "negative" right frontal area as, for example, anger does.

Does this mean that one side of my body is an eager go-getter, and the other side is an anxious coward?

Since the brain's right hemisphere corresponds to the left side of the body, and the left hemisphere to the right side, you'd expect happiness to be registered more strongly on the right side of the face, and disgust, anger, and fear on the left side. This seems to be true. (It has been speculated that the source of the "enigmatic" effect of the Mona Lisa's smile is that, in her case, it's the left side, not the right side, of the face that is smiling. Thus, the negative side of the face is happy, and the positive side is neutral—resulting in a somewhat inscrutable overall expression.) Some psychologists have argued that the right brain is the dominant hemisphere for emotions in general. This probably has some validity for the *perception* of emotion in other people's faces and other cues, but not for *feeling* the emotion itself.

Even though the left hemisphere does dominate in the *experience* of positive emotion, the right hemisphere seems to be involved in the *recognition* and processing of *both* positive and

---

  SELF-TEST: Judgment of emotion; mirror images

There's a theory that the subject of the Mona Lisa is Leonardo himself—i.e., that the painting is a self-portrait. In that case, Leonardo must have been painting his own mirror image. If we flop the image, the effect to most people is dramatic: the picture loses its "enigmatic" quality, and the subject's expression appears to become rather smirking or even lascivious than inscrutable.

Which of the two pictures below is the Mona Lisa with the inscrutable smile and which image has been reversed to reveal Leonardo da Vinci's "lascivious" smile?

negative emotional signals. The right brain also picks up positive facial expressions more than you'd think based on the left brain's dominance in feeling positive emotions. Still, the left brain does play a role in processing positive signals as well as experiencing them. Happy faces are recognized better when presented to the right visual field (left brain). Also, films shown in the right visual field tend to be rated more pleasant than ones shown in the left visual field (right brain).

So *that's* why Aunt Mary always thought I liked her fruitcake
It also happens that elderly adults are worse than younger adults at recognizing negative facial expressions—fear or disgust, for example. This finding provides support to the right-hemi-aging hypothesis—that, as we age, the right hemisphere tends to decline more rapidly than the left. Perhaps that's why certain "crystallized" left-brain abilities such as vocabulary size don't decline as fast when we age, compared to certain "fluid" right-brain abilities such as abstract spatial reasoning and facial recognition. In a recent study, young and old adults were asked to assign photographs of faces to categories of emotion ("Happy," "Fearful," etc.). Older subjects performed much worse than younger ones in identifying negative expressions, but as well as younger subjects in identifying happy faces.

Why is it that your negative-processing right brain best reads the "positive" side of another person's face?
Let's face it, the only time you can read the expression on another person's face is when you face each other. But then, the emotion that each side of the brain is specialized to perceive is in the *other* half of the brain's field of vision. In other words, when facing someone head-on, you will tend to have his "negative" side in your field of vision connected to your brain's "positive processing" skills, and his "positive" side in your "negative" field. This seeming contradiction suggests that our brains have evolved to prevent us from viewing and responding to other people in a wholly one-sided fashion.

All this has something of the flavor of a diabolical logic puzzle. If you experience frustration and disgust coupled with a desire to throttle the authors of this article, would we be dealing with right-brain-based withdrawal-oriented, or left-brain-based approach-related behavior?

EXERCISE: Getting on the "right" side of a person

Study the illustrations and the photos on these pages, then answer the following question:

If you were standing face-to-face with a stranger looking directly ahead at him or her, would you be more likely to think that person's face showed the positive or negative aspects of his or her personality?

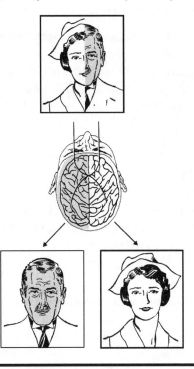

Hint: As demonstrated by the split-image diagram, the left hemisphere of most people's brains processes information their eyes pick up to the right of the midpoint in their field of vision. Similarly, the right hemisphere processes the data to the left. (For example, if your right hemisphere were damaged you might say you saw an angry man in the diagram, not a half-smiling, half-frowning face.)

Even though the left hemisphere is more specialized for the perception of positive than of negative emotion, the right hemisphere does seem to be dominant for the perception of all kinds of emotion.

The right hemisphere processes a person's own feelings of anger, disgust, contempt, fear—the negative emotions.

Each of the two hemispheres of the brain, left and right, controls the physical systems and attributes located on the opposite half of the body.

SELF-TEST: How the brain views faces

Which photo depicts the more disgusted man?

| Picture of a man expressing disgust. | **A** Composite picture in which the *right* half of his face appears on right *and* left sides. | **B** This is a composite picture of the two *left* halves of his face. |

A **B**

Which face is happy? For most people the right side of the brain is dominant for the perception of emotions. When you are looking at a person's face, the part to the left of the nose is interpreted by the right brain.

(Illus. after Julian Jaynes, 1976)

Hint for top photos: Look at the mouth of the man in photos A and B. Which mouth looks more negative? When you sneer, on which side of your face do you curl your lip?

Hint for bottom illustrations: Most people interpret emotions more strongly by what the right side of a person's face looks like—which is what they see on the left as they view that person face-to-face. Try looking at the nose of each and decide which seems happier. Most people would see face "A" as sad, and face "B" as happy.

SELF-TEST: Right-brain pattern abstraction / abstract reading

Complete the following by filling in a letter, number, or word in each blank. Total time: 10 minutes.

Example: A E I O U

1) 1 3 5 7 _

2) AB CE CD EG EF G__

3) blowhard hardhat hatcheck _____mate

4) astray stray tray ___

5) toner tone ton __

6) stone tone ton __

7) stops ____ top to

8) snit in snot on prod or mode __

9) polygram 12345678 pray 1674 ploy ____

10) gum gun bar bat sun sup lip ___

11) hole pit seed kick punt boat edge shore strengthen hurt ____clever

12) bird crane stretch sprint run snag lozenge mint new note ___ beak

13) 7913 992 488 569 72155 614__

14) Q O M K I _

15) din don fan fen pep pip cod ___

16) 289735 897352 973528 735289 _____

17) bib bib ton not 399 993 pin ___

18) JK KJ LM IH NO G _

19) 37210 2 19903 1 48737 3 52209 9 47391 _

20) retire rite strafe fart inept pen peruse ____

How to read deceit: false smiles and happy smiles

A long-standing debate in cultural anthropology is whether facial expressions match up with particular emotions on a universal or only culturally specific basis. (See p. 142.) One piece of evidence cited by proponents of the latter view is that smiles can signal so many different kinds of emotion depending on context: on the one hand, sincere happiness or pleasure, and on the other, any of a number of negative emotions such as embarrassment, chagrin, or malice.

The 19th-century French neurologist Duchenne de Boulogne observed, however, that there seem to be at least two distinct patterns of facial muscle movement which we happen to group together with the same word. One involves both the muscle which parts and raises the lips (*zygomatic major*), and the muscle which raises the cheeks and gathers the skin inward toward the eye socket (*orbicularis oculi*). He identified this as the smile of spontaneous joy. The other involves only the zygomatic major muscle around the mouth. In acknowledgment of Duchenne's insight, University of California researcher Paul Ekman has dubbed the smile of spontaneous happiness a *Duchenne* smile, while the other is sometimes called a false, social, or masking smile.

Parts of your left brain that are active when you make a sincerely happy smile are not active when the smile is false

The brain's electrical activity can be seen and measured in normal, wide-awake, active subjects using electroencephelogram (EEG) equipment. In one experiment, subjects were chosen who could make their faces create the Duchenne happy smile, as actors can. The EEG readings when they were making this genuine smile showed spots of activity in the left hemisphere normally associated with happy feelings. Activity in those areas died away, however, when the subjects changed their faces to show the false kind of smile using only the muscles around their mouth. In other words, the EEG record of their brain activity showed that they were actually *feeling* happier when they were making the Duchenne smile, but not the social smile.

You might think that this effect was due to the subjects' making themselves feel happy in order to produce the Duchenne smile, just as actors will sometimes think of something sad in order to cry. The researchers were careful to prevent this, though, by teaching the subjects to make the different kinds of expression by pointing out to them which muscles they should use; they scrupulously avoided describing the facial-muscle-movement patterns with reference to the emotions associated with them, such as "joy" or "happiness," or even referring to them as "smiles" at all.

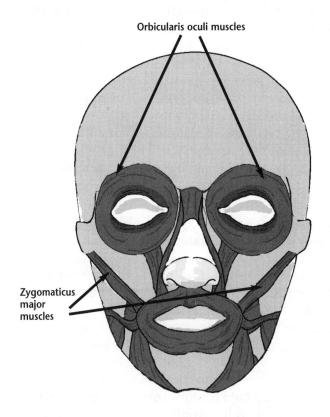

Orbicularis oculi muscles

Zygomaticus major muscles

This is important for at least three reasons. One, it shows that you can, quite simply, make yourself feel happier by smiling—as long as you make the right *kind* of smile! (See p. 141.) Two, you can tell a sincere smile from a false smile—and, in some cases, tell an honest person from a liar—by paying attention to the muscle around the eye. Third, a certain pattern of brain activity (a cerebral "map" of joy) is indeed biologically linked to a certain pattern of facial movement; those who argue that the link between smiles and emotions is arbitrary and unpredictable are confusing what are, in fact, two fundamentally different *kinds* of facial expression.

 SELF-TEST: The eyes have it

Of these four sets of eyes peeking out from behind their veils, only one goes with a "Duchenne" smile of sincere, spontaneous joy. Of the others, one belongs with a neutral expression, one with condescension and one with anger. Which is which?

On the following page the full faces are revealed down the right-hand side of the page. Only one configuration of the muscles creates the Duchenne smile. The difference is in the use of the orbicularis oculi muscle around the eye (see illustration at left), which is the only reliable indicator of sincere joy. Do the smiling mouths on the faces down the right-hand side of the following page change the way you perceive the true emotion expressed?

(cont'd on next page)

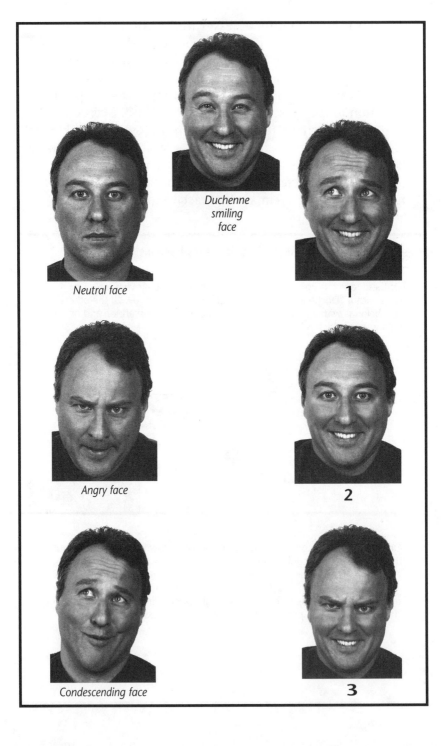

Neutral face

Duchenne
smiling
face

1

Angry face

2

Condescending face

3

How odor influences a woman's mate selection

Have you ever wondered why there are some people you feel instantly attracted to, while there are others who you have no more romantic interest in than you'd have in your pet rock? Chalk it up to chemistry. Actually, in some cases that may be more literally true than you might think.

You may not know your own mind

Over a hundred years ago, Freud had an interesting idea. Your mind isn't a seamless, unified whole. In fact, what you think of as your mind isn't even where most of the interesting action is. Beneath the placid waters of civilized consciousness, there are entire worlds of dark impulses doing battle. What emerges to consciousness is only the tip of a very large iceberg—or maybe the tail fin of a very large sea monster.

Freud's idea is no less valid today, even if neuroscientists think of it in different terms. Instead of id, libido, ego, and superego, they may prefer to talk about different brain systems—the primitive, emotional limbic system, say, and the more respectable prefrontal cortex, seat of self-awareness and socially responsible behavior.

There's no doubt that our conscious thoughts and actions are influenced by brain systems beneath our awareness. In fact, we even have direct proof of it. One recent study using brain imaging technology, for example, showed that airborne human steroid hormones can influence brain activity without the brain's owner being aware of smelling anything at all. What might those unsmelt smells be doing to us?

Something perfume manufacturers would love to know

For years, researchers have been on the trail of human pheromones—airborne chemical signals that animals use to communicate. When ants wiggle their antennae at each other, they're "talking" in a chemical language. In mammals such as pigs and mice, pheromones influence fertility and a can trigger a desire to mate. Long ago, Freud figured out that if you want to learn about unconscious impulses, there's no better place to look than things that may be embarrassing, or things many people don't feel comfortable talking about. What better candidates than smell and sex? So, here's the question: Do pheromones play a role in human sexual behavior?

It's a controversial question. But some researchers think the answer is yes. You may have heard of studies showing that women can influence each other's menstrual cycles completely unconsciously, possibly through odorless airborne chemicals that can be readily collected from their armpits. Two chemicals, which are released by a woman at different stages of her menstrual cycle, can lengthen or shorten the cycle of women around her, with the result that their cycles may end up being synchronized.

Other experiments have shown that women's response to the odor of a male hormone is influenced by their menstrual cycle. Near ovulation, when they're fertile, they'll find the hormone more pleasant-smelling than at the end or beginning of their cycle, when they're not. Not only that, they're thousands of times more sensitive to the smell of male hormones when they're fertile than when they're menstruating. (There's also evidence that women's sense of smell in general is more acute during the fertile period of their ovulation cycle.)

What women like in the scent of a man
The male hormone that women seem to find more attractive when they're fertile is amply present in men's sweat. Does that mean that a man might have better luck with a woman he meets in a bar if he doesn't wash his shirt beforehand? Not quite. The chemical in stale male sweat is not the same as the male hormone in fresh sweat. And anyway, she might think the alluring odor is coming from the guy sitting one barstool over.

One-night stands are one thing, but surely a woman will be more sensible when choosing her life partner? Maybe, maybe not. Recent experiments seem to show that a woman's choice of partner may be influenced by odors indicative of genetic compatibility. We all carry genes that help us fight diseases and infections, one group of which is referred to as MHC genes. When women are asked to sniff t-shirts worn by men for two nights in a row, each by a different man, their preferences appear to line up according to the similarity between their own MHC genes and those of the man who wore the shirt.

The question is, do women prefer a match or a mismatch? According to one frequently-cited study, women prefer the scent of a man whose genes are complementary to their own, perhaps because that would result in their offspring having a broader profile of immunity to diseases. Crudely put, this means that a woman would not want to marry someone who smells like her brother. A more recent experiment comes to the conclusion that it's actually a close genetic match that women prefer. That means that a woman would want a man who smells like her brother, or like her father.

Now, that's a finding that Freud would have found very interesting indeed.

EXERCISE: A case of confused identity

Part 1.

In the former Soviet Bloc country of "Borduria," someone has committed a series of grisly murders. The culprit has been identified and apprehended—with a couple of hitches. First, the murderer has been identified by an eyewitness, but the identified individual happens to have an identical twin brother. Both are sitting in jail, but nobody knows which one is the real murderer. Under Bordurian law, unless some evidence points decisively to one or the other having committed the murders, both must be set free. Also under Bordurian law, the state prosecutor may ask each suspect only one yes/no question to ascertain his guilt or innocence. However, here's another hitch: one brother is a consistent pathological liar, and the other brother tells nothing but the truth, but nobody knows whether the murderer is a liar or a truth teller.

Prosecutor Multinovic thinks he's figured out what question to ask each of the twins. To each in turn, he poses the following query:

"Did your brother commit the murders?"

Will this question lead him to the murderer?

Part 2.

In response to his question, Multinovic gets a response of "Yes" from the first brother, and "No" from the second.

What can the prosecutor conclude from these answers?

Part 3.

Due to his incompetence, Multinovic is replaced as prosecutor by his assistant Plavac. Under Bordurian law, a suspected murderer may be asked a second yes/no question by a new prosecutor—but the new prosecutor may assume no prior knowledge of the answers to any questions asked by a former prosecutor. In other words, Plavac must start from scratch.

If you were Plavac, what would you ask the twins? Remember, only one question is permitted for each suspect, but the question needn't remain the same from one suspect to another.

Hint: Don't forget that one brother *always* lies, even if it is to his disadvantage. What if in Part 2, the witness were mistaken or both brothers implicated? When you get to Part 3 it would help to start out by asking a question which you and the brothers know the truthful answer to.

A type of logic puzzle that often applies to real-life situations

There are relatively few different formats into which most so-called logic puzzles fit. The characters and situations within which they interact change, but the basic pattern repeats. Once that key is known it is often possible to spot a similar pattern in a dilemma a person must face in reality.

The type of logic puzzle represented by the following brain twisters is as old, probably, as the human cortex. "Familial dilemma" is a variant of the old farmer, fox, goose, and grain chestnut, which we've included in its historically original version on the following page. The "Anders" puzzle is different in detail and structure, but involves essentially the same kind of thinking.

We hope you won't ever find yourself facing these specific situations. The solutions (there are more than one) require a slight reversal of standard procedures. That is why these puzzles translate into real-life situations so applicably.

Like most logic puzzles that require the ability to plan ahead, the solution comes more easily if one can clearly visualize alternative situations. Then it is necessary to hold each of those mini-scenes in mind long enough to evaluate their consequences before retaining or discarding them.

EXERCISE: A familial dilemma

Antonio has invited his mother and mother-in-law to meet at his house so he and his wife can take them to dinner at a nearby restaurant. Since he has the only car, Antonio must drive them all to the restaurant. There are, however, some complications. His car is a Fiat two-seater convertible, so he can only take one passenger at a time. Also, his mother-in-law doesn't get along very well with his mother, and his wife and his mother have a rather tense relationship as well, so he can't leave his mother alone with either his wife or his mother-in-law at any point, either at home or at the restaurant. How can he shuttle them over to the restaurant one at a time and avoid leaving two people who dislike each other alone together? (He cannot leave anyone at a third location either.) (See "Hint," p. 38.)

EXERCISE: Fox, goose, and grain

A "familial dilemma" is a variant of the old farmer, fox, goose, and grain riddle. It goes like this:

A farmer wants to ferry a fox, a goose, and a sack of grain across a river. However, his boat is only big enough to hold one at a time. If he leaves the fox and goose alone together on either bank, the fox will eat the goose. If he leaves the goose and the grain together, the goose will eat the grain.

How can he get all three to the other side?

Hint for a familial dilemma: There are a couple of possible answers, but they both require this: Since Antonio gets along with all three women, but one of them can't get along with either of the other two, what he must do is spend most of his time with that one woman and never leave her alone with either of the others.

EXERCISE: Anders' dilemma

Anders Andert Anderson is off to an outpost in Alaska that is a six-day hike from Shungnak across a desolate expanse of snow and ice. One man can lug only sufficient food and water for four days. As you can see, one man can't go alone because his supplies wouldn't last until he reached his destination. How many people would it take carrying supplies to assure that Anders reaches the outpost and his assistants make it back to Shungnak?

Hint: No matter how many people start out at Shungnak, only Anders has to arrive at the outpost. But remember: Even assistants need to eat, so make sure the others have enough food and water to get them home.

EXERCISE: Menu please

Five old friends had a reunion at their favorite restaurant. Each man ordered something to drink, an entree, and a dessert. John and Mr. Jackson had martinis, and James and Mr. Jones ordered scotch. Mr. Jenkins had cola since he was driving. John and Mr. Jennings ordered steak. Joe and Mr. Jenkins had roast beef. For dessert Joe and Mr. Jordan ate chocolate cake, while Jerry and Mr. Jenkins had pie. The other man had ice cream. No two men sitting next to each other were served two things the same. Who had pheasant and what did Jake eat?

How to make yourself feel happier without drugs

As every actor knows, the facial expression and body language depicting any emotion can be faked. The emotional response itself, however, is usually not in the control of the person experiencing it. Emotional arousal is usually subconscious, even though many of the outward manifestations of arousal can be modified consciously by the cortex.

There is strong evidence that people are able to change mood by changing their facial expression, posture, and style of movement to reflect a different emotion from the one they are currently feeling. If someone feels depressed, for example, they can try to look and behave as if they were happy—the result will be that they actually begin to *feel* happier. The patterns of muscle and nerve action that produce an expression of happiness, in this example, also trigger other neurological changes that help a person feel happier in reality. (See p. 141.)

One element of facial expression that is a tip-off to emotional arousal is difficult to counterfeit but is easily observed by another person. Research on emotional response mechanisms conducted at the University of Chicago in the 1960's under the direction of Eckhard Hess revealed that the dark pupil in the center of the human eye grows larger when that person's interest has been aroused. Like many other physical symptoms of emotional arousal, including those measured by lie-detector polygraphs—increased heart rate, perspiration, skin temperature, for example—changes in the size of the pupil are not under the conscious control of the individual.

SELF-TEST: Interested?

Most people think that a look of aroused interest makes a person appear more attractive to others. To test this theory for yourself, look at the two faces below and select the one which appears more attractive to you, the one on the top or on the bottom.

The night a middle-aged man tackled his bureau in his sleep

In a recent study, brain scans of subjects moving a joystick in a certain pattern or simply imagining moving it in the same pattern revealed that about 80% of the circuitry used when physically moving the joystick is also used in the purely imaginary exercise. This shows that mentally picturing a physical action such as swinging a golf club or playing the piano activates most of the brain circuits used when actually performing the action, thus strengthening the brain cell connections needed for expert performance (see "What is the brain so busy doing...?" p. 177).

The role of REM sleep in reinforcing learned behaviors

In REM sleep (a phase during normal sleep in which the eyeballs move rapidly beneath the closed lids), we act out movements mentally but not physically. Normally, neurons in the spinal cord that send messages to the muscles are shut down. This makes it physically impossible to move our bodies in response to signals from the brain stem, which sends messages to muscles. (A middle-aged man with a neurological disorder is reported to have injured himself by tackling his chest of drawers while replaying a college football game in his sleep— probably during the REM phase.)

Dreaming rehearses new experiences to aid recall of them when needed

Given that the proportion of REM sleep in the sleep cycle is increased during periods of particularly active learning of new tasks, dreaming and learning seem to be linked. We've probably all had the experience of performing some repetitive physical task all day long— typing, running a cash register, house painting, sandblasting, or what have you—only to dream about per- forming that very same task that night after we fall asleep. Those dreams may be serving the func- tion of reinforcing the cell connec- tions needed to perform the task even more fluidly and effort- lessly in the future, whether we want to or not!

Why are dreams so "fantastic"?

The key to understanding the strange nature of dreams, say many researchers, lies in two different sets of neurons in the primitive brain stem that release two different kinds of chemi- cal signal.

One set releases "adrenergic" chemicals (chemicals which interact with adrenaline and adrenaline-sensitive neural recep- tors), which keep the mind alert, attentive, and free from stray images. These neurons are active when we're awake, but shut down when we're asleep.

The other set releases "cholinergic" chemicals (which interact with acetylcholine and acetylcholine-sensitive recep- tors). These chemicals stimulate the body's motor centers, emotional centers, and information-processing centers. (See p. 109.) While cholinergic neurons are active during the day, they kick into high gear when we fall asleep, sending bursts of impulses from the brain stem up into the brain's higher regions.

When the motor centers are stimulated, we visualize all kinds of movements which we would physically act out if not for the fact that the brain also sends a signal to the spinal cord which paralyzes all our muscles except for our eyes.

That's why we don't (normally) thrash out or run around while we dream, and why the dream period of sleep is associated with rapid eye movement (hence the term "REM sleep" for the phase during which we're most likely to dream).

The cholinergic chemicals' stimulation of the brain's emotional regions explains the frequency of anxiety dreams and nightmares, as well as our common dream experiences of eroticism, anger, and uplifting joy.

Why dreams often serve up such valuable insights

Perhaps the most intriguing part is the stimulation of the brain's information-processing centers. This is what accounts for the unique logic and coherence of dreams. Due in part to the suppression of the parts of our brain sensitive to adrenergic chemicals, the content of dreams seems diametrically opposed to the lines of reasoning we follow when alert and focused. As the brain stem releases its bursts of cholinergic chemicals, our stimulated information-processing centers strive to make sense out of the images generated, free of the fetters of focused concentration.

This is also why some of our most creative insights occur to us in dreams, and why scientists and artists so often attain the solution to a vexing problem while dreaming. It's not that we're more or less "smart" while we dream. Our dream intelligence is just different: more associative, more integrative, and less linear. As anyone who has watched the movie *The Last Wave* knows, many cultures believe that we ignore our dreams, and the insights gained in them, to our own peril.

Dreams and madness

That's why dreams hold such fascination for us. They give us insight into what it must be like to be a different kind of person, or even a different kind of animal. They give us glimpses of what the world may be like from the perspective of a creature that is intelligent but bizarrely lacking in self-awareness. They show us, too, how the world may look through the eyes of an insane person. In fact, some schizophrenics have an overabundance of cholinergic neurons, which may explain the hallucinations characteristic of that mental illness.

EXERCISE: Feynman's real-life exercise in dream control

The following account describes one person's successful attempt not only to control the content of his dreams, but to *see* color and *feel* sensation at will. The object of this exercise is to be inspired to try it yourself.

As a young undergraduate at MIT, the physicist Richard Feynman had a real-life waking experience of the sort of thing that runs as an anxiety motif through the dreams of countless college students and former college students. At the end of a year-long philosophy class in which he had failed to understand a single thing the professor had said, he was assigned to write an essay about what the professor had been lecturing about all year. He was at a loss until he remembered that the professor had once mentioned the term "stream of consciousness." So he decided to write about dreams.

Feynman approached the assignment as any good scientist would: not just through introspection, but through observation. The first thing he did was to observe himself during the process of falling asleep. He discovered that his internal monologues and visualizations became utterly illogical as he drifted toward sleep. He had never noticed that before simply because he had never before paid any attention. Of course, the fact of making this observation would wake him back up, so he decided to move on to other things.

Next, with enough practice he learned the trick of observing himself while he dreamed. He found that the "seeing department" of the brain could produce images as lucid and detailed as any visualization involving real external stimuli. He observed himself dreaming in color. (Do you? How do you know?) He learned that if he wanted, he could see each single hair on the head of a woman lying beside him in the dream, and that he could even reproduce the rainbow effect of the sun diffracting off the follicles. (Can you dream that vividly? How do you know?) He learned, by running his dream-finger over a dream-thumbtack, that the "feeling department" of the brain can also re-create vivid tactile sensations despite the lack of any sensory input. Not only that, he learned he could turn off one "department" at will while leaving the other one on — make the thumbtack disappear, but run his finger over the spot where it had been and still feel it.

He found, to his delight, that he could manipulate the content of his dreams at will.

How self-conscious are you?

When asked to rate their own sociability, most people's self-reports are very different from what an observer will report about their behavior in a social situation. When seated in front of a mirror, however, people tend to be much more accurate in their self-reports. In social interactions, people's tendency to view themselves as responsible for what happens during the interaction will also increase if they can see their own reflection in a mirror. When people are provoked to anger, they'll react more aggressively if they are made self-aware by seeing a reflection of themselves.

If you are rejected do you think it must be *your* failure?

Some people seem to view themselves as if a mirror were always present. If they're rejected by someone at a party, they're especially likely to hold themselves responsible for the rejection. If they give a work presentation that isn't well received, they'll consider themselves to have failed rather than viewing the audience as unreceptive. If they're provoked to anger, they'll respond more emotionally than will others who spend less time mulling over their own internal state. These people, high in self-consciousness, go through much of their life as if they were viewing their own reflection in a mirror.

Many theorists have considered what we loosely call self-consciousness to be best broken down into at least two components: private self-consciousness and public self-consciousness. Private self-consciousness is roughly what we might otherwise refer to as self-awareness or introversion: a focusing on one's internal states, moods, and motives. Public self-consciousness has more to do with others' views and evaluations. Private self-consciousness may be a prerequisite for public self-consciousness, but you can be privately self-conscious without being very preoccupied about other people's responses to you. Finally, public self-consciousness may or may not lead to social anxiety: a frequent sense of apprehension about other people's views and reactions to oneself in a social situation.

SELF-TEST: Self-consciousness inventory

Answer the following questions to determine your degrees of public self-consciousness, private self-consciousness and social anxiety. At the end of the "Self-Test," total the points as shown in the "Scoring" box.

1. You're introduced to a young woman at a party. She mentions that she works at a hospital. You ask if she's a nurse. She turns red and responds that she's a doctor. You

 (a) feel very embarrassed about your social blunder (2 pts.)

 (b) feel amused by the blunder, and/or evaluate the young woman as insecure (0 pts.)

2. Do you spend a lot of time trying to figure out the reasons you've chosen the career you have, why you give money to some people on the street but not others, and generally what your motives are for acting as you do?

 (a) Yes, very much (2 pts.)

 (b) Rarely (0 pts.)

3. When you're buying something at the supermarket, do you like to make small talk with the checker, even if you've never seen him or her before?

 (a) Rarely (2 pts.)

 (b) Often (0 pts.)

4. Do you spend a lot of time trying to figure yourself out?

 (a) Yes, very much (2 pts.)

 (b) No, that's a waste of time (0 pts.)

5. When you're walking down a commercial street, do you look at your reflection in the plate-glass windows of the shops you pass by?

 (a) Yes, frequently (2 pts.)

 (b) No (0 pts.)

(cont'd on next page)

6. Do you think a lot about how you present yourself to others?

(a) Yes (2 pts.)

(b) No, that's not very important to me (0 pts.)

7. Do you spend a lot of time trying to figure out the origins of aspects of your personality or behavior that make you less happy or successful than you otherwise might be?

(a) Yes (2 pts.)

(b) No (0 pts.)

8. Are you often anxious speaking to large groups?

(a) Yes (2 pts.)

(b) No (0 pts.)

9. When you're leaving the house, do you take a look in the mirror before walking out the door?

(a) Yes, usually (2 pts.)

(b) Not normally (0 pts.)

10. Do you often worry about making a good impression on others?

(a) Yes (2 pts.)

(b) No (0 pts.)

11. In new situations, are you often shy or inhibited at first?

(a) Yes, and it takes me a while to overcome it (2 pts.)

(b) No, what's the point? (0 pts.)

12. I'm usually aware of changes in my mood.

(a) Yes (2 pts.)

(b) I don't think so (0 pts.)

(cont'd on next page)

Scoring:

For your **private self-consciousness score** add your point totals for questions 2, 4, 7, and 12.

High: 6–8 pts.
Average: 4 pts.
Low: 0–2 pts.

For your **public self-consciousness score** add your points for questions 5, 6, 9, and 10.

High: 6–8 pts.
Average: 4 pts.
Low: 0–2 pts.

For your **social anxiety score** add your points for questions 1, 3, 8, and 11.

High: 6–8 pts.
Average: 4 pts.
Low: 0–2 pts.

If you're immoral and lazy, you may not be able to blame that on your parents

If there were any part of our mind we'd think was all "nurture" as opposed to "nature," it would be whatever part houses morality and social conscience. The next likely candidate for behavior that is learned rather than inborn might be such executive functions as self-monitoring, planning, and manipulation of oneself and others to achieve some desired goal. However, even these vaunted higher human faculties develop by way of an interaction between environment, in particular nurturing styles of the infant's caregiver, and inborn tendencies. Here's one model that explains how it works.

Individual differences in temperament begin to show themselves at a very young age. Even newborns exhibit different levels of distress, and different degrees of frustration and fear as these emotions emerge during the first few months of development. (In fact, one of the five physiological indicators of shyness is evident even before birth: Children who turn out to be shy have a higher-than-average heart rate in the womb.) At about six months of age, infants learn to approach and interact with their environment in a more positive way—they learn so-called approach-related behavior. Shortly thereafter, infants begin to learn to inhibit their approach-related behavior, to control their interaction with things and people around them through effort of will. This learning process continues through much of childhood and, arguably, beyond.

EEG readings show different baseline levels of activation of the "motivating" and "inhibiting" parts of the frontal lobes of the brains of infants, corresponding to differences in the degree to which they are characterized as "inhibited," "shy," or "anxious." Even though all infants enter a period of "behavioral inhibition" at around the same age (seven months), some infants just seem to be more predisposed than others to view their environment with caution.

Are some temperaments "good," and others "bad"?

From one perspective, it's wrong to view temperament in absolute terms. A given temperament may translate into a well or poorly adjusted individual depending on how well matched that temperament is with the demands and expectations of others—a concept sometimes referred to as "goodness of fit." Different societies place different values on different temperamental profiles, and different occupations or subcultures may reward or punish temperament types at variance with the norms of the dominant culture.

On a developmental level, what this means is that an infant's innate temperamental predisposition will tend to elicit a different response from the mother or caregiver depending on the culture or individual temperament of the mother herself. Distress-prone infants tend to develop different personalities depending on whether their mothers are German or Japanese, since German mothers are more likely to expect their children to deal with emotional challenges on their own.

We can only go so far, however, in our liberal-minded relativism. All humans, regardless of culture, have a negative biological stress-response to the sound of a screeching baby. To a point, this serves a useful purpose, since it elicits attempts to soothe, comfort, and bond. But too much screeching can also cause a mother to avoid or even dislike her baby. Regardless of culture, distress-prone infants whose mothers avoid or dislike them are far more likely to become maladjusted than those whose mothers respond with soothing behavior. The child's future behavior is influenced by the reactions elicited by its inborn temperament, and certain temperaments tend to carry with them inherent risks.

A little anxiety is a good thing...

If a child were somehow unable to learn to inhibit his or her impulses, he or she would have serious problems later in life in almost any culture. While guilt, shame, and anxiety may *seem* to be unhealthy traits in a child, they are in fact helpful in the learning of effortful self-regulation and the acquisition of moral behavior.

If a child has a highly active "anxiety" center in the right frontal lobe, then she may well be quicker to learn this process of self-regulation. She may also, of course, grow up to be a social phobic. It is no coincidence that phobics and obsessive-compulsives tend to be empathetic and highly sensitive to the needs and feelings of others.

On the other hand, if the child has low baseline activation levels of the right-frontal "anxiety" center, and a high threshold for anxiety, guilt, and shame, it seems to be much more difficult for him to develop impulse control, a social conscience, and moral standards of behavior. (The choice of masculine gender for this child, and feminine gender for the overly anxious one, is not arbitrary; boys and girls seem to have a tendency to differ along these lines.)

Again, temperament doesn't determine morality; it just carries with it certain predispositions and risks. A child who is anxious and inhibited by nature won't develop a strong social conscience in the absence of appropriate models in the environment—a caregiver who helps her understand the consequences of her actions, and the reasons why she should or shouldn't do certain things. And even a child with an extraordinarily high threshold for anxiety and guilt can internalize moral standards if the caregiver treats him with patience and understanding, rather than simply punishing, threatening, or ignoring him.

...but too much anxiety is bad

Given the relationship between anxiety or inhibition, and the development not only of morality but also of executive functions of self-regulation, attention, and planning, one might suppose that anxious infants might be more likely to develop into high-achieving adults. It does seem to be true that young children who have a highly developed faculty of effortful self-control perform better scholastically when they get older. On the other hand, children who are *too* anxious may develop an avoidant behavioral style, and may be so preoccupied with monitoring imagined threats that they have difficulty focusing their attention on complex new information.

EXERCISE: Frontal lobe logic

One ability associated with the frontal lobe of the brain is that of holding one option in your mind while you track its sequential entailments. Remembering options is a crucial prerequisite to forecasting the consequences of your actions and planning and manipulating future events.

Part 1.

The CEO of a certain Silicon Valley corporation was faced with a familiar problem of the times: downsizing.

"We have to cut our payroll in half," he explained to his assistant. "But how do I make sure the ones I lay off won't return the favor with an Uzi? There's a lot of that going around, you know."

"No problem," replied the assistant, who knew a thing or two about both logic and human psychology. "Don't lay anyone off. Let them lay themselves off. That way they can't blame you. Just let me handle it."

The assistant invited each employee into her office, one by one. As each employee entered, the assistant explained that she had on her desk two envelopes. One contained a pink slip, while the other contained a contract renewal.

"All you have to do," she would tell each employee with a wink, "is pick the right one."

"How do I know which is which?" the employee would ask.

"Simple. Just read what's written on the envelopes."

The envelopes had the following instructions:

Envelope A

Pick me! I have a contract renewal inside me.

Envelope B

Either I or the other envelope contains a pink slip.

(cont'd on next page)

"Are these instructions true and accurate?" the employee would ask.

"Only one," the assistant would reply.

"Which one?"

"If I told you that," the assistant would answer in an admonishing tone, "then I would be denying you the opportunity to prove your value to the company. If you can't figure it out on your own, then surely you don't deserve a contract renewal."

If you were the employee, which envelope would you choose, and why? (See "Hint," p. 56.)

Part 2.

The next day, the CEO was still not satisfied.

"You've given ten employees a shot at your puzzle, and they've all picked the correct envelope. I don't think you're making it hard enough."

So the assistant agreed to crank it up a notch. Now, she explained to each employee that she had two envelopes; both might contain pink slips, or both might contain contract renewals; or one might contain a pink slip and the other a contract renewal. She presented one of the envelopes with her left hand, and one with her right. If the left-hand envelope contained a contract renewal, the instructions on the envelope would be correct, but if it contained a pink slip, the instructions would be wrong. For the right-hand envelope, if a contract renewal was inside, the instructions would be false; if a pink slip was inside, the instructions would be true.

The envelopes had the following instructions:

Left Envelope   **Right Envelope**

It doesn't make any difference which envelope you pick.

The other envelope has a contract renewal inside.

If you were the employee, which envelope would you choose, and why?

Part 3.

The third day, the CEO was even more agitated.

"Twenty employees have now had a shot at your puzzle, and they've all passed! This is not helping me solve my payroll problem. You have to make the puzzle harder!"

The assistant thought for a moment.

"The remaining employees are all very smart. I don't know whether I can make the puzzle hard enough. And even if one or two should make a mistake, the payroll won't be cut in half. There is, however, one solution I haven't tried yet."

"By all means then, try it. And if it hasn't worked by the close of tomorrow's stockholders' meeting," the CEO added with a threatening glare, "I know of at least one head that will roll!"

At the next day's meeting, the assistant rose to explain the problem to the assembled major shareholders. She concluded her presentation with the following remarks:

"As yet, our payroll is still twice what it should be. The problem is, all the employees so far have been too smart to pick the pink slip. However, the shareholders will observe," she said, gesturing with a pointer to a piechart she had prepared the night before, "that half the payroll is taken by the salary of a single executive."

The CEO blanched.

"If," she continued, "we could find a legitimate way to rectify this situation, then our payroll problems would be instantly solved. I therefore propose to present the hardest puzzle yet to the one who makes the most money: the CEO!"

The assembled shareholders murmured their approval.

Turning to the CEO, the assistant explained as follows:

"I have here, sir, three envelopes."

(cont'd on next page)

"Three envelopes!" exclaimed the CEO. "That's not fair! The others only had to choose between two!"

"True, but you told me to make the puzzle harder. And," the assistant added with a sly wink, "surely you're at least 50% smarter than the rank and file. After all, you earn fifty times as much."

The CEO glared, but held his tongue.

"Of these three envelopes," continued the assistant, "one contains a contract renewal. The others contain pink slips. As usual, each envelope has a statement written on it. No more than one is true. Which envelope do you choose?"

The three envelopes had the following statements:

Envelope A

This envelope has a pink slip.

Envelope B

This envelope has a contract.

Envelope C

Envelope B has a pink slip.

(cont'd on next page)

Which envelope would you choose, and why?

Part 4.

By the end of the meeting, the company's payroll problems were solved and the shareholders went home happy.

The final puzzle: Did the CEO choose the right envelope?

Hint: The shareholders were so pleased with the assistant's solution that they promoted her to the recently vacated CEO position.

 EXERCISE: If-then thinking

Here are five statements:

1. *Only one of these statements is false.*

2. *Only two of these statements are false.*

3. *Only three of these statements are false.*

4. *Only four of these statements are false.*

5. *All five of these statements are false.*

Which, if any, of the statements is true?

"Show me the child at seven and I'll show you the man": a genetic clue to personality

Midwives often claim to be able to predict the temperament of a child as soon as it is out of the birth canal. Those who prefer to believe in the malleability and improvability of human character reject such notions out of hand; personality, they argue, is influenced by environment, not determined by genetics. It turns out that they're both right. New evidence confirms that some aspects of personality—those aspects traditionally referred to as "temperament"—are indeed strongly molded by our genes. Other aspects—what we might call "character"—are more a product of upbringing, environment, and values we choose for ourselves in a self-willed process of emotional maturation. Together, both sets of components contribute to our personality as a whole. (See "If you're immoral and lazy...," p. 51.)

Four inherited "temperaments" and three learned "characters"

One version of this model of personality, developed by Robert Cloninger at Washington University of St. Louis, posits four basic building blocks of temperament, and at least three dimensions of character. The four building blocks of temperament are *novelty seeking, harm avoidance, reward dependence*, and *persistence*. The three character dimensions are *self-directedness, cooperativeness*, and *self-transcendence* (as opposed to self-centeredness). The four temperaments tend to be stable from childhood to adulthood and constant across cultures, while the three character dimensions may change significantly in a manner that appears to be influenced by environmental factors. Overall, based in part on studies of twins, it is estimated that about 50% of what we call personality is genetically determined.

Do you have a "novelty seeking" temperament?

Each of the four temperament variables is associated with different structures in the brain and different brain chemicals. Novelty seeking is modulated by the neurotransmitter dopamine, which is linked to pleasure-seeking behavior. Patients with Parkinson's disease, which is marked by a depletion of dopamine in the brain's basal ganglia, become rigid, stoic, and uninterested in novelty, but remain otherwise unchanged in temperament. People high in novelty-seeking behavior tend to have a higher-than-average tendency to indulge in alcohol, nicotine, and cocaine, which stimulate dopamine transmission in the brain. Harm avoidance is associated with the neurotransmitter serotonin, while reward dependence is modulated by norepinephrine.

Recent research has even identified specific genes which contribute to novelty-seeking behavior and to harm avoidance. The novelty-seeking gene, which encodes the instructions for one of five dopamine receptors in the brain, tends to be longer in individuals who habitually seek the thrill of adventure. They are impulsive, quick to latch onto new ideas, and equally quick to become bored with them, and are impatient with structure and monotony. The harm-avoidance gene, which is involved in serotonin regulation, also comes in two versions, with the more common version predisposing most of us to chronic but mild anxiety—part of the typical human condition. The less common variant—a "natural Prozac," as it were—contributes to an unusually cheerful and outgoing temperament.

Taken one by one, low or high values for the four different temperament variables correspond to different personality traits. (See "Self-Test" on following pages.) Anyone may have high, low, or average values for each.

Each one of these parameters varies independently of the others, and different combinations yield different behavioral tendencies. Someone high in novelty seeking but low in harm avoidance will have a marked risk of self-destructive behavior such as alcohol abuse. High novelty seeking combined with high harm avoidance may give rise to conflicted or neurotic behavior, such as bulimia (binging and purging). In all cases, though, the contribution of "character"—those aspects of personality most strongly influenced by upbringing and environment—is crucial. For example, someone low in reward dependence—say, a nonconformist personally contemptuous of others' opinions—may still be high in cooperativeness and self-transcendence, and thus act with tolerance, respect, and compassion for others, and have high moral principles. Adolf Hitler didn't have bad temperament; he had bad character. Nobody is born evil.

 SELF-TEST: The temperament identifier

High or low levels of the following four different outlooks on life are thought to be built into a person's genes at birth. Most people's temperaments show either high or low tendencies toward more than one of the out-looks. Do you assign the highs and lows to your own temperament the same way someone else does? The description below and charts on the following three pages provide a guide to the high vs. low relationships among the four genetically based temperaments identified by Robert Cloninger.

Novelty Seeking

High: *Thrill-seeking, adventurous, disorderly, intuitive, impatient with structure, impulsive, histrionic, fickle with friendships.*

Low: *Orderly and organized, self-controlled, analytical, detail-oriented, direct, loyal, stoic.*

Harm Avoidance

High: *Anxious, pessimistic, inhibited, given to depression, easily fatigued.*

Low: *Uninhibited, carefree even in the face of imminent risk, confident, optimistic, highly energetic.*

Reward Dependence

High: *Dependent on the emotional support and feedback of others, highly sentimental, sensitive to social cues and the needs of others.*

Low: *Socially detached, content to be alone, nonconformist, cynical, socially insensitive.*

Persistence

High: *Eager, ambitious, determined.*

Low: *Unambitious, uninterested in achievement.*

(cont'd on next page)

High Harm Avoidance

High Novelty Seeking

Excitable
Quick-tempered
Extravagant

Hypothymic
Neurotic
Easily distressed
Conflicted/wavering
Uncertain/indecisive

Cautious, apprehensive

Fatigable, inhibited
Serenity-seeking

Passive
Unassertive
Inactive
Patient
Quiet
Introverted

Stoic
Slow-tempered
Frugal

Low Novelty Seeking

Impulsive
Exploratory
Fickle

Danger-seeking
Aggressive
Competitive
Overactive
Impatient
Talkative
Extraverted

Confident, carefree

Uninhibited, energetic

Hyperthymic
Cheerful
Unwavering/stubborn
Boastful/overconfident

Reflective
Rigid
Loyal

Low Harm Avoidance

(cont'd on next page)

High Novelty Seeking

Reward Dependence

Excitable
Quick-tempered
Extravagant

Attention-seeking
Self-indulgent
Passionate
Insecurely vain/narcissistic
Conflicted/wavering

Ambitious

Sentimental

Authoritarian
Unassertive
Unaffected/candid
Warmly direct
Traditional

Stoic
Slow-tempered
Frugal

Low Novelty Seeking

Impulsive
Exploratory
Fickle

Libertarian
Opportunistic
Skillfully charming
Coolly poised
Talkative

Reflective
Rigid
Loyal

Privacy-seeking
Self-effacing
Dispassionate
Modest
Unimaginative

Detached
Tough-minded

Reward Independence

(cont'd on next page)

Reward Dependence

High Harm Avoidance

Low Harm Avoidance

Reward Independence

Cautious, apprehensive

Fatigable, inhibited

Confident, carefree

Uninhibited, energetic

Sympathetic/warm
Sentimental
Moody

Passive avoidant
Submissive/deferential
Indirectly manipulative
Dependently demanding

Cunning/devious
Ineffectual/reserved
Underachieving
Alienated/cynical

Tough-minded
Detached
Emotionally cool

Ambitious
Industrious
Persistent

Heroic
Persuasive/pushy
Perseverant
Gullible

Oppositional/defiant
Directly controlling
Detached/indifferent
Imperturbable

Unambitious
Self-willed
Practical

Physical exercise helps keep your brain young

People usually think of regular workouts as something they should do to keep their bodies healthy and youthful. Exercise may do that, but it can also play an important role in keeping the brain healthy, and in helping the brain retain a youthful ability to create new neurons and make new connections for learning new things.

Studies have long shown a correlation between level of physical activity in the elderly and retention of mental function, but it hasn't been clear exactly what's causing what. Is the exercise somehow helping the brain to maintain its neurons in good working order, or does physical activity simply correlate with other factors which interact in some other way with mental function, such as level of education, diet, maintenance of a mentally active lifestyle, and so on?

New evidence points to a direct causal relationship. Physical exercise promotes production of a growth factor which plays a critical role in the function and survival of brain neurons. Experimental studies with rats show that the growth factor, brain-derived neurotrophic factor (BDNF), is not only increased with exercise, but may be selectively increased in parts of the brain associated with memory formation and the translation of cognition into action.

Rats like to run 1–2 K's a day (at their own pace)

In the experiment, rats were provided free access to running wheels; since rats seem inherently to enjoy physical activity, they automatically fell into a pattern of running 1-2 kilometers each night, with each rat choosing and consistently maintaining its own preferred activity level. The BDNF messenger RNA in various brain structures of the rats was measured following 0, 2, 4, and 7 nights of free access to the wheel. After two nights BDNF RNA was found to be significantly increased over control levels (i.e., the level before any exercise), and to remain elevated over the full seven-night period. Also, there was a positive correlation between distance run per night and BDNF RNA levels in the hippocampus and caudal neocortex.

One of the most exciting findings of the study is that the greatest effects of exercise on BDNF occur in precisely those highly "plastic," or changeable, areas implicated in degenerative age-related diseases

Exercise increases BDNF levels in the hippocampus, which in turn transports the growth factor to cholinergic neurons of the forebrain—a locus of Alzheimer's and similar age-related degeneration. The authors of the study from which the information in this article is drawn arrived at a finding with a practical application for everyone over 40 years old: *"Exercise-induced upregulation of BDNF could help increase the brain's resistance to damage and degeneration through BDNF's support of neuronal growth, function, and survival."*

As you age, physical debility is no more inevitable than mental dementia

Growth factors like BDNF are one of a class of chemicals called neurotrophic factors that the brain uses to keep its cells alive and healthy. Young brains are awash with growth factors, which act like neural nannies to nourish brain cells and help them behave properly—for example, make the right kinds of connections with other brain cells.

Grown-up brains have growth factors, too, but in smaller quantities. Growth factors continue to nourish and maintain brain cells, and to help the brain form new connections as it learns new things, but not at the same explosive rate as in a young brain. That's probably one reason older brains recover from injury more slowly, and less completely, than young brains.

Neuroscientists are discovering more about the special powers of neurotrophic factors at a rapid rate. Stem cell researchers have identified them as the chemicals that switch on the genes in newly-generated cells to help them turn into the appropriate kind of specialized cell in the right part of the body—blood, liver, skin, or brain, for example.

Your brain uses new brain cells to make new memories

Until just a few years ago, neuroscientists believed that the adult brain lost its ability to regenerate brain cells, a process known as neurogenesis. It now turns out that the conventional wisdom was wrong. Adult brains do produce new neurons, at least in the hippocampus. In fact, there's evidence that new memories are formed by generating brand-new brain cells, rather than just by reconfiguring old ones. Since the hippocampus is a brain structure so important for learning and memory, that seems like a good place for the brain to be able to renew itself.

The brain performs this remarkable feat of self-renewal by drawing on its supply of neural stem cells (sometimes also called progenitor cells). Those stem cells have the ability to become any of several types of brain cell, including neurons as well as other cells that help to nourish and protect the neurons. (See "New hope for those at risk...p. 133.)

How to help your brain retain its youthful learning curve

Recent experiments have also shown that physical exercise can have the effect of doubling the rate at which the brain creates new specialized brain cells from its stem cells. So what exercise helps the brain to do is, essentially, stay youthful. It increases the number of those neural nannies so important for nurturing and protecting brain cells. It also makes an old brain act more like a young one in its ability to generate new neurons of the type needed for learning and remembering new things.

Apparently an active life *and* attitude are common among humans who have lived to unusual ages

The following is a selective list of people who have lived long. Some of them are known primarily for other achievements. The fact that those people excelled suggests that they pursued the interests from which they took personal satisfaction and that they invested their energies in those interests aggressively and constantly through their lives. For example:

- *Red Grange, a famous football player and superb athlete, lived to the age of 87.*

- *Pablo Picasso, the Spanish painter and sculptor, worked in his studio up to the age of 91.*

- *Grandma Moses taught herself to paint quite late in life and continued until her death at 101.*

- *Gabriel Erazo claimed to have worked in his garden every day until his death at 130.*

- *Gabriel Sánchez, who farmed for 120 years, died at 135.*

- *Zabo Agah lived more years than any of the above, and for 100 of his years he worked as a porter.*

   EXERCISE: On the fastest track

The 100-meter run in the Olympics is a thrill to watch. It is over in seconds and requires a young lifetime of unremitting training and constant physical conditioning. Over the last 100 years the time it takes to run 100 meters has steadily decreased by about 20%.

Examine the two columns below. One shows the dates of Olympic 100-meter races. The other shows the winning times, but their order is incorrect. After you have matched the times with the dates—an easy task—you will see that it took 54 years, between 1906 and 1960, to shave one second off the winning time. Assuming that same rate of improvement from the '84 Olympics, which broke ten seconds for the first time, in what year can we expect to see 100 meters run in less than nine seconds?

OLYMPIC YEARS	WINNING TIMES
1. 1896	A. 10.30 Seconds
2. 1906	B. 11.20 Seconds
3. 1920	C. 9.99 Seconds
4. 1932	D. 10.80 Seconds
5. 1960	E. 10.20 Seconds
6. 1984	F. 12.00 Seconds

memory
function

MEMORY

Memory is a partner in developing all other mental skills. The key to learning is the brain's ability to convert a current experience into code and store it so, later, the experience can be recalled for your benefit. The brain codes some kinds of inputs from the senses permanently with no conscious effort on your part. It can also store other kinds of data because you consciously pass that data through a rehearsal loop repeatedly—which, incidentally, can also take place during sleep.

The brain codes some kinds of experiences indelibly, instantly, and without any conscious effort. It reads that kind of experience as so closely linked to raw survival that your conscious mind has to stand aside so instincts, which trigger emotions, can take over. Other, less crucial data earns permanent storage for its code by passing that experience through a rehearsal loop again and again. There is some evidence that is what dreams do. During sleep, while the cortex isn't busy sorting out data coming in through the senses, it can rehearse bits of recent experience to help them become permanent memories. Remember the multiplication tables?

And so, the more experiences the brain is exposed to, the more its cells send out branches from their axons and dendrites to link those cells with as many other cells as possible to help solve current problems. The more links that are available, the easier the brain can spot similarities between parts of a new experience and old experiences it already knows about. That way, the brain doesn't have to create all new codes to store the new experience — only the unfamiliar parts of it. Apparently it's true that the more you know, the easier it is to learn even more.

But first you must pay attention. If you don't focus your attention on new experiences they can never make it into memory. Fortunately, to life-threatening experiences, the brain pays close attention automatically without our having to focus consciously at all. It pays such close attention that when it thinks it has a crisis on its hands, it ignores anything else going on. That may explain why self-conscious people have difficulty noticing the forest around their own tree, so to speak. However, when you use your short-term memory system to recall someone's name so you can say "good night" after a party, for example, you have to make an effort. Even when you look up a phone number just to dial it right away, you must concentrate to fix it in immediate memory even if you needn't rehearse it consciously.

These are the three kinds of memory: Immediate, such as remembering only the next step in a current process such as, in knitting, "purl 3"; Short-term, such as recalling what you had for lunch yesterday; Working, which is data coded, sometimes unconsciously, so you can call it up anytime. The meaning of a word is a good example.

The exercises in this chapter help develop memory skills in two ways: First, they will force you to concentrate, which builds mental stamina. Second, they introduce so many different kinds of data—math, verbal, spatial, logic, etc.—that some of it is bound to be new to you. That new data and, more important, experience with how to organize data so you can locate a solution, will build links among your brain cells that, later, can help you learn new data and find a pattern to cope with it.

Your "memory" is, in fact, many processes that occur in different parts of the brain

An injury to one part of the brain may affect the conscious recall of facts and events (declarative memory), while leaving intact various forms of unconscious (nondeclarative) memory, including skill and habit learning. It is even possible to show that someone with apparently complete amnesia for pictures shown to him only minutes earlier may nevertheless retain an accurate memory of them, as demonstrated by a tendency to pick out those same pictures from among other ones on a repeat showing. Part of the brain has registered and stored the images, even though another part of the brain can't bring that knowledge to conscious awareness. Recent studies have shown that a structure responsible for retrieving memories is the part of the medial temporal lobe called the hippocampus, which acts to bring together widely distributed sites in the brain in the formation of a conscious memory.

The brain stores the components of a personal experience near the senses that registered the event

Memories themselves—as opposed to the structures that retrieve them—seem often to be localized, with some redundancy, in the very same regions where the sensory perception of the related stimulus first occurred. The neurologist Oliver

When the senses pick up impressions from the outside world, those inputs travel along neural pathways from the organ that took in the data to the section of the brain that interprets input from the eyes, or ears or nose or skin. From there the information is normally shunted to the hippocampus for short-term storage—a matter of weeks, usually. If the data seems to be important somehow—often because it is consciously rehearsed—the hippocampus sends code for the various aspects of that memory to the part of the cortex that specializes in each aspect. For example, codes to recognize a face, or to attach a

The hippocampus routes, retrieves and sometimes stores data picked up by the senses.

use to a tool, to reconstruct a musical phrase or to visualize a familiar street are aspects that would be stored at different spots in the cortex. If that spot is damaged, the ability to recall that aspect is lost.

Sacks describes a painter who suffered neurological damage to the visual cortex, which robbed him not only of the ability to perceive color, but of any memory of color whatsoever.

The distinction between explicit, declarative memory and implicit, nondeclarative memory can also be illustrated with an experience familiar to all of us. We've all had what is called "infantile amnesia"—the inability to recall events that happened before our third year of life. Obviously, we do remember things as infants—we learn to recognize faces and voices, we learn to perform certain tasks—but we somehow can't remember learning these things, nor can we recall any events at all from before about age two. Apparently, events experienced before the development of the brain system supporting declarative memory can't be consciously retrieved even after that system has developed.

SELF-TEST: Nondeclarative memory

Notice this display of five playing card designs.
Don't look at the other page until you've
finished reading the text on this page.

(cont'd on next page)

Don't look at the preceding page where these five cards are shown face-up.

Try to remember which of these five cards shown face-down would reveal the same design, if you turned it over, as the one shown below them. Follow your instinct. Very likely you stored a "nondeclarative" memory (which means you know it but cannot say it because you don't know you know it) of the image of those cards face-up when you first saw them on the preceding page.

You may not know why you retain visual memories for a while rather than erase them immediately, but you do. That may be why instinctive trust in the accuracy of the "mind's eye" works in this test. (But not always. The brain can persuade itself that it experienced something it did not if it has a reason to believe the fantasy can better protect the body the brain loyally serves. This can happen, for example, when you unconsciously incorporate a false image into your memory in response to the suggestion of another person in order to avoid invoking their ire.)

EXERCISE: Card senses

Rearrange these 16 playing cards so that no 2 of the same value or the same suit are in the same row either vertically, horizontally or diagonally. The small white boxes in the lower right corner of each space allow you to write in the initials (JH for jack of hearts, QS for queen of spades, etc.). If you prefer, lay out cards the same way as shown below, using your own deck of playing cards.

This exercise uses short-term memory skills and builds concentration because you must hold certain possible locations in memory while testing other possibilities in your mind's eye. About five minutes is a reasonable norm for completing the task. A "Hint" appears below to get you started on the right track, if you need a little help.

Hint: Put these cards in the four corners: ace of spades in the upper left, jack of clubs lower left, king of diamonds upper right, queen of hearts lower right.

Imagine a memory-enhancing drug that would make you remember EVERYTHING the first time it happens. Would you want to take that drug?

While it is an old truism that practice makes perfect—that repeated practice and rehearsal aid in the long-term memory of a skill or knowledge—it is also true that, sometimes, a single salient event is seared permanently into memory because that event has triggered an emotional response. Recent advances in the understanding of the molecular underpinnings of long-term memory shed light on this apparent paradox and even suggest ways we might manipulate our powers of learning through "smart" drugs.

In memory formation, the brain works at two levels, *immediate* recognition of an event, and long-term memory retention. The formation of those long-term memories involves a process of protein synthesis. (See the "Research" box on page 80 for more details on how this affects your ability to learn and retain information you want to remember.)

The fly that at 12:41:06 p.m. passed through the right extreme of your field of vision. This event had no emotional impact. Your brain secreted a chemical that prevented you from remembering that you even saw it, much less what it looked like.

If you think about it, you are subjected to millions of individual data bytes that your senses pick up even in an "uneventful" day. Don't blame your senses. They are just trying to protect you by keeping your eyes, ears, nose, mouth and skin open. But how does your brain decide which of these data bytes are worth remembering, and which aren't?

The reason you can remember some things the first time is linked to forgetting everything else

With most events, the brain processes the information, allowing you to cope with that information as it is occurring. If your brain perceives the event as affecting your ability to survive—in whatever ways you have defined survival for your-self, from charging mastodons to your boss's refusal to reply to your cheery "Good morning!" greeting—your brain kicks in with a mechanism that transmits action messages to the rest of your body. Because it sees the situation as a kind of crisis, these *emotion-driven* responses cause the event to be stored for future reference (see "What is the brain so busy doing...," p. 177).

However, if an event like a fly buzzing off packs no danger-wallop, you forget it. Current research suggests that the same mechanism that codes an event as a crisis also erases most other events to prevent overload. But, how can you overrule your brain's decision about what's worth remembering? What if you *want* to learn something that's not emotionally charged?

How can I erase the eraser?
Try repetition. Maybe that can make your brain "change its mind," so to speak. Maybe your brain will say to itself, "This person I am trying to protect seems to be paying a lot of attention to an 'event' that my early programming didn't equip me to recognize as a 'crisis' worth remembering. But I am nothing if I can't adapt to protect the boss, so OK, 2 + 2 = 4. I'll store this event away also since it seems to be so important it keeps coming up."

Do I really want this drug?
Recent experimental work hints at another way we might one day be able to outsmart our brain's gatekeeper. The brain mechanism responsible for preventing events from being encoded in long-term memory can be temporarily switched off by administration of an antiserum. Thus far, this "CREB

EXERCISE: Word Overlapping

Directions: Just as one word leads to another, words lead into each other, or overlap. If you start in slot #1 with the right word, you should have little trouble completing the circle with 9 additional overlapping words. Each word starts in a numbered slot that corresponds to the number of the clue.

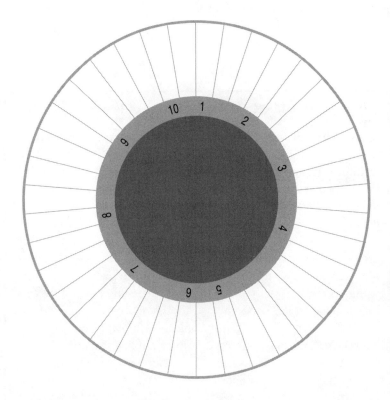

1. Collette wrote with one
2. Rubeola
3. Brain injury
4. New York neighbor
5. _____ up (admit)

6. Brain cell
7. Beginning
8. Teapot brouhaha
9. Mark of disgrace
10. Traveler's aid

HINT: #9 is stigma.   HINT 2: #2: causes quarantines

cocktail" (see the "Research" box below and the diagrams on pp. 81-82) has only been served to white mice and sea slugs. The implications, however, are tantalizing: imagine memorizing any facts you want—quickly, automatically, and without so much as an ounce of self-discipline. On the other hand, think about this: would you really want to take a "smart" drug that wreaks havoc on the brain's tried-and-true system for separating life-essential experiences from inconsequential trivia?

THE RESEARCH—The chemistry of learning

It has been known for some time that the formation of long-term memories requires protein synthesis, perhaps because a permanent alteration in nerve dendrites is involved so that future transmission across a synapse is enhanced. Cyclic AMP (cAMP), a gene regulator within the cells, and a protein called CREB, which responds to cAMP, appear to be involved in the cellular basis of this process. CREB also has a repressor version, which has the opposite effect of the protein-synthesis-stimulator version. Normally, a single training episode releases both the stimulator CREB and its repressor twin; the function of the repressor version of CREB may be to hinder over-memorization of unnecessary details encountered only once.

However, the repressor version deactivates more quickly than the stimulator version, so repeated training or encounters interspersed with rest intervals result in an overall accumulation of stimulator CREB and maximally effective learning. When the repressor version is experimentally blocked by an antiserum, equivalent long-term memory formation occurs after a single training session.

Normally, lasting long-term memories following a single event occur only when that event is particularly emotionally charged. This may occur because the same systems in the brain which mediate the processing of emotional stimuli may also inhibit that repressor version of CREB.

"To store it or ignore it": that is the question that CREB responds to.

1. Child sees scary tiger, which sends impulses racing from eyes through nerve cells in brain.

2. Inside nucleus of cells the CREB action molecules push aside the "forget-it" CREB.

3. Action CREB flips switch on DNA, which tells its genes to spit out protein molecules.

4. Proteins rush down dendrites of nerve cells to strengthen and lengthen them so the next time she sees a tiger she'll get the picture right away and RUN!

(cont'd on next page)

However, if the child experiences something not worth noticing, the "forget-it" CREB molecule routinely hits the "OFF" button. No switch, no proteins, the dendrite backs away limp.

1. Mother calls, "Time to turn off the TV, dear." Sound sends impulse racing from ears through nerve cells in brain.

2. Inside nucleus of brain cell the "forget-it" CREB routinely flicks the OFF switch—as it always does unless an experience is emotional or the person consciously repeats an experience to memorize it.

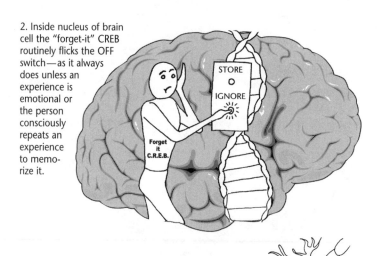

3. No proteins are released to strengthen connections between cells. Child forgets what mother just said because experience had no emotional impact to deactivate the "forget-it" CREB.

Moral: If you need to learn a lot about something, you can replicate the memory-enhancing effect of emotional arousal by working in repeated practice sessions interspersed with periods of rest. This way, your "action" CREB molecules rise to the point that they outnumber the "forget-it" CREB.

You can still use some kinds of knowledge even if you don't know you have them

Imagine the following scenario:

A patient with amnesia is shown a list of words. Within minutes he is unable to remember not only any of the words on the list but even the fact that he has been shown a list at all. And yet, when asked to do an exercise in which his memory is primed—such as filling in blanks with the most appropriate words—an amnesic patient so frequently uses the same words from the earlier list he saw that it is impossible to conclude that he does not somehow remember them.

This kind of experiment shows that the normal, conscious recollection of facts and events—called declarative or explicit memory—is a quite different thing from unconscious, implicit, nondeclarative memory. Explicit memory tasks usually require the participation of implicit memory, but damage to the medial temporal or diencephalic regions of the brain may cause a loss of explicit memory while leaving implicit memory intact.

The Man Who Mistook His Wife for a Hat by Oliver Sacks contains a case history of a patient suffering from an extreme form of prosopagnosia.

A similar kind of unconscious memory has been shown to occur in patients exhibiting what has been called "blindsight." Such patients, who have suffered damage to the visual cortex, are blind in the straightforward sense that they are completely unaware of being able to see anything. For example, if shown a bright light in their right visual field, they will report having seen nothing at all. However, when pressed to *guess* where a light *might* have been shown, these patients will indicate the correct area with well above chance frequency, and sometimes nearly perfectly.

People who can't recognize familiar faces

Other parallel findings come from the study of patients with prosopagnosia, an impaired ability to recognize familiar faces. When they are shown pictures of faces of famous and unknown people they say they don't recognize any of them. Surprisingly, though, they are just like normal people in coming to a quicker evaluation of whether two simultaneously presented faces are the same or different when the faces are famous compared to when they are not.

Research shows practice and tricks improve explicit memory

All of these pathologies represent extreme forms of the memory lapses everyone suffers from. Even without damage to any part of the brain, we all have different degrees of skill in consciously recording and accessing knowledge and perception. The ability of human brains to consciously retrieve knowledge from memory evolved relatively recently and is still imperfect. But those declarative memory skills—first, the learning of new material, and second, the retrieval of it—appear to be improvable with practice.

 SELF-TEST: Retrieval of implicit knowledge

This simple test will show you just how difficult it can be to retrieve knowledge even if we are intimately familiar with it from daily experience reinforced over many years. Try to answer these questions:

1) On a traffic signal light, which color is at the top, red or green?

2) Try to visualize a telephone keyboard. Sketch the configuration of all the numbers, plus the star and the pound sign.

3) On the spine of a book, is the title rightside up or upside down when the book is laid face-up? (Hint: American and British books have different conventions.)

4) What are the highest and lowest numbers on your oven dial?

5) On a penny, which direction is Abraham Lincoln facing?

6) Of all the former statesmen on the bills between $1 and $100, two are non-presidents. Name them. Next, name all the former presidents on the other bills. (Hint: One was ambassador to France, the other Secretary of the Treasury.)

7) We all know how many stars there are on the U.S. flag. But how many rows are they arranged into, and how many stars are in each row? Next, how many of each of the red and white stripes are there, and which color is the top-most stripe?

SELF-TEST: How to remember people's names

Learning personal names is an ability which appears to vary considerably across individuals, and forgetting names is the most frequent memory complaint among the elderly. Even poor name memorizers, however, can overcome this deficit through the use of simple mnemonic tricks based on an understanding that when information is encoded in a personally meaningful way (which is sometimes referred to as the memorization being more *elaborated*), the memory is more likely to be enhanced.

A. Roundy

C. Bins

A. Miller

J. Richardson

For each of the following face-name pairings:
1) Identify a prominent facial feature.
2) Transform the person's name into a concrete, visually vivid object.
3) Mentally picture the facial feature combined with the transformed name-object.

(Examples: A man with long hair named O'Brien; transform "O'Brien" to "lion," and visualize a lion's mane emerging from his head. A woman with heavy eyebrows named Crocker; transform "Crocker" to "cracker," and visualize a cracker on her eyebrows.) This technique can be further strengthened by performing the final step of making an emotional judgment of the pleasantness or unpleasantness of the image association.

EXERCISE: Memory terms

Work this exercise in the same way as a crossword puzzle. In this case it tests recall of seven key words related to memory. All seven have been used and defined in the preceding article.

ACROSS

3. Inability to recall past events

7. Inability to recognize familiar faces

DOWN

1. Ability of neurologically blind people to correctly identify objects shown to them

2. Adjectival form of "memory"

4. The normal, conscious kind of memory for past events

5. A non-declarative kind of memory one is not aware of having

6. A way to help recall by supplying clues to questions or blanks to fill in

Hint: Seven Across is "prosopagnosia."

A major cause of forgetting

If you've ever been to a movie double feature, you know that you'll have a hard time remembering the plot and details of the first movie immediately after seeing the second. This can't be explained by the greater amount of time since viewing the first—in fact, your memory of the second movie remains stronger a couple of hours later.

This phenomenon is called *retroactive inhibition* or *interference*, and it has been demonstrated to apply to a wide variety of learning and memory tasks, with greater similarity between the first and second task correlating with a greater degree of forgetting. Knowledge of this phenomenon has led to a view of interference of one body of material with previously-learned material as a fundamental cause of forgetting.

Another kind of forgetting that's not your fault either

Interference also works the other way. If, say, two lists of words are memorized in succession, retention of the second list will be worse than if only one list were memorized. This is called *proactive inhibition*.

"I forgot... again!"

Retroactive inhibition has one rather bizarre aspect: it actually *fades* with time. Experiments have shown that the apparently extinguished memory of the first of two tasks will undergo a spontaneous recovery over a 24-hour period. As memory of the first task recovers, it will interfere with memory of the second, and vice-versa, until the amount of forgetting produced by proactive inhibition will be about as great as that caused by retroactive.

Could these two naturally-occurring causes help explain why people approaching middle-age think their memories are failing when they are only having to deal with greater amounts of data in their work and personal lives?

SELF-TEST: Retroactive inhibition

Study the **(A)** word-pairs for five minutes. Then cover them with a piece of paper and look at the list at the bottom of the page, which includes all the first words of the pairs below, arranged in a different order.

Keeping list **(A)** covered, write down each word's matching half from memory as best you can. After writing down as many items as you can remember, uncover the list and note the number correct. Repeat with a fresh piece of paper. Continue until you've memorized all the pairs.

(A) BUG — ONION   BASEBALL — LOCK
WATER — ZEBRA   PAINT — MINT
PAPER — LAMP   GUM — CLOCK
TONGUE — CAR   FAN — CANDLE
HOUSE — SUN   COLLAR — BEE

COLLAR —   FAN —
PAINT —   GUM —
WATER —   PAPER —
BUG —   HOUSE —
TONGUE —   BASEBALL —

Next, study and memorize the **(B)** list of word-pairs. This list matches a different right-hand column of words to the first list's left-hand column. If it takes you longer than it took to learn the first, this is due to proactive inhibition.

(B) BUG — GLOVE   BASEBALL — BELL
WATER — POSTCARD   PAINT — ROCK
PAPER — PHONE   GUM — SHINGLE
TONGUE — BOX   AN — BEACH
HOUSE — MASK   COLLAR — FIRE

Once you've memorized the second list, re-test yourself on the first list of pairs. If you can't remember those first pairs, what you're experiencing is the effect of retroactive inhibition.

Finally, wait one day and re-test yourself. If you come up with a mix of the first and second lists' pairs, this is due to a spontaneous recovery of the details of the first memorization task, which will inhibit, but in return be inhibited by, the details of the second. On average, this will result in a wash: you'll forget (or remember) the details of the two lists more or less equally.

What your eyes reveal about how hard you're thinking: LEMs and pupil size

Have you ever wondered why people often look away when they're answering a question? Or why do they sometimes look right, other times left?

One theory is that different kinds of thinking trigger lateral eye movements (LEMs), when activity in one of the brain hemispheres spread into the "eye fields" on that side of the brain. The eye field on the right side of the brain is linked to the left field of vision, and controls eye movement to the left, while the left-brain eye field connects to the right field of vision and controls rightward LEMs.

To come up with the right word, look up to the right

Some psychologists have proposed that "left-brain" thinking, such as trying to remember the meaning of a word might trigger a rightward LEM. Similarly, a "right-brain" task, such as visualizing the layout of the rooms in a house, might make people look to the left. Be careful, though; if you ask someone "How are you related to your father's sister's son?" they will usually look to the left, even though they will answer with a word ("cousin"). It is a right-brain task because they are following a path of relationships in their mind's eye. They can remember the word "cousin," a left-brain task, perfectly easily.

Harder questions are more likely to result in LEMs, whether rightward or leftward, because LEMs reflect the question's difficulty. Why?...to block out distractions. It is hard to do two things at once, such as to concentrate on a book if someone's talking. Averting your gaze allows you to cut yourself off from a particularly attention-getting and distracting environmental stimulus—the questioner's face—in order to focus on the answer. If something prevents you from averting your gaze, you'll have a harder time answering a question.

You can test the idea that more difficult questions are more likely to trigger LEMs by asking someone the questions on the next page. They increase in difficulty, making it more and more likely that people trying to answer them will look to the side while thinking. Notice the size of their pupils, too: the harder the question, the larger the pupils become.

SELF-TEST: Memory Test

Psychologists at the University of Washington and University of California, Irvine, compiled a list of general-knowledge questions and posed them to their undergraduate students in order to get an idea about how a person with a "normal" memory would perform on this memory task, so that the questions could be used to test other people's memory. These questions start out easy, but get harder as you go along. The number next to each answer shows the percent of college students who answered that question correctly. If you can answer more than 20, that puts you in the top third of the sample of college students the questions were tested on.

What's the name of the:

1. Comic strip character who eats spinach to increase his strength?
2. Bothers who flew the first airplane at Kitty Hawk, North Carolina?
3. Crime of purposely setting a building or property on fire?
4. Dorothy's dog in "The Wizard of Oz"?
5. Man who rode horseback in 1775 to warn that the British were coming?
6. Last name of the famous magician and escape artist who died of appendicitis?
7. Thick layer of fat on a whale?
8. Sport in which riders on horseback hit a ball with their mallets?
9. Largest desert on earth?
10. Italian city known for its canals?
11. Mythical Island-City said to have sunk into the ocean?
12. Small Japanese barbecue used for outdoor cooking?
13. One-eyed giant in Greek mythology?
14. Last name of the general who lost the battle of Little Bighorn?
15. Chapel in Rome whose ceiling was painted by Michelangelo?
16. Unit of measure referring to a six-foot depth of water?
17. Woman who began the profession of nursing?
18. Quick-reflexed animal that attacks cobras?
19. Roy Rogers' horse?
20. Last name of the author of "1984"?
21. Roman emperor who supposedly fiddled while Rome burned?
22. Poison Socrates drank when he was executed?
23. Alexander Graham Bell's assistant?
24. German who began the Protestant Reformation?
25. King Arthur's sword?
26. Ship on which Charles Darwin made his famous voyage to the Galapagos?
27. Capital of Finland?
28. Mountain range separating Asia from Europe?
29. First person to run the mile in under four minutes?
30. Cuban leader overthrown by Castro?
31. Artist who painted "American Gothic"?
32. Town through which Lady Godiva supposedly made her famous naked ride?
33. Highest mountain in South America?

If you want to remember complex data, visualize it—geniuses do

Those rare wizards with incredible memories or prodigious powers of mental calculation have something to tell us about how to use our brains more effectively. Their seemingly super-human skill—acquired through training or compensation for some cognitive disability—may be useless as a practical matter. If we can write things down and if we have access to mechanical calculators and computer databases, why do we need to do all this in our head? Still, such geniuses will always retain a certain fascination even if some of their most remarkable abilities lose their practical value. Who among us wouldn't love to know just how they do what they do—and, perhaps, even learn how to do it ourselves?

Great memorizers often perform their feats by having a special knack—either by gift or hard practice—of translating information into a *visual* mode. British mnemonist Leslie Waugh set up a real-life filing cabinet for all the major sporting events spanning the previous half-century, which he then internalized in his mind's eye. When asked a question about the date of an event or about events that had occurred on a given date, he would picture himself thumbing through the files and then opening one to find the requested information.

The right and left lobes of the brain transmit instructions and process data to and from the opposite sides of the body.

To an extent, Waugh's feat seems within the grasp of most of us. For example, we all presumably have a memory of the layout of our house, and even of a previously lived-in house, which allows us to mentally walk through room by room visually inspecting things as we go. Under the right circumstances—under hypnosis or in a dream perhaps—these recollections are so rich and detailed that we can almost literally touch, smell and stumble over the objects as we perform our mental virtual-reality tour.

In such a case, we've visually internalized information in a manner which almost seems to go beyond memorization. The neurologist Oliver Sacks relates the story of a man with right-hemisphere damage rendering him blind in his left visual field. This affected his visual *memories* just as strongly as his vision: when asked to recall the landmarks in a familiar city square by imagining entering the square from the south end, he could recall nothing on the square's west (left) edge. When asked to imagine entering from the north, his recall of the shops on the west edge returned in full clarity, and it was the east edge that became a complete blank.

The trick is, however, to internalize the sort of information Waugh does at will, in the degree of detail he does, and to recall it whenever we like. This, presumably, is more than just a matter of practice.

"S," a patient of A.R. Luria's, had the keenest memory of all. But the fact that he could not ignore any data often overwhelmed him

"S," the man whose memory the great Russian psychologist A.R. Luria described as "one of the keenest the literature on the subject has ever described," had such overwhelmingly clear and powerful images of visual and auditory stimuli that this almost superhuman ability, which lay at the basis of his seemingly inexhaustible memory, also became something of a handicap. Despite his unsurpassed mnemonic brilliance, he often conveyed the impression of being muddled and dull-witted, since his visual images had nothing to do with the plot or structure of what he was being told, only with individual words or sounds. The result was utter confusion: "No," he would say. "This is too much. Each word calls up images; they collide with one another, and the result is chaos. I can't make anything out of this." S's problem was the opposite of what most of us face: the challenge for him was reining in these images, and learning procedures (such as writing phone numbers down on a piece of paper, which he then burned) for forgetting information he didn't want to retain.

The amazing linguist and calculator Hans Eberstark remembers both words and numbers by the sounds they make

Austrian-born simultaneous interpreter Hans Eberstark has a genius for both languages and numbers, in a manner which makes the two abilities seem intimately related. Once he registers in memory the sound and meaning of any word in any language—that *duk'as* means "abalone" in Kashaya Pomo, for example—he never forgets it.

Eberstark is also a phenomenal mental calculator and number memorizer. A crucial feature of his personal technique is to translate numbers into "words" in a language of his own invention. The words are based on sounds that the numbers' images might suggest—for example, the number seven is an L, since it looks like an L upside-down. Numbers in sequence then become a string of sounds. With this straightforward and completely automatic translation from the domain of numbers into the domain of sound (like dialing a touch-tone phone), combined with his photographic auditory memory, Eberstark is able to memorize pi to over 10,000 places!

Alexander Aitken committed data to memory with incredible speed and accuracy by noticing how new data is somehow related to other data already in memory

The great mathematician, mental calculator, and all-around genius Alexander Craig Aitken also relied on an "auditory-rhythmic memory" of numbers, but in addition had a gift for imbuing even the most arbitrary-seeming data with rich relationships to other facts and patterns in his vast mnemonic store. Thus, he described his associations with the number 7 in terms far richer than a simple visual or auditory image:

> The line of poetry "They passed the Pleiades and the planets seven"—mysteries in the minds of the ancients—Sabbath or the seventh day—religious observance of Sunday—7 in contrast with 13 and with 3 in superstition—7 as a recurring decimal .142857 which, multiplied by 123456, gives the same numbers in cyclic order—a poem on numbers by Binyon, seen in a review lately—I could quote from it. (Hunter 1977:163)

As Ian Hunter put it in a biographical essay:

> It is clearly misleading to draw a firm line around certain of Aitken's activities, call them "memory," view them as an

isolated "faculty," and attempt to understand them without going outside the circle we have drawn. Aitken's memory was one aspect of an immensely complex, many-sided, highly-integrated system of mutually supporting activities cumulatively developed over the years. (Hunter 1977:159)

Doing what comes naturally

For geniuses such as Eberstark or Aitken, their gifts seem so natural that they believe anyone can accomplish the same feats with a little practice. Of course, this would only be true if we possessed the same sorts of minds such prodigies take for granted. Could you learn to perform mental calculations as quickly and flawlessly as Aitken? For example, could you learn to multiply 2 three-digit numbers—say, 123 by 456—in two seconds? We return to Aitken's own remarkably self-aware account of his method in a passage from another of Hunter's biographical pieces, and you can decide for yourself:

I do this in two moves: I see at once that 123 times 45 is 5535 and that 123 times 6 is 738; I hardly have to think. Then 55350 plus 738 gives 56088. Even at the moment of registering 56088, I have checked it by dividing by 8, so 7011, and this by 9,779. I recognize 779 as 41 by 19; and 41 by 3 is 123, 19 by 24 is 456. A check you see; and it passes by in about one second. (Hunter 1978:341)

Strategies for passing the mail carrier exam

Try your hand at the mail carrier exam on the next page. Unless you have a photographic memory, you'd flunk this test without the assistance of some mnemonic technique or other. In fact, people who do well on this invariably avail themselves of tricks of visual association. They devise straightforward methods for translating numbers and meaningless names into familiar concrete images. (See "Hint" on page 96.) In this way, with a little practice, anyone of average intelligence can ace the test.

SELF-TEST: Could you be a mail carrier?

Memorizing tricks, useless though they may sometimes seem, do have their practical applications. If you want to become a U.S. Postal Service clerk, carrier, or letter-sorting machine operator, you first have to pass a memorization test, just like the one here. Take a look at it. Try your hand at it if you like. (Good luck!) Once you're feeling nice and humble, read the "Hint" following the exam to see how the people who pass it actually do it.

Directions: Each of the five boxes labeled A-E below has three sets of number sequences associated with street names, and two unnumbered names. You have five minutes to memorize which number sequences and names are associated with which box.

A	B	C	D	E
2900-3299 College	2000-2099 College	6100-7299 College	4100-4899 College	1300-1599 College
Wellmann	Shike	Kaytron	Britt	Farne
8500-9199 Bancroft	3200-3399 Bancroft	9900-9999 Bancroft	2400-2899 Bancroft	4300-4399 Bancroft
Sextor	Dandle	Remy	Funt	Perl
5300-5399 Addison	7200-8499 Addison	6300-6799 Addison	5800-6099 Addison	4500-4799 Addison

After five minutes, cover the boxes. You're not allowed to refer back to them. Working from memory, as quickly and accurately as you can, write the box letter beside each of the addresses below. You have five minutes.

1. 2000-2099 College
2. 7200-8499 Addison
3. Sextor
4. 5800-6099 Addison
5. 4300-4399 Bancroft
6. Funt
7. 2900-3299 College
8. 6300-6799 Addison
9. 8500-9199 Bancroft
10. Kaytron
11. Farne
12. 9900-9999 Bancroft
13. 1300-1599 College
14. 7200-8499 Addison
15. Wellmann
16. 2400-2899 Bancroft
17. Britt
18. 6100-7299 College
19. 6300-6799 Addison
20. Dandle
21. Shike
22. 4100-4899 College
23. 3200-3399 Bancroft
24. 4300-4399 Bancroft
25. 5300-5399 Addison
26. Remy
27. Perl
28. 1300-1599 College
29. Farne
30. 2900-3299 College
31. 2400-2899 Bancroft
32. Wellmann
33. 1300-1599 College
34. 9900-9999 Bancroft
35. Dandle
36. 6300-6799 Addison

(cont'd on next page)

37. 7200-8499 Addison	45. Kaytron	53. Wellmann
38. 1300-1599 College	46. Sextor	54. Remy
39. 6100-7299 College	47. 2900-3299 College	55. 4100-4899 College
40. 3200-3399 Bancroft	48. 4300-4399 Bancroft	56. 8500-9199 Bancroft
41. Shike	49. 2400-2899 Bancroft	57. Funt
42. 4500-4799 Addison	50. 1300-1599 College	58. 4500-4799 Addison
43. 5800-6099 Addison	51. 9900-9999 Bancroft	59. 4300-4399 Bancroft
44. Perl	52. 7200-8499 Addison	

Hint: Try visualization tricks like these. Note first that no number sequence is re-used for more than one street or lettered box, so you don't have to bother with memorizing the end of a number sequence or the numbered street names at all.

Let's take the first item in box "A" in the preceding page. "2900-3299 College." The trick is to translate the number into sound, and then into an image. Let the sound corresponding to an initial 2 be "t" (the first sound in the name of the number) and the sound corresponding to 9 be "ine." This gives you "tine," which is logically visualized as a fork. To remember that the number sequence beginning "29—" is in box "A," combine the fork with an easily-visualized object beginning with that letter. A fork stuck in an apple works perfectly well.

The next item in the box is "Wellmann." Picture a well on an apple, or for that matter an apple in a well—it makes no difference as long as the image is clear and easily remembered—and you've got it. This may seem cumbersome, but such is the nature of mnemonic techniques which rely on visualization. The more you practice the number associations, the more automatically the image comes into your mind when you see any two-digit number. In other words, you quickly enough learn to bypass the compositional step, even though you can always fall back on it if you need to. In this way, you can learn the same sorts of visualization techniques that come automatically to mnemonic geniuses such as Luria's "S."

SELF-TEST: Test yourself against the best

You will need a timer.

A) How long would it take you to memorize the entire table to the far right? Luria's "S" needed just three minutes of study for perfect recall. (As usual, he then retained perfect recall of it, along with thousands of other such tables and number and nonsense-syllable sequences, for the rest of his life.) "V.P.," the mnemonic genius studied by Hunt and Love (1972), took six and a half minutes.

B) The table to the right took "V.P." four minutes and six seconds:

1	6	4	3	5	9
2	6	6	5	5	9
4	1	3	2	6	4
9	6	2	4	0	4
0	3	7	4	2	8
5	1	9	7	2	3
5	4	8	4	6	5
6	5	1	3	0	0

6	6	8	0
5	4	3	2
1	6	8	4
7	9	3	5
4	2	3	7
3	8	9	1
1	0	0	2
3	4	5	1
2	7	6	8
1	9	2	6
2	9	6	7
5	5	2	0
x	0	1	x

C) How many trials would it take you to memorize this list of 25 words? When he had the entire list read aloud to him at a rate of one word per second, Aitken required four trials; the first trial, he got 12 correct, the second trial 14 correct, the third trial 23 correct, and the fourth trial all correct.

> HEAD, GREEN, WATER, SING, DEAD, LONG, SHIP, MAKE, WOMAN, FRIENDLY, BAKE, ASK, COLD, STALK, DANCE, VILLAGE, POND, SICK, PRIDE, BRING, INK, ANGRY, NEEDLE, SWIM, GO.

(Aitken, by the way, never used the standard mnemonist's trick of associating each word with a visual image in a story. He simply proceeded by "sound.")

D) How many trials would it take you to memorize a list of 16 three-digit numbers? When the following list was read aloud to him at a rate of one word every two seconds, Aitken needed four trials. In the first trial, he got 6 correct, the second trial 10 correct, the third trial 14 correct, the fourth trial all correct.

> 194, 503, 876, 327, 714, 961, 583, 259, 487, 364, 950, 613, 294, 437, 182, 659.

DON'T TRY THIS ALPHABET GAME DURING
YOUR NEXT FAMILY ROAD TRIP

You might think just visual distractions would make it harder to drive, but it's also a matter of what you're doing with your mind.

In a recent study funded by the Spanish Department of Transportation, researchers recorded drivers' eye movements under actual driving conditions when they were assigned verbal and visual tasks of equal complexity. Both tasks resulted in a reduced "visual inspection window," increased "eye freezing responses" while the participants were thinking, and overall diminished attention to what they were supposed to be looking at. The visual task had a significantly greater impact than the verbal one.

For the verbal task, the participants were told to think of and say words beginning with whatever letters of the alphabet the researchers prompted them with. For the visual task, this is what participants were instructed to do:

Imagine the letters of the alphabet one by one, from A to Z. For each letter, say:

(a) whether it remains unchanged when you rotate it vertically;

(b) whether it remains unchanged when you rotate it horizontally;

(c) whether the letter is closed, or

(d) whether the letter is open.

As examples, if we were talking about numbers 0 and 9 would be closed, and 3 and 7 would be open.

Giving your undivided attention helps you think, remember, and react effectively

How do you remember who won Wimbledon in 1980, or figure out in your head what the square root of 676 is? Everyone knows it helps if you can give the problem your undivided attention. That's why people take tests in rooms where proctors pace the aisles enforcing strict silence.

There are some things you just don't do at the same time. You don't knit while riding a bicycle. You don't read the newspaper during an interview. You don't watch TV in church. And judging by the number of "Shut Up and Drive" bumper stickers you see, many people have added something new to the list: You don't talk on the phone while driving.

Why you can walk and chew gum at the same time

Some things are easy to do at the same time. Others aren't. Tap your foot while you sing? No problem. And your mother would never have had to scold you about talking while you were eating if it hadn't come naturally. But try patting your head and rubbing your stomach at the same time, and you're liable to end up rubbing your head and patting your stomach (or an entertaining mix of the two). And talking while reading is a lot harder than talking while eating.

Why the difference? In the parlance of neuroscience, it's partly due to how much of your *attentional capacity* the two tasks demand (see box). It's also a matter of how similar their *processing requirements* are. If two things depend on the same part of your brain, it's harder to do them at the same time than if they depend on different parts—it's as if the signals cross. So it's easy to rub your stomach while you talk, or pat your head while you read.

Many of the hardest things to do simultaneously are two tasks of the same type. There's a standard test of short-term memory known as *digit span*—repeating back a random series of numbers. The task becomes much harder when a psychologist claps a pair of headphones on you and plays one string of numbers into your left ear and a different string into your right. A more natural example might be when your spouse is telling you about what happened that day at the office while you're trying to have a conversation with a friend on the phone.

Are you aged 30–40? Starting to have trouble with conversations in noisy restaurants or cocktail parties?
More often, we have to try to *ignore* one thing while paying attention to another. That's what happens when you're trying to read the paper while your neighbor has *Tosca* turned up way too loud. It gets harder the older you get. Even by the time you're middle aged, your ability to tune out distractions and focus will have started to decline.

Now, how about that suddenly popular pet peeve—people who talk on a cell phone while driving? What are the facts? Is it really hard to talk on the phone and drive at the same time?

Keep your mind on the road
Those certainly seem to be different things, plausibly handled by different parts of your brain. Once you pass driver's ed, you don't have to pay attention to the relative movements of the steering wheel, brake pedal, gas pedal, gear shift, and clutch. All that's in your muscle memory. While you're driving, if you're doing something else that requires your conscious attention, it's usually no problem—you can talk or listen to the radio while driving, for example, perfectly easily.

But there's good evidence that talking on a cell phone while driving is indeed a risky business, and statistically may even be as dangerous in terms of actual accidents as drunk driving. Why might that be?

It's not just what you do with your eyes, it's what you do with your brain
The common-sense explanation would be that a phone diverts your eyes and hands from watching the road and steering the wheel. So hands-free cell phones should be OK, right?

Not quite. True, hand-held cell phones can distract your eyes and hands. But cognitive distractions are responsible for even more accidents than the other two. The brain doesn't segregate mental imagery from actual visual perception as neatly as you might think. A lot of the same neural networks are used for both. So whatever mental visual imagery your brain conjures up while you're on the phone will distract you from your ability to pay attention to what's right in front of your eyes (or in the rear-view mirror, as the case may be).

Another recent study found that talking on a cell phone doubles your chances of missing a red light regardless of whether the phone is a hand-held or hands-free model. So it seems that the very fact of having a conversation on the phone, regardless of what your hands or eyes are doing, diverts too much of your attention from driving.

It isn't just any kind of conversation that makes it that much harder to drive. Talking to someone who's sitting in the passenger seat may be distracting. But it's less of a distraction to your attention at those crucial moments when you need all of it, partly because everybody in the car tends to pipe down as soon as driving conditions get worse, and to warn you if they see a potential hazard.

Pretty much every study on the topic has concluded that older people have a harder time with divided attention tasks than younger people. So it's harder for an older person to talk while driving—or, rather, it's harder to drive well while talking—let alone talk on a cell phone while driving.

Of course, cell phones are a recent enough phenomenon that not many older people like to use them anyway. (Or maybe they're just too polite, or too smart.) As of the most recent count, there are over 120 million cellular phone subscribers in the United States. With any luck, if the results of current research hold up and are heeded, talking on the phone while driving will be about as common as knitting while bicycling long before all those younger cell phone addicts get much older.

+ ÷
− ✳
EXERCISE: Divided attention

Here are two variants of a divided attention task. The second one is harder because the two things you're trying to do at the same time have processing requirements that match more closely than the two tasks in the first one.

(1) Go through the letters as quickly as you can, and cancel out each one that's curved (e.g., B but not N) as well as each A:

(2) Go through the letters as quickly as you can, and cancel out each G and each A:

N K D S O A P E W A B

D Q I P J A A D C E J M

Z X U E O L Q A S W E

G B U K P A F E B N E

H K E U I G A H A J P

E C O L N A T K A G B

M X Y P W K X Z D A H

CONSERVING YOUR LIMITED COGNITIVE RESOURCES: HOW TO PAY ATTENTION

What you call "paying attention" is something psychologists break down into several categories. There's focused or selective attention, which means focusing on just one thing while ignoring other things that might distract you. (That's what's commonly known as concentration.) Then there's sustained attention (or vigilance), divided attention (paying attention to two things at once) and altering attention (shifting between two different things.) Whichever category we're talking about, there are limits to your attentional capacity. In other words, you can't concentrate on one thing forever, you can't tune out all distractions, and you can't pay attention to an unlimited number of things at once.

Attentional capacity is like two tanks linked by an overflow pipe. You can fill half of one and still have room in the other for an additional task. If you fill one too high, it overflows into the other and reduces your capacity for doing anything else.

What can affect your attentional capacity? Fatigue can: if you're tired it's harder to concentrate or focus. Age can, too: kids take a while to learn to pay attention, adults can focus pretty well, but as we age our attentional capacity tends to go downhill again especially for complex or mentally challenging tasks. Of course brain damage, including dementia, can wreak havoc on your attentional capacity. Depression can too. Problems with mental focus are often falsely attributed to dementia or old age when it's actually depression that's at fault.

Why are stories easier to recall than lists?

With the exception of some idiot savants, or those rare individuals endowed with a photographic memory, most of us will memorize information much better if we can tack that information to something we already know. Any story, for example, will be much easier to recall if we can match it to what are called *schemata* or *scripts:* generic structured outlines of familiar events or routines.

A simple example will illustrate: Anyone familiar with the general rules and structure of chess will find it much easier to remember an account of the details of a particular match than will someone who has never learned how to play the game. According to one point of view, many people with good memories owe their ability simply to the fact that they have such a large store of knowledge that they can rely on it to contextualize new information and make it personally meaningful. That explains why they find it easier to organize and manage new facts.

Your mind tries so hard to fit new data into the patterns it already knows that it may substitute what "probably" happened for what really happened

Our urge to integrate new information into a prior knowledge base—to go beyond the simple objective facts themselves and, as it were, turn mere stimuli into knowledge—is so strong, and so automatic, that it may sometimes lead us to err in our understanding or recollection of events. If we hear a story in which a friend hands over his credit card to the waiter and then asks for the check, we are very likely, when prompted to repeat the story, to unconsciously "correct" the sequence to fit the familiar restaurant script. And the fact that the reference to a "restaurant script" in the previous sentence is sensible rather than confusing to you, the reader, results from your *assumption* that someone asking a waiter for a check has just finished a meal in a restaurant—even though that was never mentioned.

Consider, too, the following mini-story:

A man and his young son were struck by a hit-and-run driver while crossing the street. The father was killed instantly, and the son critically injured. The boy was taken to the hospital and rushed immediately into the emergency room, where the doctor exclaimed, "I can't operate on my own son!"

The confusing effect of this story relies crucially on an *assumption* we make about the doctor being a man, rather than a woman and therefore the boy's mother. Most people will cling to this assumption so tenaciously that they will go to great lengths to make sense of the story without questioning their image of the male doctor—and yet, nowhere is it stated that the doctor is in fact a man.

Why stereotypes come in handy
Even though we are often criticized for maintaining stereotypes of this sort, they are just one of many types of generalization without which we could surely never function effectively in the world. Using strict logic it is unjustified to assume that, just because we got burned once by putting our finger in a flame, the same thing would happen should we do it again— but imagine how quickly an organism would die if it failed to make this sort of inductive leap. No such logical organism would ever get the chance to pass on its genes.

Our need to turn mere stimuli into coherent knowledge is so strong that true non-sequiturs—conversational contributions that simply have *nothing* to do with the previous comment (literally "don't follow")—are rarely interpreted as such. The listeners try their darnedest to find something in their past experience that makes the comment relate *somehow*. Imagine that a young woman has applied for a job with your computer software company, and you contact her previous employer to verify her qualifications. When you ask about her ability as a programmer, her former boss replies, "Ms. Widget always came to work on time and dressed appropriately." You will naturally interpret this as a tactful indictment of her skills—"damning with faint praise," as the saying goes—and you won't hire her. Perhaps, though, the poor woman's former employer was simply saying whatever came into his mind without really trying to respond to your question. Sometimes, as even Freud had to admit, a cigar is just a cigar.

The worst part of your memory to lose is your ability to relate a new experience to old ones
In the field of clinical memory rehabilitation, one of the most difficult kinds of amnesia to overcome involves the inability of the patient to integrate new information into previously-acquired knowledge. Laird Cermak and colleagues describe a severely amnesic patient who, though able to learn a few memory aids, is absolutely unable to profit from them. When he memorizes facts at all, he does so in a parrot-like manner, with little or no understanding of them. Without the ability to give meaning to mere stimuli by bringing to bear a rich knowledge base, this patient has lost a much more fundamentally human ability than memory alone.

 SELF-TEST: Memorizing meaningful vs. random patterns

Memorization skill relies on the integration of data into familiar patterns. When presented with a configuration of 28 chess pieces from an actual match (below left), grandmaster-level players are able to memorize about 16 pieces after only five seconds, while beginners memorize only about four. When presented with a board featuring the same pieces arranged randomly (below right), experts and beginners perform the same. If you know the rules of chess, study the board on the left for one minute and memorize as many of the positions as possible. Next, try the same thing with the board on the right.

SELF-TEST: Memorizing lists as stories

A typical trick for memorizing arbitrary lists is to connect the items in a meaningful way, by stringing them together into a story. For example, take the following list of apparently unrelated items:

airplane	ball
hyena	grease
cream cheese	monument
moon	mailman
volcano	lunch

Most people, when presented with such a list, would find its memorization to be a tedious or even daunting task. However, consider an alternative mode of presentation (based on Bower and Clark 1969; Higbee 1977; and Crovitz 1979):

The first word is airplane. Just remember that however you like. The next word is hyena, because all the passengers sitting in the seats are hyenas. The next word is cream cheese, because each of the hyenas is taking bites out of a cream cheese sandwich. The next word is moon, because the moon is really made out of cream cheese. The next word is volcano, because there is a volcano on the moon. The next word is ball, because when the volcano on the moon erupts, it spews out balls. The next word is grease, because the balls are covered with grease. The next word is monument, because the balls have so much grease on them it flows all the way to the Washington Monument. The next word is mailman, because a group of mailmen is touring the Washington Monument. The last word is lunch, because when the mailmen finish their tour they go have lunch.

After being presented this mini-story, most people can recall the ten words embedded in it in both forward and backward order. This sort of mnemonic method, which promotes what is nowadays referred to as "elaborate" encoding of the material, can be traced back two and a half thousand years to the Greek poet Simonides.

(cont'd on next page)

A mnemonic technique which does *not* work well for memorizing arbitrary lists involves what is sometimes called "first-letter mnemonics." For example:

hammer

slipper

peach

trunk

leopard

By taking the first letter of each word and filling in vowels where needed, you can form a word such as "HOSPITAL." An effective trick for coding and retrieval? No. This sort of mnemonic technique is only useful for memorizing the *order* of otherwise known items, as in the use of the phrase "Richard of York Gave Battle in Vain" for memorizing the order of the colors of the rainbow.

 SELF-TEST: The effect of context on memory

Not only are stories much easier to remember than lists, but the easiest kind of story to remember is one that is made meaningful by contextualization. Knowing ahead of time what a story is going to be about makes its details much easier to recollect after the telling.

Consider the following story:

A hundred happy faces dreamed of friends and lovers waiting to the north. Deep within, a container of the stuff we breathe sparked to life, burst, burned. Out of life came death. All choked within the darkening cocoon. The nether world of scaled creatures rushed to greet them, and mud filled their eyes. A nation reeled in shock. The friends and lovers watched lit boxes and cried.

After reading the story, how much of it can you remember? Chances are, not much. Now, consider that the story is about a disaster in the Florida Everglades in which a jetliner full of passengers crashed into the reptile-infested swamps. Now read it through once more. How much can you remember this time?

A little stress helps memory but too much destroys it

Recent work on the neurological underpinnings of cognitive deficits in the elderly bolsters yet another piece of traditional wisdom: *too much stress makes you old before your time!*

Memory, as we now know, is anything but a passive capacity. Many factors can influence whether we form a long-term memory of a specific fact or event. One such factor is our emotional state: an emotionally-charged, stressful event will much more likely be remembered than one that occurs in the absence of emotional arousal.

Why memory improves after a meal...

One of the many theories as to why this happens runs as follows: Physical and psychological stress stimulates the sympathetic nervous system to release neurotrans- mitters such as epinephrine. These neurotrans- mitters increase the brain's utilization of glucose, and—while research reports differ as to *why* glucose has this effect—it has been shown conclusively that glucose enhances memory, even in Alzheimer's patients. This is why memory formation is better after a meal.

...but stress interferes with memory

In addition to memory-enhancing epinephrine, stress also releases a slower-acting wave of hor- mones called glucocorticoids, generally known as *cortisol*. In low levels, such as those that occur naturally during the day, cortisol enhances long-term memory formation. In higher, stress-induced concentrations, however, they have an inhibit- ing effect on memory and a toxic effect on neurons.

Once the role of cortisol in neurons is fully understood, the hope is that drugs that manipulate the levels of these hormones will help slow the effects of aging and, in particular, forestall the decline in powers of memory. In the meantime, follow your mother's advice and *relax* already. Too much corti- sol can even kill brain cells by causing an excess of calcium intake into neurons.

Cortisol is as destructive to the brain as cholesterol is to the heart. A recent study shows that higher-than-average levels of the hormone cortisol are correlated with cognitive defects in the elderly. A group of healthy elderly subjects were tested for blood levels of cortisol, then tested on a battery of cognitive functions including memory, attention, and language ability. Those subjects who had relatively high cortisol levels, and whose cortisol levels had been increasing over a four-year period, scored the lowest on memory and attention tasks. Elderly subjects with *decreasing cortisol levels,* however, performed as well as healthy young subjects on the cognitive tasks. Coincidentally, independent studies reveal that high evels of cortisol are seen in people afflicted with Alzheimer's disease.

How cortisol destroys memory
We all know what it's like to be unable to think clearly or to learn or remember things when under stress. One of the reasons is that cortisol, which is released in stressful situations, reduces the blood sugar energy supply to the hippocampus and the rest of the brain. If the hippocampus is temporarily out of commission, short-term memories can't be created and we feel mentally confused.

Another reason for mental confusion under stress is that cortisol interferes with the brain's neurotransmitters, preventing us from laying down new memory pathways and from retrieving pre-existing memories from long-term storage. That's why it can be so hard to access facts during the stress of an exam or while public speaking.

Thalamus (right and left)

Hippocampus (right and left)

The hippocampus and the two egg-like thalami are parts of the primitive "limbic system," where emotions and lasting memories are aroused and retrieved. The hippocampus is crucial to humans' ability to learn about things, ideas, and the events that make up life — hence, damage to it affects memory. Without it, the mind cannot learn new data or access information learned in the past — precisely the kind of memory loss suffered by high-cortisol subjects.

Your brain was not designed for facing daily stress

The human brain has evolved to release cortisol when serious danger stimulates the adrenal glands which releases a neuro-transmitter called epinephrine. They heighten awareness, focus attention and cause other physical changes that prepare the body to protect itself or escape in time. But exposing yourself to *chronic* stress kills brain cells and may hasten the onset of Alzheimer's. The crucial word is "chronic." The levels of cor-tisol compounds in your hippocampus caused by a stressful situation naturally decline to their normal set-point after the situation is resolved. However, if the stress is repeated, say, daily for over four months, the levels in the hippocampus remain so high their toxicity begins to destroy those brain cells. Damage to the hippocampus and related organs in the limbic system weakens memory formation.

How you can lower your cortisol levels and enhance your prospects for brain longevity

The trick is to control your *response* to stress by avoiding it or adjusting to it emotionally so it is no longer perceived as a threat. Stress reduction techniques like yoga, meditation, and biofeedback can play a crucial role in helping you keep cognitively fit.

Regular aerobic exercise also helps. Physically fit people tend to have a milder stress response and their cortisol levels are generally lower. A half hour of sufficiently vigorous aerobic exercise can have a tranquilizing effect that lasts for several hours. Increasing blood flow to the brain helps release neuro-transmitters essential to good mood and memory.

Excess cortisol also creates free radicals which can be blunted by antioxidant vitamins A, C, and E. An adequate supply of choline in your diet, by taking lecithin, for example, helps ensure that you have enough of the essential building block of the "memory" neurotransmitter acetylcholine.

THE RESEARCH

There are two types of glucocorticoid receptor cells in the hippocampus (a part of the brain crucially involved in some kinds of memory—see "Your 'memory' is, in fact, many processes," p. 73). One type, which stimulates increased memory function, is activated by low levels of the hormone. Once these receptors are saturated, higher levels will activate a different type of receptor cell which has an opposite, inhibiting effect on memory. (Imagine how few women would want to experience a second childbirth if this didn't happen!) One possible way that this second set of cells may inhibit memory function is by interfering with glucose transport and uptake.

If glucocorticoids are kept at stress-induced levels for periods up to a few weeks, they will cause atrophy of the dendritic branches of hippocampal neurons. (Dendrites are the branching structures that convey signals toward the cell body of a neuron.) This damage is, however, reversible.

If, on the other hand, stress levels of glucocorticoids are maintained for a period of months, irreversible loss of hippocampal neurons occurs. In experiments with rats, the effects of this kind of loss mimic the effects of aging at a rapidly accelerated rate. In addition, the older the animal, the more vulnerable it is.

 SELF-TEST: Emotion-enhanced memory formation

Here's an experiment you can run to test the claim that emotional arousal enhances memory formation. On the following pages are two stories, equal in length and complexity, but different in the emotional arousal they evoke. The experiment doesn't take long, but you'll need a few willing participants.

To avoid interference effects, choose a different person for each story, rather than presenting them both to the same person or group of people.

Don't reveal ahead of time that the participant will be asked about the details of the story. On the pretext of wanting to find out what kinds of emotions the story evokes, read the neutral version to a friend while he follows along with the accompanying illustrations. Try the same thing on a different friend with the emotion-arousing version.

(cont'd on next page)

NEUTRAL VERSION

1. A grandmother and her young grandson are leaving home in the morning.

2. She is taking him to the bus stop, where he will catch a bus to visit his mother at work.

3. His mother works in a big chemical research lab in the suburbs.

4. They walk to the bus stop.

5. While the grandmother is studying the bus schedule, a bus pulls up to the stop.

6. Two women get out of the bus.

7. One greets the boy and pats him on the head.

8. When the grandmother asks the woman if this is the right bus to the chemical research lab, she says yes.

9. The woman walks away and the grandmother puts the boy on the bus.

10. The bus takes the boy to the suburbs.

11. When the boy gets out, he is in a pretty area with lots of trees and birds.

12. The bus driver calls down to the boy that if he wants his mother to pick him up, he should call her from a pay phone.

13. He finds a pay phone near the bus stop and calls her.

14. She picks him up, and takes him to her workplace.

(cont'd on next page)

EMOTION-AROUSING VERSION

1. *A grandmother and her young grandson are leaving home in the morning.*

2. *She is taking him to the bus stop, where he will catch a bus to visit his mother at work.*

3. *His mother works in a big chemical research lab in the suburbs.*

4. *They walk to the bus stop.*

5. *While the grandmother is studying the bus schedule, a car pulls up to the bus stop.*

6. *Two men jump out of the car.*

7. *One man grabs the boy and knocks him unconscious.*

8. *When the grandmother begins to scream, the other man shoots her.*

9. *The two men jump back in the car with the boy and drive off, leaving the grand-mother bleeding on the sidewalk.*

10. *They take the boy to their hide-out.*

11. *When the boy wakes up, he is in a dark basement with lots of rats and cobwebs.*

12. *One of the kidnappers calls down to the boy that if he doesn't want the two men to hurt him, he must call his mother and tell her to bring them ten thousand dollars.*

13. *They give him a phone, and he calls her.*

14. *She pays the ransom, and the boy is returned to his mother.*

(cont'd on next page)

You'll have to wait about a week before asking each of the subjects an open-ended question about what details he or she recalls from the story. As an additional check, ask the following multiple-choice questions:

TEST FOR THOSE WHO HEARD THE NEUTRAL VERSION

Question #1 [refer to Picture #1]: <u>Who are these two people?</u>
A) a mother and her son   **B)** a nanny and a little boy   **C)** an aunt and her nephew   **D)** a grandmother and her grandson

Question #2 [refer to Picture #2]: <u>What is one woman asking the other?</u>
A) what time the bus comes   **B)** whether she knows the boy's mother
C) where the bus came from   **D)** where the bus is going

Question #3 [refer to Picture #3]: <u>What is the driver saying to the boy?</u>
A) that the boy should call his mother from a pay phone and she will pick him up   **B)** that the boy forgot to pay his fare   **C)** that he should wait by the tree for his mother   **D)** that he hopes he has a nice day

TEST FOR THOSE WHO HEARD THE EMOTION-AROUSING VERSION

Question #1 [refer to Picture #1]: <u>Who are these two people?</u>
A) a mother and her son   **B)** a nanny and a little boy   **C)** an aunt and her nephew   **D)** a grandmother and her grandson

Question #2 [refer to Picture #2]: <u>Why is the man shooting the woman?</u>
A) because she tried to grab the boy   **B)** because she started screaming
C) because he wants no witnesses   **D)** because she said she would call the police

Question #3 [refer to Picture #3]: <u>What is the man saying to the boy?</u>
A) that he should stop yelling   **B)** that he will never see his mother again
C) that he should call his mother for the ransom money   **D)** that he will be killed if he says anything to the police

"Now, where did I put my Prozac?"

We all know that failing memory goes hand-in-hand with aging. While forgetfulness may be forestalled to some degree, we generally accept that older people won't be quite as sharp memory-wise as children or young adults. Right?

Yes and no. A growing body of evidence shows that in many cases, a decline in the power of memory may be due not simply to inevitable age-related neurological changes, but—at least in part—to psychological depression. Depression appears to correlate with an increased risk for developing Alzheimer's disease and other senile dementias—along with a poor prognosis for recovery from stroke or heart attack.

Of course, the complexity of the interaction between mood and memory shouldn't be underestimated. Gifted memorizers, as discussed elsewhere (see "Why are stories easier to recall than lists?" p. 103), are often individuals who apply such a formidable body of interests to their environment in general that new information is readily encoded in a per-sonally meaningful and "elaborated" way. This kind of active *engagement* with the world is almost by definition the very opposite of psychological depression. Standard symptoms of depression, according to the diagnostic manuals, include apathy and a lack of interest in usually enjoyable hobbies or activities.

Depression destroys memory faster than age

Conversely, withdrawal from participation in challenging mental activity may lead to depression. This is why depression often follows hard on the heels of retirement.

The lesson to be drawn from this is simple. Since happiness and mental acuity are if anything faster friends than forgetful-ness and aging, the best way to be happy is to keep yourself on your toes whether you think you want to or not. Of course, if the things that challenge you intellectually are the things that you love doing, so much the better. And the best way to keep your mind sharp is to keep yourself surrounded with what psy-chologists call an "enriched environment"—challenging activ-ities and interesting acquaintances—which will in turn make you a happier person.

SELF-TEST: Geographics

Here are seven Middle Eastern nations in the news. Their boundary conflicts can be quickly resolved by drawing only three straight lines from any side of the box to any other without touching any nation. When you are through, each nation must be completely enclosed in its own area. Write the name of each of the seven nations next to one of the numbers in the box below the map. Then write that number in the circle next to that nation's shape.

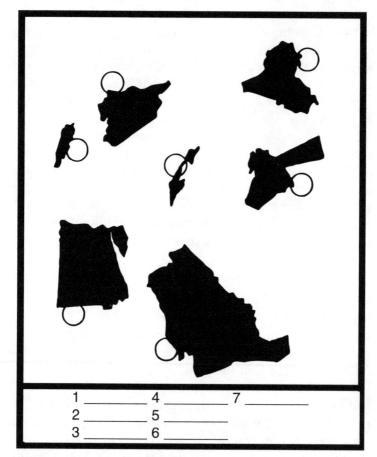

1 _____ 4 _____ 7 _____
2 _____ 5 _____
3 _____ 6 _____

Norms: Seven correct answers — excellent
Five correct answers — good
Four correct answers — fair

Hint: Lebanon, the small one on the far left, and Israel, the small one in the center, are each enclosed by a different small triangle. The first line you draw should divide Saudi Arabia and Egypt and fence Syria off from Iraq.

Can challenging mental activity throughout life forestall age-related cognitive decline?

Yes! In a study of cognitive ability and aging in university professors, older professors showed the usual declines in reaction time and some aspects of memory, but no decline at all in the acquisition and organization of conceptual knowledge. This indicates that the pursuit of demanding intellectual activity throughout life may counteract the usual age-related decrement in planning, organizing, and manipulating information.

Younger (age 30–44), middle-aged (45–59) and older (60–71) professors at the University of California at Berkeley were shown prose passages and tested for their recall of the content. Unlike older subjects in the general population, older professors recalled the facts as well as their younger peers. (See "As they age...," p. 123.)

Working memory

In a test of this short-term memory process involved in on-line monitoring or control of information, older professors showed no effects of "proactive inhibition"—the interference of the details of one learning task with performance on a second similar one. Generally, older individuals show a marked decrease in their ability to exclude extraneous details from their minds while performing this kind of task. The older professors, however, appeared to have use of strategies to overcome or prevent this.

The findings of this study are consistent with others showing a correlation between lifelong intellectual activity and freedom from dementia in old age. What's meant by "intellectual" isn't necessarily high-brow or sophisticated. Intellectual activity really just means challenging your mind by asking it to cope with new experiences, like learning Spanish, tackling a new kind of crossword puzzle or joining a singing group. It does *not* mean doing the same old things over and over again, like watching the same sitcoms every evening.

Of course, correlation isn't the same as causation, and it doesn't identify what might really be happening in the brain. Why is it, exactly, that using your mind helps to keep it healthy?

SELF-TEST: Prose recall

Don't read the italic type below. If possible, have a friend read the passage below to you. The reading should not be rushed, but no long pauses are permitted and nothing may be repeated. After hearing the entire passage, you should re-tell the story as accurately as you can remember it. Be as specific as possible. Include all details, not just the general outline or plot. Your friend should keep track of how many of the facts you remember as you re-tell the passage you just heard him or her read to you. When you have finished, check your score against the norms shown at the bottom of page 121.

This self-test can also be done unassisted if you have a timer. Read the unsegmented passage (below) once through at normal reading speed; do not take longer than 30 seconds. Next, write down the story from memory to the best of your recollection, and assign yourself points with reference to the segmented version, below.

Jimmy Johnson, a track star from West Los Angeles, was buying clothes one day in Beverly Hills. A 15-year-old from the suburbs mugged a 70-year-old woman five feet in front of him. Jimmy chased the mugger five blocks, caught him and returned the woman's 10 dollars. The old woman told him that she needed the money for her grandson's Bar Mitvah. She gave him a 15-cent reward.

Segmented Versions:

Jimmy Johnson/, a track star/ from West/ Los Angeles/, was buying/ clothes/ one day in Beverly Hills/. A 15-year-old/ from the suburbs/ mugged/ a 70-year-old/ woman/ five feet/ in front of him/. Jimmy chased the mugger/ five blocks/, caught him/ and returned/ the woman's 10 dollars/. The old woman told him/ that she needed the money/ for her grandson's/ Bar Mitvah/. She gave him/ a 15-cent reward/.

Mental exercise builds more brain cells

Recent findings from Princeton's Elizabeth Gould may provide an answer to that question. In experiments with rats, Gould found that mental stimulation doubled the rate of brain-cell regeneration, a process known as neurogenesis (see "Physical exercise," p. 65). For the rats, mental stimulation meant figuring out how to negotiate a new and different maze every day. The experiment's method required Gould to kill the rats to examine their brains, which obviously couldn't be done with humans. But it's pretty certain that parallel findings would hold for humans, too.

A mere few years ago, it would have been regarded as nonsense to talk about the regeneration of brain cells at all. Now, we know that adult human brains can and do grow new brain cells. It's still true that young brains grow new neurons much more readily than old brains. But the process of neurogenesis never really ends. In fact, hard though this may be to believe, brain researcher Fred Gage of the Salk Institute has even found evidence that human brain cells continue to develop after death—for a short time, of course.

What mental exercise can help you do, then, is keep the rate of neurogenesis closer to what it was when you were much younger. Those newly-generated brain cells can, in turn, be put to use for doing and learning new things. That, as Gould points out, is a perfect example of the "use it or lose it" principle applied to the brain.

A BC **SELF-TEST: Why testimony may be inaccurate but not a lie**

Read this list to a friend and have him repeat back to you every one of the words he remembers:

> *bed, slumber, dream, drowsy, pillow, tired, nap, yawn, doze, snore*

Chances are, your friend will not only remember some of the words on the actual list, but will also falsely recall the one obvious word you didn't say: *sleep.*

In experiments using lists like this, PET scans show that the auditory cortex is activated every time a previously-recited word is recalled, but not when a word is incorrectly recalled.

A
BC ✷🖐   **EXERCISE: Neuron and off**

1	2	3	4	■	5	6	7	8	■	9	10	11
12				■	13				■	14		
15				■	16				■	17		
■		18		19	■	20		21				
22	23			24	■	25			■	■		
26			■	27	28				29	30	31	
32		33		34			■	35				
36			37			38	■	39				
■		40			■	41	42					
43	44	45			46	■	47			■		
48			■	49		50	■	51		52	53	
54			■	55			■	56				
57			■	58			■	59				

ACROSS

1. Neuron signal conveyance process
5. Whatnot case
9. Sash
12. Pierre's dream
13. Wallet contents
14. Tommy follower
15. German river
16. No ifs — or buts
17. Palindromic conjunction
18. Unchangeable computer memory
20. Nervous system functional units
22. Ribbed
25. Meadow
26. Unit of work
27. Ascertain
32. Enzymes
34. — King Cole
35. Pet
36. Examined again
39. — Cat (winter vehicle)
40. Cruelest mo.
41. Abase
43. French white wine
47. Describing 43 Across
48. Black dog

(cont'd on next page)

49. Story about a duo
51. Castro's realm
54. Sleeve resident
55. Greek cheese
56. Bone up on in a hurry
57. Washington crossed it (abbr.)
58. Several Peters were one
59. Before plane or drome

DOWN

1. "All the things you —"
2. Deleted
3. Surpluses
4. Fiddler and pianist
5. Greek letter
6. Volunteer state, for short
7. Not removed
8. Creator of a bond
9. Cookie
10. —— Free
11. Residential suffix
19. Pre —- courses
21. Butts
22. Rip
23. Gaelic
24. Neuron signal conveyance processes toward the cell

28. Mai —
29. Anxious
30. Ship of 1492
31. Collar or jacket
33. Pierce
37. Kind of bra
38. — Plaines
42. Hadj target
43. Apparelled
44. "He does" in Madrid
45. Cain's victim
46. Bristle
50. Deface
52. Pub
53. Latin I word

(See Self-test, page 118)

Scoring: This passage is divided into 25 "facts" or significant details, as indicated in the segmented version (in which the phrases that contain a fact are separated by slashes). Each such fact must be correctly remembered in order for maximal points to be obtained. If you recall all 25 facts, then your score is 25/25, or 100%. Fifteen remembered facts would yield a score of 15/25, or 60%.

Norms (when the passage is read aloud to the subject): The norm for younger subjects is 15 correct, or 60%; for older subjects, 11 correct or 44%.

EXERCISE: Personal pairs

Make the 10 most logical pairs out of these 20 different items. Use each picture only once and don't leave any picture out. Pair them so all 10 are the *most likely* combinations of similarities. There is no "correct" answer. This exercise requires that you keep specific images in short-term "working" memory while you work through the 10 pairings without writing notes as you go. Two possible sets of 10 pairs are shown in the "Solutions" section.

For fun, try this with a friend, and see if you can match the items in the same way you think your friend would. Score two points for each pair of yours that matches your friend's answer and one point for each pair not matching his or her answer. If you have to leave any picture out, subtract one point for each.

After completing this exercise try the matching exercises on pages 124–127. Even if you have already done those exercises once, you may be surprised to find that proactive inhibition interferes with your ability to match those pairs of faces, words or symbols correctly without restudying them.

As they age, most people tend to notice problems with their "working" memory

Everybody knows that some things are easier to remember than others. It's hard to forget the time you tripped over your graduation gown just as you were about to receive your high school diploma, but easy to forget the principal's remarks of just a few minutes before. You can bet that the oldest grandparent in the audience remembered your pratfall better than the speech, too. The ability to remember one bit of data for a short time does not falter with age, such as the amount of late fees the video store clerk just said while you pull out your wallet and count out the bills. As long as they're not too distracted, people's short-term memory can handle daily events like that, whether they're 20 or 80.

As people move into their 60's their short-term "working" memory normally begins to fail. For example, a phone number just looked up may be confused with another number recently memorized.

The gap between young and old brains shows when mental "processing capacity" of working memory begins, literally, to shrink with age. The dendritic fibers that allow cells to connect into circuits shrink with disuse or age and sometimes the whole cell dies. This weakens the circuits that process data for memory. Especially vulnerable are the circuits used to remember new data consciously, bare facts with no dramatic or emotional kick to them and "Executive Function" tasks in which a sequence of independent items must be kept in mind and alternative solutions evaluated while processing them (like multiplying 34 x 81 in your head).

The kind of things that strain this kind of capacity tend to be hard at any age. Anyone will fumble mentally with an unfamiliar task when distracted by TV, or have a hard time trying not to forget a phone number while struggling to remember a new calling card number. Even getting the point of a joke often uses more processing capacity than you might guess.The old Groucho Marx line, for example: "Time flies like an arrow, but fruit flies like a banana" requires a double-take, as you hold the words in your mind long enough to go back over them and get the joke.

A little absent-mindedness is a natural part of aging

It's the kind of mental agility demanded by tasks like these that first starts to falter as you get older. In general, the fragile memory skills go under the *working memory* (WM) heading. These are skills that you use pretty much all the time as part of the process of thinking, focusing, or figuring things out. You may not even realize they're considered memory skills. It is your short-term memory system for storing, but also for manipulating information "on line," just as long as you need it to solve a problem. For example, you use your WM to figure out what someone's saying to you, add up numbers in your head, or even do something as straightforward as remember a phone number you just looked up long enough to dial it.

Temporary failures of WM are common and it is one of the first areas to show lapses consistently with age—forgetting where you put your car keys, or what you just came into the kitchen to get, or even what you were just in the middle of saying in a conversation.

More specifically, older people have a harder time avoiding *interference* (also called *inhibition*) of one memory by another. (See "A major cause of forgetting," p. 87.) For example, interference explains why it is easy to get distracted by whatever it is you start thinking or doing after you put down your keys, or before you open the fridge door. Typically an 80-year-old has a harder time filtering out distractions than a 20-year-old will. (That's assuming, of course, that the 20-year-old *wants* to filter them out.) This is also a reason people find it more and more difficult to do two things at once as they enter their senior years. (See "Undivided Attention," p. 99.)

Multiple choice or fill-in-the-blank?

Professors in big lecture courses like to give multiple-choice exams to test their students' mastery of the course material. Why? Because they're easy to correct and grade. But a multiple-choice exam can also be a big relief to the students—especially the ones who tended to doze off during lecture. What's that fancy name for someone who collects coins? If you're not sure, is it a *philologist, proctologist, numismatist,* or *polygamist*? You are more likely to recognize the correct word in a list than you are to be able to search and retrieve it from scratch.

Psychologists who study the difference between *recall* and *recognition* point out that recall, which is harder even when you're young, gets harder and harder the older you become. Recognition, on the other hand, tends not to change as much. Recall uses up more of that ever-shrinking "processing capacity" mentioned above. But that way of putting it seems pretty circular. What's really happening in your brain to explain the difference?

The older you get, the more likely the "record" and "replay" buttons on your mental VCR will start to stick

Harvard memory researcher Daniel Schacter has used brain scanning technology to answer that question, and he's found that a part of the brain people use when making the effort to remember a piece of information so it can be recalled later, or when retrieving that information from memory, switches on more automatically in younger brains than older ones. For the same level of activity in that particular brain region, healthy older test subjects have to put more conscious effort into it. (That difference shows up only during attempts to memorize or recall lists of words, but not during attempts to recognize whether or not a word was on a previously-seen list.) The brain difference correlates with a difference in memory performance: older people do about as well as younger people on tests of recognition, but not as well on tests of recall.)

How are those findings useful? They show that this kind of common age-related memory difference isn't due to the loss of any ability or the death of neurons in a part of the brain used in memorizing and remembering. Instead, it's due to how automatically and effortlessly that brain region kicks into action when its services are required.

The older you get, the more you have to concentrate on committing a phone number or a name to memory, and the more effort you have to put into recalling it later. If you can't recall it, don't panic! If you focus calmly, it will come—or maybe you'll just have to go back to it and put a little more effort into memorizing it the second time around. And it's perfectly OK to make use of mnemonic strategies to compensate

SELF-TEST: **Recall and recognition**

It's a lot easier to realize that you've seen a face before than it is to "place" it—to remember when or where you saw it, let alone remember the name that goes with it. Recall is harder than recognition, and tends to get harder the older you get.

It would be a pretty easy task to study the faces below, look at another group of faces, and pick out one you saw here. That would be a simple test of recognition.

It would be a lot harder to close the book and describe each pair of faces from memory. That would be a difficult test of recall.

This self-test falls between those two. Your task will be to remember which faces go together, but you'll be allowed to see all the faces again, just not in pairs.

First, study the six pairs of faces here for about half a minute. Then, turn to page 128 and pair up the faces up to match these pairings. Don't spend longer than a minute trying to match them up. Repeat the task twice, observing the same time limits.

(cont'd on page 128)

for that natural change in brain function. (See "How to remember people's names," p. 85, and "Could you be a mail carrier," p. 95.)

How to be better than "normal"

At any age, a good memory is as much a matter of habit and attitude as a raw cognitive skill. If you get into the habit of making the effort to focus, your memory will, as a practical matter, improve. And you may be able to do even more than that. A recent study of professors of all ages at the University of California showed that the older professors appeared to have the ability to overcome the effects of memory interference as well as the younger ones did. These results suggest that individuals whose minds have been kept active into old age (60–71 years of age in this study) may not show this kind of "normal" decrease in mental ability. If that's the case, you might be able to maintain your processing capacity, and your working memory, through practice.

In addition, very recent evidence supports the idea that mental exercise can boost *neurogenesis,* or the generation of new brain cells, in your hippocampus. The hippocampus is a part of your brain that has a central role in making and retrieving memories. So if you get into the habit of using your memory in ways that may take a little extra effort, you may be less likely to lose it.

Norms:

First trial: two correct for older subjects
(60–71 years), three correct for
younger subjects (18–23 years)

Second trial: two correct for older subjects,
four correct for younger subjects

Third trial: three correct for older subjects,
five correct for younger subjects

1___
2___
3___
4___
5___
6___

SELF-TEST: Proactive inhibition (graphic)

Below are two grids of 36 boxes, with a pattern in each box. Some patterns appear in more than one box. Your task is to work rapidly through the first grid, marking each pattern *once* the first time it appears. To prevent looking back at previous rows, cover upper rows with a piece of paper as you progress down. By the time you reach the bottom right, you should have marked each pattern once and only once. You have one minute to complete the task.

After completing one trial, add up your errors and repeat on the second grid.

On this task, older subjects generally do worse on the second trial than on the first. The increased errors made by the average older subject on the second trial is due to proactive inhibition—the interference of an earlier task with performance on a subsequent task of the same type. In general, older people have a harder time with this phenomenon and with filtering out extraneous information on tasks like this.

Normal decline of very short-term memory shows up in some tests of older people

The brain produces a chemical called acetylcholine to carry messages between cells that are involved in recall and strategy-making. The availability of such neurotransmitter chemicals appears to increase in brains which are frequently used to meet problem-solving challenges. This may account, at least in part, for the fact that some older people do not lose these abilities as much as others as they age. Neuropsychologists use variations of the exercise shown on pages 130–131 to measure such changes.

The ability to find the most efficient strategy changes too

In a study of correlations between age and problem-solving strategies for the exercise on the following pages, older people (60 years and older) were shown to be much less likely to use the optimal strategy than were younger people (14–35 years). Also, among a group of 64 participants divided evenly into young and old, only the older group members ever used the least efficient strategy. For a related study, see the articles beginning on pages 117 and 123.

A self-test similar to the age-related memory research

For this exercise, you need a playing partner. The two extra grids printed on page 131 allow you to experiment with different strategies. However, you may want to photocopy the grids so you can play this brain game again with the same or other partners. You can then keep track of the difference in the target square the "examiner" had in mind.

In some ways this is similar to the game called "Battleship." For each grid, an "examiner" must select one square without telling the "examinee" which square has been chosen. (Numbers and letters have been written along the edges for easy reference and identification.) The examinee's task is to find the chosen square by asking a series of yes/no questions. The fewer the number of questions asked, the higher the score.

To solve a problem like this, there are essentially three possible types of strategy

The simplest but least efficient strategy is to ask, for each square in turn, "Is this the right square?" This strategy is not too bad for very small grids, but quickly becomes hopelessly inefficient for larger ones. For example, for a 2 x 2 grid, you'd always get the right answer after no more than three questions, but for an 8 x 8 grid you might have to ask as many as 63; and for a 100 x 100 grid, you may need 9,999 questions before hitting the chosen square.

Of course, with the least efficient strategy you might get lucky and hit the right square on the first question. For a really large grid, this would be as likely as winning the lottery. With the optimal strategy, you'll never get the right square on the first question. But on average, for any grid 2 x 2 or larger, you'll be better off with the optimal strategy. A "Hint" appears below. A description of the most efficient, optimal strategy appears in the "Solutions" section.

Hint: A somewhat more efficient strategy is to proceed row by row and then, once the right row is found, square by square until the correct one is reached. For a small, 2 x 2 grid, this works as well as any strategy (maximum number of questions = 2), while for a larger, 8 x 8 grid the maximum possible number of questions required will be 14. For a 100 x 100 grid, you'll need up to but never more than 198 questions.

EXERCISE: Eliminating possibilities

Here are three boxes of fruit, one containing one dozen bananas, one with a dozen lemons, and a third with six bananas and six lemons. But all the covers have been switched. Now imagine that you can select one box. Shut your eyes, open the box, take out only the first fruit you touch. Don't feel around inside the box. Close the cover. When you see what fruit you have, can you tell which fruits, or combination of fruits, are in each box?

New hope for those at risk for Alzheimer's: stem cell therapy and vaccines

It's been said that if the human brain were simple enough for us to understand, we'd be too simple-minded to figure it out. You hear a lot these days about futuristic technology like neuroprosthetics—brain-embedded electrodes that allow quadriplegics to move cursors with nothing more than their thoughts. Some scientists even predict that before long we'll walk around with bits and pieces of man-made machinery spliced into our brains and bodies, in a bionic improvement on nature's design.

And yet, let's face it, even our most impressive technology for doing nature one better often works by harnessing the brain's own powers to heal itself. The thus-far modest success of neuroprosthetics, for example, depends on the spontaneous ability of brain cells to grow around and link up with the implanted electrodes, thereby enabling the natural electricity generated by thoughts to run the artificial machinery.

Using stem cells to help the brain help itself

Some researchers think that a cure for Alzheimer's might be found in the regenerative powers of stem cells. Stem cells are generalist cells that can divide without limit and produce specialized cells, including brain cells. They can be collected from aborted fetuses, or even from the discarded umbilical cords of newborns. One hope is that such cells may be coaxed into generating any of a number of kinds of more specialized cells, and then implanted into the body or brain of a person with a

Compare this picture of brain cells called neurons with the one below. The difference is not the number of cells—they both show about seven—but the number and length of the dendrites that branch off of them. The more dendrites that branch out to touch other cells, the better they can combine forces to recall information or solve problems fast.

This pictures healthy active neurons. The adult human brain has billions of them, and each has thousands of contacts with other neurons. Estrogen may cause brain cells to expand these contacts. Also, a brain that is kept busy grows more dendrites than an idle one.

disease of a corresponding cell or organ type, such as diabetes (pancreatic cells), heart disease (heart cells), or Parkinson's or Alzheimer's (brain cells).

But stem cell technology wouldn't exist without the regenerative powers that the brain and body already possess. Some stem cells continue to produce specialized cells after you're born—indeed, all your life. Until very recently, scientists believed that adults don't have brain stem cells—that, in other words, cells in the brain can't regenerate the way that the cells in our skin, blood, and other body systems do. As with so much other long-accepted knowledge about the brain, that conventional wisdom turns out to be wrong.

The success of stem cell treatments for Alzheimer's may depend more on finding out how to coax the brain into boosting the production of brain cells from its own neural stem cell supply (a process known as neurogenesis) than on invasive implant procedures. Some of the most recent research suggests that the key to neurogenesis may lie in cells called astrocytes, which appear to have the ability to trigger the growth of new brain cells. It might be possible, then, to use astrocytes from some parts of the brain to create new neurons in brain regions affected by Alzheimer's.

Fighting plaque buildup in the brain

The buildup of a pattern of protein amyloid "plaques"— typically in the hippo- campus—accompanies the beginnings of memory loss for recent events.

Another important current focus of AD research is something called amyloid plaques (also known as senile plaques), which are abnormal protein deposits in the synapses between brain cells.

There seem to be many possible reasons for amyloid plaque deposits, just as there are many possible causes of Alzheimer's. Some people inherit a defective gene for a protein known as APP, while other Alzheimer's cases result from a mutated form of a gene called presenilin, resulting in overproduction of the plaque protein. And there are many other cases of amyloid plaque buildup, and of Alzheimer's, that result from as-yet-unknown factors unrelated to genetics. In fact, most cases of Alzheimer's lack a clear genetic basis.

Even though Alzheimer's seems to have so many different possible causes (in this sense, it's like a disease such as cancer), the amyloid plaque buildup is a sure sign of the disease. But is it only a sign or symptom, with no causative role in the deterioration of mental function? If so, treating the plaques would do no good, since it would mean just treating the symptom without addressing the cause.

Apparently, the plaques are more than just a symptom of Alzheimer's. They appear to be an integral part of the process of the malfunction and eventual death of brain cells leading to problems with memory, reasoning, and social behavior characteristic of the disease. Many of the most promising Alzheimer's treatments are intended to work by helping the body to cure itself by combating senile plaque buildup.

You may have heard reports of an Alzheimer's vaccine. One vaccine, which has been tested successfully in mice and has undergone preliminary clinical trials in humans, works by stimulating the body's own immune system into clearing plaques out of brain cell synapses. Another, which has so far just been tested in mice, introduces antibodies against the amyloid protein. Other treatments target proteins and carbohydrates that serve to protect the amyloid deposits from destruction by natural processes in the body. Yet others bind to metals that appear to accelerate amyloid plaque accumulation.

In the meantime, you might want to take note of the fact that researchers have recently discovered that physical and mental exercise can double the rate at which new brain cells are generated from neural stem cells. This sort of mechanism may be at play in the studies that indicate a self-challenging lifestyle may have a preventive effect against Alzheimer's. So just don't let the promise of futuristic brain technology lure you into a state of complacence about the state of your mind.

EXERCISE: Singles only please

The point of this exercise is to stretch your short-term memory slightly. There are two of almost all the objects. What makes it interesting is the "almost." It should not take you more than four minutes to count how many objects there are only *one* of.

Try to find the solution by keeping track of the images in your mind's eye only—without making marks on the page or taking notes. When you have the answer you may write down the names of the single objects, if you like, before you check the hint at the bottom of the page or the answer in the Solutions section. Before you start get a timer ready and allow yourself four minutes.

emotional function

EMOTIONAL

Neuroscience is revealing the loci in the brain of our emotional faculties, and the neural pathways linking emotion to the "intellectual" functions of the mind. Emotion is intimately linked to cognition, and to the maintenance of the health of our brain cells as well as our body's immune system.

In the past, neuroscience has focused more on the brain's role in cognitive processes like memory than on emotion. That viewpoint is changing. We now know that emotion—dependent on structures in the brain itself—plays a crucial role in memory formation. Scientists have discovered that there's a neural pathway directly linking the brain's emotion and memory centers. The cortex—housing "higher," more complex and conscious faculties—may join in the act of interpreting or evaluating a threatening stimulus, but only after the emotionally-charged experience has been seared into memory. In fact, emotional memories are very hard to extinguish. It may seem like some particularly traumatic ones are banished from the conscious mind, but thy reappear years later in times of stress.

Mood and temperament fluctuate with levels of neurotransmitters, chemicals involved in the transmission of messages between brain cells. Some of the most philosophically challenging medical research of the last decade has centered on the manipulation of mood through the pharmacological manipulation of the brain's levels of neurotransmitters such as serotonin and norepinephrine. For the first time in human history, changing your emotional profile and, in a real sense, your personality seems as safe and easy as taking an aspirin.

We're also learning more, at a rapid clip, about the complex interactions between emotion and health, including the function of the immune system. Depression is linked to heart disease and reduced immunity, while laughter boosts your T-cell count. One of the most exciting recent discoveries is that stress, through the release of the hormone cortisol, can destroy brain cells and may lead to Alzheimer's. The more we know about this, the better our prospects for controlling our stress-response, counteracting the cognitively destructive effects of stress, and keeping both our body and mind healthy.

Acting as if

The way you arrange your facial muscles and posture can change your feelings. If you don't believe it, next time you're feeling blue stand up straight, walk with a spring in your step and compose your facial muscles into a smile. Things will look better. The reverse is also true. If you're in a happy frame of mind, try slumping your shoulders, looking down, and frowning. Soon you'll be feeling worse. Commiserate, anyone? In fact if a mood-altering drug as effective as "acting as if" were discovered it would probably be illegal to sell without a doctor's prescription. In the next section you'll find out why and how emotion and physical expression are so closely linked.

It's cheaper than gin

What would you think of someone who could control his or her emotional state with the same ease with which you comb your hair or stick out your tongue? You'd probably think they had a special gift, or an unusual power of the sort only attainable through years of practice or training. It turns out that the trick of manipulating your emotions is probably far simpler and more obvious than you'd ever imagined—so obvious, in fact, that it's been staring you in the face your whole life and you've never even noticed.

You have more control of your emotions than you think

We typically think of emotions as things that "happen" to us, that exist independently of us, that rise up inside us (and sometimes come out of us) whether we like it or not, or that come from outside and involve us in an event in which we're a purely passive participant. Consider the way we talk about emotions: we are "overcome by anger," "paralyzed by fear," "thrown into a state of confusion," or "overflowing with joy." A University of California researcher has accumulated an impressive body of evidence over the last several years that challenges this view. Among other things, he's shown that by consciously manipulating your facial muscles, you can actively generate whatever emotion you like—anger, fear, disgust, sadness, or pure, sweet joy.

You can change your mood by changing facial expressions

Paul Ekman, in collaboration with colleagues in the psychology and psychiatry departments at U.C. San Francisco, U.C. Berkeley, the University of Wisconsin at Madison and elsewhere, has performed experiments showing that subjects who simply manipulate their facial muscles according to his instructions frequently show many or all of the physiological correlates— increased heart rate, higher finger temperature, etc.—of the emotions associated with those facial expressions. EEG measures, too, show that manipulation of the facial muscles associated with happiness results in the same left-frontal brain activity known to correlate with spontaneous joy. And for all expressions, subjects report subjective feelings of emotion corresponding to the expression they're making.

Facial expressions and emotions are biologically linked
This fits well with Ekman's independent findings of the universality of facial expressions of emotion. In fieldwork with preliterate, isolated cultures of New Guinea, he found that members of those cultures matched descriptions of emotions to photographs of facial expressions just as Western subjects would match them.

This sort of evidence indicates that there are hard-wired, innate links between certain universally recognized facial muscle movements and autonomic motor activity (heart rate, skin conductance, etc.) and brain activity. This literally means that, if we want to feel different, we can change our facial expression into what we want our mood to become. Facial expression, which we usually think of as a mere *signal* of the emotion, actually can *create* the feeling.

How to feel teal: color and mood

If someone were to ask you to choose among different hues to find the ones that were most soothing or calming, you'd probably pick colors in the blue range, including perhaps indigo, violet, and maybe blue-green. For colors that are exciting or energizing, you'd probably draw on the red range, including orange and yellow. Are those just arbitrary culture-specific associations, the way that different languages match different speech sounds to meanings?

Apparently not. At least some color symbolism is deep-seated and deep-rooted, probably grounded in the natural effects of colors on the human brain and body.

Eyes, superhighway to the soul

Most neuroscientists consider eyes to be an extension of the brain—not separate sense organs that convey information to the brain, but parts of the brain itself protruding through the skull and lying naked to the world. As discoveries in neuroscience erode the barrier between mind and brain, it seems more apt than ever to call eyes a window into the soul. When your mother-in-law drops by unexpectedly and you greet her with a welcoming smile, it's the muscles around your eyes that betray the fact that you'd rather be watching a Seinfeld rerun (see "How to read deceit," p. 29. And if you tell the antique shop owner that you're really not that wild about the Victorian settee she's asking $1500 for, it's your pupils that might tell her you're lying (see "How to make yourself feel happier," p. 41).

There's very recent evidence for the existence of a hitherto unknown class of receptor cells in the eye's retina. You've probably heard of the other two types of receptors, *rods* and *cones*. Rods are used for night vision, and three types of cones (red, green, and blue) are what you use for color vision when the light's bright enough. Now, it turns out there are also light-sensitive cells whose job it is to gather information that the brain uses to set its own internal clock and mood.

The most solid knowledge about how the eyes' sensory input can affect brain states comes from research into Seasonal Affective Disorder, or SAD (see "Why are women more affected," p. 173). Natural sunlight raises levels of serotonin, the same neurotransmitter raised by antidepressants such as Prozac, as well as levels of dopamine, the brain chemical boosted by pleasurable drugs such as cocaine and alcohol.

Feeling blue? Try red instead

What about color? There's good evidence that colors in the red, orange, and yellow range stimulate what's called the sympathetic nervous system, raising pulse rate, blood pressure, and the overall level of the body's arousal. Blues tend to have the opposite effect, triggering the parasympathetic system to slow the body down. The sympathetic and parasympathetic systems are both part of what's called the autonomic nervous system, which regulates automatic, unconscious bodily functions like heart rate, blood pressure, appetite, sex drive, and body temperature.

Color isn't just a matter of hue, but intensity as well. We've all heard people in a really good mood say that colors look brighter, more vivid, more intensely saturated. People who talk like that aren't just speaking metaphorically. Depression may be correlated with impaired color sensitivity—that is, if you're depressed you'll tend to see the world as more washed-out, drab, colorless, and gray. If that's really true, then this would be just another way that vision can affect mood If you're feeling under the weather, try surrounding yourself with intense, saturated colors to improve your mood.

Is a blade of grass still green in the dark?

It's easy to overlook the fact that color is light. Something is green because it absorbs all visible wavelengths of light except the ones corresponding to what we call green; those wavelengths are reflected back to us and the cones in our eyes process them as green.

Colors are different frequency vibrations of light, and light is energy. Different colors correspond to different frequency vibrations of energy—of electromagnetic energy, to be precise—reaching your brain through your eyes. Another way that physicists think and talk about light and color is to say that one photon of light in the blue part of the spectrum has more energy than one photon in the green part.

The atoms and molecules of all the objects around us absorb light, which is another way of saying that they absorb different frequency vibrations of light energy, or photons with different energy levels. Different kinds of atoms and molecules absorb different parts of the spectrum, which means they absorb different levels of electromagnetic energy. Since your body is made of atoms and molecules, you can absorb light energy through your skin. The burn you get on a sunny summer day is your skin's reaction to the absorption of too much ultraviolet radiation for its own good. But only your eyes contain light and color receptors, which means only the eyes convey the energy of the visible light spectrum directly to the brain.

So different colors correspond to different wavelengths and energy levels of light. The light energy strikes your retina, reconverts to electrochemical energy, and travels to your brain by way of the optic nerve. It makes sense that your brain activity might be affected by the colors of things around you—the walls of the room, the carpet, or the upholstery.

Does that mean that you can be a more productive worker in a room painted a certain color, or get a room full of venture capitalists to fund your start-up if you wear the right color of clothes? You've probably heard of classrooms painted in colors to help students learn better, or pink holding cells calming down otherwise violent criminals. Does all that really work?

Yes and no. Even if it's true that certain colors have predictable effects on your brain, if you're in a room with teal-green walls, ceiling, and carpet, other colors will be impacting your brain whenever you see anything that isn't teal-green— your desk, your clothing, your own body. Even more important, the light from the light source itself will provide wavelengths corresponding to all sorts of colors besides teal-green, combining to make light that is more or less white. If, on the other hand, the light source offers the energy of only a limited portion of the visible spectrum, then the potential of a single color to affect the brain is stronger, especially if that light source is intense. That's what would happen if, say, you were to shine an intense red light directly into your eyes in a dark room.

That may shed some light on one of the most common mood-manipulating applications of color. Who would know more about manipulating mood than an actor or stage director? In an otherwise dark room, colored stage lights have a particularly powerful impact. That's true not just for the audience, but perhaps even more so for the actors. To get in the mood for her passionate romantic scenes in the movie Grand Hotel, Greta Garbo insisted on rehearsing under colored lights on an otherwise darkened stage. What color? You guessed it— red. You can bet she would never have won an Academy Award for that role if she'd used blue.

Self-illusions are good for you

Common sense has it that an accurate self-perception is essential to good mental health. By this view, "normal" people have a realistic understanding of who they are, what they are capable of, and what will happen in the future. People who lack such a balanced understanding, by contrast, may be unwell or, in extreme cases, insane.

The facts show that the opposite may be true. The healthiest and happiest people, it seems, are the ones who have unrealistically positive illusions about their own good qualities, their control of chance events, and their future prospects. The realistic ones have a tendency to suffer from some degree of depression.

Do you view yourself as happier, healthier, luckier, more virtuous, and more skilled than others?
People who score low on inventories of depression tend to exaggerate their own positive qualities. They'll rank themselves as having a stronger sense of ethics than most others, as being more creative, imaginative, and intelligent. Their assessment may not be true statistically, but they believe it and so are happier people than those who are more realistic in their self-evaluation.

THE
ANSWER
TO YOUR
PRAYERS

Do you think your good qualities are unique, and your flaws common?
Well-adjusted people tend not to focus on negative aspects of themselves to begin with. But pressed to acknowledge their flaws, they dismiss them as unimportant, often because "everybody's like that." Positive aspects, on the other hand—abilities, talents, and virtues— are perceived as rare and distinctive. Depressed people tend to have a more even-handed view of themselves and others.

Do you think your future will be better than your past?

Most people characterize themselves as more oriented toward
the future than the past, and most people believe the future
will be better than the past. There's really no way to know
beforehand whether such beliefs will turn out to be justified
or realistic. But some things point clearly to the fact that most
of us are simply not facing reality.

Why is life insurance such a hard sell? Because most of us
cultivate comforting illusions about our mortality. Far fewer
people believe that they'll ever be in a serious automobile accident, or be a victim of violent crime, than statistics indicate is
realistic. Why would otherwise happy and intelligent people
indulge in life-threatening activities—cigarette smoking or
tailgating at 80 miles per hour—if they were being realistic
about the risk involved? Happy and optimistic people aren't
realistic—they think *other* people will get lung cancer or die
in a car accident.

People with mild depression and low self-esteem tend to
have views of their prospects more in line with statistics and
hindsight, and tend to be more sober and analytical about
their future. It's a telling comment on the pervasiveness of
unrealistic optimism that the sober realists are often accused
of being pessimists. It is, in fact, *depressing* to be realistic, and
indulgence in realism about the future is even considered
socially unacceptable. And woe betide any politician who
admits that the future might not be better than the past.

Do you indulge in magical thinking?

It appears to be a good sign for your mental well-being if you
have an exaggerated view of your control of events and people
around you. "Normal" people indulge in this kind of thinking
much of the time. In games involving pure chance, we imagine we can somehow influence the outcome even though we
can't—by rolling the dice softly if we want low numbers and
hard if we want high numbers, for example.

Many people select lottery tickets with personally meaningful numbers—birth dates, anniversary dates, and the like—
rather than buying a randomly generated "quick-pick" ticket.
Rationally, this makes no sense. First, there's no way that a
personally meaningful number sequence will stand a greater

chance of winning in a random drawing. Second, "quick picks," while admittedly not more likely to win, are likely to result in a greater prize if they do win: certain date-based numbers (1 through 31) tend to be picked by people who take that approach, thus increasing the chances of having to share a prize with like-minded others. We may speculate that it might be possible to identify those at risk for mild depression by the fact that they choose the rational approach, rather than the irrational "magical" one. On the other hand, given that your chances of winning the lottery are probably less than those of finding buried treasure in your back yard, the very fact of buying the occasional lottery ticket may be indicative of a healthy temperament.

Illusions aren't just comforting—they improve performance
People like to have the illusion of control. Businesses have recognized this for many years: Employees are less likely to resist change if they're informed beforehand of what's happening and included in the decision-making process— even if they're given no real authority to change the ultimate outcome.

But there's more to it than just this. Having an unrealistically positive self-image and an exaggerated sense of control over events may be construed as a sort of egocentricity. Coincidentally, memory is organized egocentrically: The more personally meaningful something is, or the more self-relevant it is, the easier it is to remember. Therefore, positive self-illusions may have cognitive benefits for memory.

Even more important, positive illusions feed back into performance. People with unrealistically high self-perceptions, belief in personal control, and optimism about their future are often more motivated and persistent, and may perform better because of this.

SELF-TEST: Illusions inventory

The object of taking this test is to measure the types and degrees of the illusions you maintain about yourself. As the foregoing article explains, the higher your self-esteem the more likely you are to escape depression— up to a point of course.

At the end of this self-test you will find a scoring legend based on the number of points you have earned by totaling those allocated to each answer to the questions that follow.

Do you think you're more honest than others?

(a) Yes,very much so (2 pts.)

(b) Maybe a little (1 pt.)

(c) No (0 pts.)

You and a friend each buy a quick-pick lottery ticket. You ask him to hold your ticket while you tie your shoe, and you later realize the tickets must have been jumbled: the one you have is not the same as the one you originally had. Does this bother you?

(a) Yes, very much so (2 pts.)

(b) Maybe a little (1 pt.)

(c) No, it makes no difference (0 pts.)

Of all your talents and abilities, which one do you think is best or most important? _____

What percentage of other people in the country do you think share your level of skill in this ability?

(a) 0-30% (2 pts.)

(b) 30-70% (1 pt.)

(c) 70-100% (0 pts.)

(cont'd on next page)

Do you think you're a better driver than other people?

(a) No doubt about it (2 pts.)

(b) Better than average, but not dramatically (1 pt.)

(c) No (0 pts.)

Do you think that the success you've had in life is due more to hard work than just being in the right place at the right time?

(a) Very much (2 pts.)

(b) Somewhat (1 pt.)

(c) No (0 pts.)

Of all your flaws, which one do you think is worst or most significant?

_____

What percentage of other people in the country do you think also have this flaw?

(a) 70-100% (2 pts.)

(b) 30-70% (1 pt.)

(c) 0-30% (0 pts.)

Do you think you're more sincere than others?

(a) Very much so (2 pts.)

(b) Somewhat (1 pt.)

(c) No (0 pts.)

How true do you think the following is?

Most people act out of self-interest, but I try to help people rather than hurt them.

(a) Very true (2 pts.)

(b) Somewhat true (1 pt.)

(c) Not true (0 pts.)

(cont'd on next page)

Do you think that good things happen to people who do good, and bad things to people who do bad?

(a) Definitely (2 pts.)

(b) To some degree (1 pt.)

(c) No (0 pts.)

Do you think that people who get in automobile accidents are bad drivers?

(a) Almost all of the time (2 pts.)

(b) Only occasionally (1 pt.)

(c) No, it's basically random (0 pts.)

Scoring:
Add up your point total.

15–20 pts. =
You probably have very strong happiness-enhancing illusions.

8–14 pts. =
You have moderate happiness-enhancing illusions.

0–7 pts. =
You're a sober realist, and quite possibly at greater risk for mild depression.

How the brain recognizes fear

Mounting evidence indicates that different emotions are processed by distinct neural networks, rather than in a single part of the brain. At the same time, some brain structures seem to play an important role in processing a range of emotions. The amygdala, an almond-sized structure buried deep in the temporal lobe, serves to process social signals of emotion, with a particularly central role in generating and recognizing feelings of fear.

People whose amygdala has been damaged due to disease or invasive treatment of epilepsy lose the ability to discern fear in another's face, and are unable to match pictures of facial expressions with names of emotions or with other pictures of faces displaying the same emotions. The ability to identify the direction of another person's gaze also seems to be affected. These patients, however, have no difficulty recognizing the *identity* of a familiar person's face.

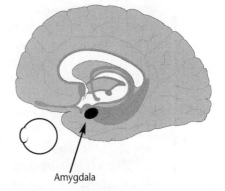

Amygdala

These new studies corroborate previous experimental evidence of the amygdala's role in social communication. Experiments with cats in the 1950's monitored the neurons in their amygdalas while they were interacting with each other or with humans. The amygdala neurons fired while the cats were miaowing and flank-rubbing, but did not fire when social interaction stopped. Experiments in the 1970's also implicated the amygdala in various aspects of social behavior in monkeys, including discrimination of the direction of another monkey's gaze.

Organic damage to the amygdala, it is speculated, may explain certain mental illnesses, including those involving a paranoid delusional state: if you're unable to ascertain a person's emotions by examining their facial expressions, then paranoia about their intentions may follow.

WHAT'S SO FUNNY? A role of the right frontal lobe

"...you make her laugh, you got a life." Jack Nicholson in *As Good As It Gets*, Gracie Films/Tristar Pictures, 1997

Most people know the feeling of "being in need of a good laugh" to raise their spirits. Unfortunately, for some brain-damaged people, the ability to appreciate humor can be so seriously impaired that, while they may retain some understanding of what constitutes humor, they no longer experience it to the same degree or with the same sense of satisfaction as do the rest of us.

Working at the University of Toronto, scientists Shammi and Stuss used tests to assess the ability of brain-damaged patients to appreciate various forms of humor: verbal humorous statements, longer verbal jokes, and cartoon-jokes that relied on purely visual details to impart their humor. In order to be able to distinguish which area of the brain was implicated, either CT (Computed Tomography) or fMRI (functional Magnetic Resonance Imaging) techniques were used.

With the verbal joke tests, Shammi and Stuss found that it was specifically damage to the right anterior region within the right frontal lobe of the brain that impaired humor. In the absence of a punchline, these patients were able to select a logical ending to the stem of a joke, thus demonstrating that they understood, if you will, a non-joke. But when asked to complete a joke by choosing between a logical ending, an unfunny (non-sequitur) ending, a slapstick ending, and the correct punchline, they were apt to choose the slapstick ending. While choosing slapstick showed that the patients understood the need for the element of surprise in a joke, they couldn't establish a relationship between the ending and the stem of the joke—like saying, "I think this should be funny but I don't know why." They were also unable to select the correct punchline, showing this requires a cognitive ability they appear to have lost. Moreover, it was only those patients with right frontal damage that displayed a deficit in the appropriate emotional responses to humor.

SELF-TEST: Facial expressions and emotions

There is good evidence that there are six basic emotions that correlate universally with facial expressions, regardless of culture. These emotions are happiness, sadness, anger, fear, surprise, and disgust. Even though much finer-grained emotions may be recognized on a culturally specific or language-specific basis (e.g., German Schadenfreude, "the feeling of pleasure you derive from someone else's misfortune"), these six basic emotions are recognized in every culture and universally recognizable from facial expression.

Match these six words for emotions with the expressions in the six illustrations:

Sadness	**Disgust**	**Anger**
Surprise	**Fear**	**Happiness**

Could you make a life or death decision based on someone's facial expression?

Picture this true story: Two policemen are on patrol at 2 a.m. in South Central Lost Angeles. One cop, Officer John Yarbrough of the Los Angeles County Sheriff's Department, gets out of the patrol car, gun drawn, to check the license and registration of a sports car they've pulled over. Suddenly a 17-year-old gets out of the passenger side of the stopped vehicle and points a gun directly at the officer. Yarbrough and the young man freeze, separated by no more than 10 feet. Yarbrough, clearly in danger, has a gut reaction—don't shoot the young man. Trusting his instinct, the officer lowers his weapon. The young man backs down.

What did Yarbrough find in the young man's facial expression that told the seasoned cop to hold his fire? Was it a lucky guess?

The library of facial expressions

Apparently Officer Yarbrough is one of the handful of virtuosos who can spot the truth in a person's face, despite what the person says or even how they act. But what about the average person? If she wanted to learn how to read the subtleties in peoples' expressions, where would she begin?

She could start with the work of Paul Ekman and Wallace Friesen. The two psychologists have assembled over 3,000 facial expressions, and the rules for reading and interpreting them, into the Facial Action Coding System, or FACS. Researchers have used the system to study diseases from schizophrenia to heart disease—FACS has even been used by computer animators at PIXAR and Dreamworks.

Facing practice

So how can you practice reading faces more deeply if you can't pore through the 500-page FACS manual or study the videos? One way is to turn off the sound and watch, say, Court TV. As long as no one's been injected with Botox, you'll be surprised at what you read between the lies.

"Watch two Marx Brothers movies and call me in the morning"

Science is finally catching up to what we knew all along: Laughter is good for you. Or, as Proverbs 17:22 puts it, "A cheerful heart is a good medicine."

Laughter improves your blood circulation, exercises your abdominal muscles, increases your heart rate, expels stale air from your lungs, aids digestion, and releases muscle tension. After a bout of laughter, your blood pressure drops to a lower, healthier level. According to laugh researcher William F. Fry, one hundred laughs provide the same cardiovascular benefit as ten minutes of rowing.

Why *Duck Soup* may be better than chicken soup

In addition, researchers working in the new field of psycho-neuroimmunology—the study of the effects of psychological status on immune function—have determined that laughter has a beneficial effect on the immune system. While stressful emotions trigger the release of cortisol and aldosterone, which may reduce immunity by lowering your T-cell count, laughter does just the opposite. It also activates virus-fighting killer cells and interferon-gamma, lowers your levels of the stress-related neurotransmitter epinephrine (a.k.a. adrenaline), raises your levels of immunoglobins, and increases the production of natural pain-reducing neuropeptides such as endorphin. Laughter is good medicine—and it's free!!

What happens when you laugh?

Psychologist Peter Derks, using EEG readings, has done more than anyone to improve our understanding of the neurological underpinnings of laughter. When you're presented with a joke, your left hemisphere's language centers begin the task of processing the words. Within milliseconds, "emotional" regions of the frontal lobe kick in, followed instantaneously by regions of the right hemisphere responsible for posing the juxtaposition or finding the incongruity involved in getting the point of a joke. (Stroke patients who have lost the function of this region will be unable to get the point of a joke or story, or will laugh inappropriately at any non-sequitur.) This is followed within milliseconds by the participation of the sensory-processing region of the occipital area, and finally—still only a fraction of a second, typically, after hearing the punch line—negatively charged delta waves wash over your entire cerebral cortex as you "get" the joke and start laughing. Some have speculated that the creativity-jogging potential of humor is a direct result of the complex and integrated brain stimulation triggered by good jokes.

Women tend to laugh more often during conversation

All humans in all cultures have the capacity to laugh. Human babies universally begin to laugh at around two to three months, and primate researchers tell us that chimpanzees respond with breathy, pant-like laughter when tickled or chased. Even anacephalic infants, born with nothing but a brain stem, will appear to laugh when tickled. Laughter is, then, an automatic and innate behavior. However, there are also some interesting cultural variations.

In our culture, the number of laughs per day peaks at around age six, and then declines as we move into adulthood. This is a culturally specific fact. Also specific to our culture is the fact that, when a man is talking to another man, speaker and listener tend to laugh roughly equally. When a woman talks to another woman, the speaker tends to laugh more frequently than the listener. This effect is much stronger when a woman is talking to a man. But when a man is talking to a woman, the listener will laugh more frequently than the speaker.

It's an open question, however, whether this sort of polite social laughter produces the same physiological and psychological benefits as a laugh of abandoned joy. And is derisive laughter as salubrious as mirthful laughter? Apparently not. What about laughter at another's expense? Perhaps initially, but subsequent guilt or other negative repercussions may outweigh any initial stress-reducing effect. True mirthful laughter is surprisingly difficult to fake. It is not simply the physical act, but also the emotional state underlying it that is important.

There do exist largely innate (see "Show me the child at seven...," p. 59) individual differences in temperament which predispose some people to laughter more than others. But the humorous insight underlying mirthful laughter is more a matter of perspective than biological determination. Anyone can develop this perspective, and sometimes all it takes is allowing oneself the indulgence of a moment's irreverence for a stressful event to release itself in a cathartic appreciation of life's absurdity. Shakespeare exploited this in his alternation of serious scenes with humorous ones. For Goethe, humor was one means of releasing emotional blockages that could harm both mind and body, just as in oriental medicine certain physical or emotional states may block flow of life's energy, or Chi.

 ### EXERCISE: Pick the punch line

Read the story below and pick what you think would be the funniest punch line. There is no correct answer. However, absence of an ability to detect humor is often linked to the right hemisphere of the brain, where the components of poetry and music are also synthesized.

 A politician campaigning yet again for reelection arranged to speak at a full-care retirement facility seeking the senior vote. When he rose to start his speech he asked his audience, "Do you know who I am?"

After a brief silence a quavering old voice spoke from the audience:

1. "No, but we won't remember later anyway."

2. "Yes, that's why those of us who came are all sitting near the door."

3. "No, but if you go to the front desk they'll tell you."

Are you phlegmatic or bilious? Do you suffer from choler? Would you choose to be more sanguine if it were as easy as taking an aspirin?

If mood were determined purely by identifiable events in our life—good news from the boss or bad news from the IRS—then we could view our emotional life as a canvas upon which our environment paints a picture of anxiety, depression, elation,

Melencolia I by Albrecht Dürer, 1514. (See Exercise on page 164.)

or optimism. But this is clearly the wrong way to look at it. Our moods seem to fluctuate from hour to hour and day to day in a way that can't be reduced to external events. And some people just appear to have a dour or melancholy outlook, while others are naturally optimistic. If the painter metaphor is at all appropriate, then it seems to be our inner mood which is coloring our environment, not vice versa.

In medieval European medicine, fluctuations and individual differences of temperament were attributed to the effects of various bodily *humors* (literally, "moistures" or "fluids"): blood (associated with optimism, hence "sanguine"); phlegm (apathy—hence "phlegmatic"); bile (melancholy or irascibility—hence "bilious"); and yellow bile or choler (anger—hence "choleric"). An imbalance of phlegm, then, would cause apathy, and to cure this all you had to do was bring the phlegm into proper balance with the other fluids. A person with just the right balance of each was said to be in "good humor."

The traditional approach captures the idea that mood is an internal state that may fluctuate independently of external circumstances. Current wisdom differs from the "humor" theory, however, in the substances viewed as responsible for this state.

sending neuron

neurotransmitters

receiving neuron

Mood is in the brain, not the spleen
The dominant theory at the moment is that the locus of mood is in the brain, and the precise substances implicated in mood fluctuation, as well as in states of chronic depression and mania, are chemicals called biogenic amines—otherwise known as neurotransmitters.

The way it works is this:
The cellular basis of mood lies in the transmission of messages across the synapses of certain brain neurons. Chemicals that facilitate this kind of transmission are called neurotransmitters.

One important member of their class is called amines, a group of chemicals with a structure resembling that of ammonia.

When amines are released by a nerve cell into the synapse, a message is conveyed to an adjacent cell. (A particular nerve cell will produce just one kind of amine neurotransmitter, and hence send just one kind of message; however, any given nerve cell may have receptors for more than one neurotransmitter, and hence receive more than one kind of message.) This process is terminated when the amines are reabsorbed into the transmitting cell and deactivated by "janitorial" enzymes.

An excess of amines is considered to cause mania, and a deficiency, depression. One way of treating chronically depressed individuals, then—those who once would have been considered to suffer from an excess of bile or phlegm—would be to increase the level of amines either by slowing their reabsorption back into the nerve cell or blocking the janitorial enzyme that deactivates them. This is, in fact, precisely how most antidepressants work, such as imipramine, iproniazid, Elavil, Norpramin, and Prozac.

Like the "humor" theory that preceded it, the biogenic-amine theory is far from perfect. One problem is that, while imipramine blocks the reuptake of amines within a matter of minutes or hours, it takes weeks before a patient actually begins to *feel* less depressed. Second, some effective anti-depressants have no direct interaction with amines, and others actually decrease the level of amines in the brain. Clearly, then, the facts are somewhat more complex than the amine theory would indicate.

Should we interfere with nature?

One reason it's risky to treat mood disorders with drugs like these is that the interactions of brain chemicals are so complex that it's hard to isolate and treat just one problem without causing other problems elsewhere. In this respect, the environment of brain structure and chemistry is not unlike the external ecosystem. For example, a class of monoamine-oxidase inhibitors (MAOIs), still in common use in Great Britain, work by blocking the amine-digesting janitorial enzymes. But some amines raise blood pressure, and these same amines are present in foods such as aged cheeses, some wines, ripe figs, and other foods. So when a patient on MAOIs eats these foods, blood pressure may shoot up to dangerous and sometimes life-threatening levels.

Antidepressants such as Prozac are considered by many physicians to be superior to other amine regulators precisely because they're so specific in their effects: they interact with just one single amine—serotonin—by blocking its reuptake into the nerve cell. This results in elevated serotonin levels—ideally resulting in greater self-confidence, lessened anxiety, improved optimism, and enhanced energy and mental clarity—but few other side effects, and with none of the distortions of perception or mood crashes caused by alcohol or cocaine. True, Prozac is not quite as "clean" a drug as one could imagine. Serotonin has at least fifteen different kinds of receptors in the brain, only some of which have to do with mood; others regulate different functions such as digestion and sexual appetite. Prozac, in inhibiting the general reuptake of serotonin rather than in stimulating or blocking serotonin-sensitive sites, affects all of these receptors. Clinical trials of a new generation of "cleaner" antidepressants—ones which target specific receptors rather than raising neurotransmitter levels throughout the brain—are in fact already under way in both Europe and the United States. (The French, by the way, consume more antidepressants than Americans per capita; so much for the myth of the low-stress Mediterranean lifestyle.)

Prozac even appears to have beneficial effects on the mood and temperament of many individuals who fail to meet the criteria for true clinical depression—people who traditionally might have been viewed as having levels of depression or anxiety well within the "normal" range, or as suffering from extremely mild personality disorders. This has given rise to the uniquely modern dilemma of "cosmetic" psychopharma-cology: Is it right to take a drug that has the sole effect of making you more like the kind of self-confident, outgoing, optimistic, energetic person you always wished you could be, or should you simply accept your inborn temperamental constitution as the hand that nature dealt you?

EXERCISE: "Melencolia I"

Albrecht Dürer's engraving on page 160 is based on the writings of Marsillo Ficino, who claimed that anyone who excels in the arts is a "melancholic." He distinguished between "black bile" and "white (or yellow) bile" melancholy, with black being mania and white being brilliancy.

Architects, artisans, and artists (all of whom used mathematics as a tool) were inclined toward the "imaginative" melancholic temperament as depicted in the engraving. Clearly, the medieval meaning of the word *melancholy* was not sadness, as it means now, but an enlightened frustration over the attempt to understand and design a meaningful order from observation of the chaos and contradictions of nature.

Without looking back at page 160, list as many of the objects in the engraving as you can that relate to art, architecture, the artisans' crafts, and mathematics. This is an exercise in observation, memory, and imagination.

 EXERCISE: Emotions

ACROSS

1. Brain part that perceives emotion in another's facial expression
3. Be offensive to
5. Be afraid of
6. Emotional response to the unexpected
7. A state of well-being and contentment

DOWN

2. Rage
4. Grief or unhappiness

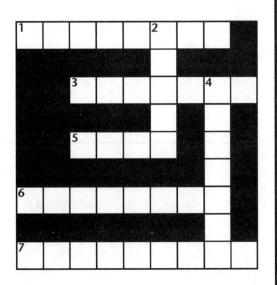

Hint: 1 Across is amygdala.

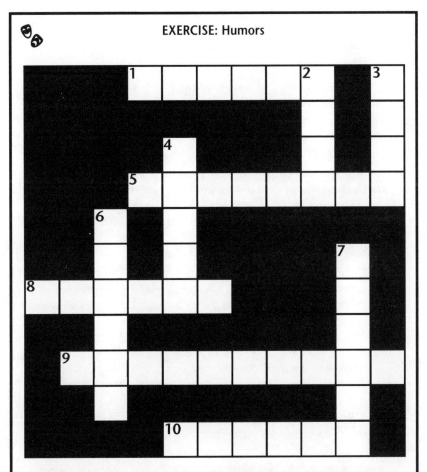

EXERCISE: Humors

ACROSS

1. Humor identified with an apathetic temperament
5. Adjective describing temperament formerly associated with blood
8. Antidepressant that blocks serotonin from being reabsorbed into a cell
9. Emotional condition caused by insufficiency of amines
10. Class of neurotransmitter having chemical structure similar to ammonia

DOWN

2. Blocks enzyme that digests amines
3. Humor identified with melancholia
4. Emotional condition caused by excess of amines
6. Humor identified with an angry temperament
7. In medieval medicine, fluids in the body that determine temperament

Hint: 9 across is depression.

SELF-INVENTORY: Neuroticism, extraversion, openness, agreeableness, and conscientiousness

One of the most widely used tools for categorizing individuals according to basic personality traits is called the NEO-Personality Inventory, short for Neuroticism, Extraversion, and Openness to experience; a more recent revised version adds Agreeableness and Conscientiousness.

It's easy to be judgmental about someone's "definition" with respect to these traits. For example, nobody would want to characterize himself or herself as basically moralistic and uncomfortable with complexities, as opposed to introspective, creative, and open to new experiences. It's therefore always necessary to find a less direct way of eliciting such information, either by interviewing friends or family members or by asking the person how he or she would think, feel, or act in a given situation, without ever mentioning the loaded adjectives themselves.

It's also important to realize that high or low values in any of the dimensions don't necessarily mean the person has a "good" or "bad" personality, or is well or poorly adjusted, successful or unsuccessful, and so on. Fighter pilots are high in Extraversion, but low in Agreeableness. Modesty and tender-mindedness may be good qualities in some walks of life, but certainly don't represent the "right stuff" when it comes to flying an F-14. It may well be that there has been evolutionary selection for a wide range of personality traits in different individuals, since different kinds of people with different modes of action and interaction may enhance the survival prospects of the social group as a whole.

There is persuasive evidence, by the way, that some of these variables are strongly determined by birth order. Oldest siblings may tend to rate higher in Conscientiousness than youngest siblings, while the youngest tend to rank higher in Openness. Whether you think a high Conscientiousness ranking is "good" or "bad"—whether it means the person is ethical and responsible or simply a moralistic goody-goody—may well depend on whether you yourself are a youngest or oldest sibling.

See where you rate by answering the following questions and adding up points in each section. There is a key at the end to give an idea of what personality traits you most likely have.

(cont'd on next page)

A.

1. When you travel on vacation, do you like to plan an itinerary in advance and make reservations for each night's stay, or do you prefer to leave your options open?

a) plan an itinerary (1 pt.)

b) leave options open (2 pts.)

2. When you go to a new restaurant and get a dish that you really like, will you order that dish again on a repeat visit, or will you try something different?

a) order dish again (1 pt.)

b) try something different (2 pts.)

3. Ralph Waldo Emerson once wrote that "a foolish consistency is the hobgoblin of little minds." Do you think that people tend to adhere to consistency too uncritically, or do you feel we'd all be better off if consistency were more highly valued?

a) consistency should be highly valued (1 pt.)

b) people adhere too uncritically to consistency (2 pts.)

4. If you see a child displaying acrobatic skills on his bike in the middle of a busy sidewalk, would you be more likely to be angry at him for endangering others or to admire him for his skill?

a) angry (1 pt.)

b) admire (2 pts.)

5. If your child were to ask to put an unusual condiment or topping on her food—say, parmesan cheese on her breakfast cereal or jam on her spaghetti—would you be inclined to let her try it, or would you forbid it outright?

a) forbid it (1 pt.)

b) let her try it (2 pts.)

(cont'd on next page)

B.

1. If a coworker made a clearly phony excuse to stay home sick one morning, would you be irritated at her duplicity or concerned that she might have some problem that she feels she has to hide?

a) irritated (1 pt.)

b) concerned (2 pts.)

2. Imagine you order a dish at a restaurant and find it to be overcooked and oversalted. When the waiter comes by and asks, "How is everything today?" would you be more likely to tell him what you don't like about the dish or to say, "Fine, thank you"?

a) tell him (1 pt.)

b) say, "Fine" (2 pts.)

3. Which would you say better characterizes your attitude toward friendship?

a) it is good to push your friends to their limits, and to make them question their satisfaction with themselves and their own performance or behavior, in order that they achieve more in life (1 pt.)

b) it is important to show friends that you like and support them, and to avoid making them feel insecure or hurting their feelings (2 pts.)

4. If someone you're talking to uses or pronounces a word incorrectly, would you be more likely to correct them or to ignore the error?

a) correct them (1 pt.)

b) ignore the error (2 pts.)

5. When you're driving on the freeway and someone pulls in front of you, do you automatically slow down to make room between you and him, or do you ever stay on his tail for a while or pass him to show your irritation?

a) stay on his tail or pass him (1 pt.)

b) slow down (2 pts.)

(cont'd on next page)

C.

1. If a close friend were to tell you that she's concerned about you because you seem to be depressed, would you feel upset or flattered that she cares enough about you to tell you?

a) flattered (1 pt.)

b) upset (2 pts.)

2. If you were to meet a graphologist (handwriting analyst) at a party, do you think it would be fun to show him a sample of your handwriting, or would you be anxious or self-conscious about the conclusions he might draw about you?

a) fun (1 pt.)

b) anxious (2 pts.)

3. When you express anger or irritation with someone, do you usually later feel that you did the right thing, or do you sometimes feel guilty or worry that you might have overreacted?

a) feel I did the right thing (1 pt.)

b) feel guilty (2 pts.)

4. Do you think that a stranger would be able to tell much about you after a single encounter, or do you feel that your projected personality changes enough from one setting to another that any such evaluation would probably be incorrect?

a) would be able to tell (1 pt.)

b) evaluation would probably be incorrect (2 pts.)

5. Do you ever have the experience of feeling guilty or mortified about something you've said in the past, or are you more likely to have the attitude that everyone makes mistakes and that all you can do is learn from them and try to avoid making the same mistakes in the future?

a) everyone makes mistakes (1 pt.)

b) feel mortified (2 pts.)

(cont'd on next page)

D.

1. When arriving at or departing from a dinner party given by close friends, do you prefer to hug or shake hands?

a) shake hands (1 pt.)

b) hug (2 pts.)

2. If given a choice between cooperating on a project with a group of others, or finishing a task on your own, which would you usually choose?

a) finish on my own (1 pt.)

b) work with others (2 pts.)

3. When you buy something that turns out to be defective, does it bother you to go back to exchange it, or do you think it's silly to feel shy about it?

a) bothers me (1 pt.)

b) silly to feel shy (2 pts.)

4. If someone wants to take your picture at a party, do you usually feel that they should just go ahead and take it without making a fuss, or do you think it's fine for them to interrupt what you're doing and ask you to pose and smile?

a) just go ahead (1 pt.)

b) OK to interrupt (2 pts.)

5. Orson Welles, in a certain wine commercial which aired in the 1970's, once said he liked to "cast" parties the way he casts a play. Would you like to attend such a party, or would you resent the host's manipulative expectations and prefer to stay home?

a) prefer to stay home (1 pt.)

b) like to attend (2 pts.)

(cont'd on next page)

E.

1. Let's say a package arrives on December 10 addressed to you and your spouse. You open it, and find dozens of cunningly crafted Swiss chocolates in red and green Christmas foil. Would you go ahead and taste one, or feel compelled to save them all until Christmas?

a) go ahead and taste one (1 pt.)

b) wait until Christmas (2 pts.)

2. While waiting in line at an automated bank teller, you step on a small brown paper bag, pick it up, and find $500 in 20-dollar bills inside. There's no name or identification of any kind. Would you keep it, or go inside the bank and give it to the teller with your name and telephone number in case nobody claims it?

a) keep it (1 pt.)

b) give it to the teller (2 pts.)

3. Would you be more inclined to agree with those who opine that a neat desk is the sign of a sick mind, or that a messy desk betrays a lazy nature?

a) a neat desk is the sign of a sick mind (1 pt.)

b) a messy desk betrays a lazy nature (2 pts.)

4. Do you think that laws should always be obeyed by everyone, or that rules are made to be broken?

a) rules are made to be broken (1 pt.)

b) laws should always be obeyed (2 pts.)

5. If you're halfway through a book, do you usually finish it even if your interest flags, or do you see no point in finishing it if you're no longer interested?

a) no point in finishing (1 pt.)

b) finish it even if no longer interested (2 pts.)

(cont'd on next page)

Key:

*A: 10 pts. = Rebellious, nonconforming, imaginative, liberal-minded:
high in Openness to experience*

*5 pts. = Conventional, conservative:
low in Openness*

*B: 10 pts. = Sympathetic, compassionate, compliant:
high in Agreeableness*

*5 pts. = Suspicious, critical, antagonistic:
low in Agreeableness*

*C: 10 pts. = Temperamental, self-pitying, thin-skinned, vulnerable:
high in Neuroticism*

*5 pts. = Calm, self-assured, objective:
low in Neuroticism*

*D: 10 pts. = Gregarious, assertive, socially poised:
high in Extraversion*

*5 pts. = Quiet, reserved, most comfortable alone:
low in Extraversion*

*E: 10 pts. = Well-organized, dependable, ethical, dutiful:
high in Conscientiousness*

*5 pts. = Disorganized, self-indulgent, capricious:
low in Conscientiousness*

Why are women more affected by seasonal fluctuations in day length?

When lengthening shadows send the squirrels scurrying to hoard nuts for the winter nights ahead, your own brain chemistry is adjusting to the waning daylight hours in a way that may explain seasonal affective disorder (SAD)—at least, if you're a female of the species.

SAD, also known as winter depression, typically occurs during the winter months of temperate or high-latitude climates, and affects far more women than men.

Women respond to melatonin more than men do

As the summer solstice comes and goes and the nights begin to lengthen, women experience a proportional increase in their levels of melatonin, a hormone secreted by the brain's pineal gland. (Melatonin is involved in the regulation of the body's biological clock; that's why it's taken in pill form by frequent flyers who have difficulty adjusting to time-zone changes. It's also an increase in melatonin production, in response to the lengthening nights, that prompts squirrels to gather nuts for the winter.) Other hormones adjust to the shortening days as well; prolactin, which induces a sense of well-being during what nature intended to be a long night of rest, experiences a lengthened nightly surge.

If left to follow their internal adjustments to the seasonal rhythms, most women would presumably fall quite naturally into a winter pattern of long nightly slumbers. As it is, in our modern world, they must instead force their bodies to adhere to what is in effect a year-round summer pattern of long days and short nights.

Men, on the other hand, appear relatively immune to seasonal changes, permitting their bodies to be convinced by artificial light that summer never ends. In order to experience the sort of hormonal fluctuation that women do, they must be isolated at night from the yellow glow of the electric bulb and the shifting blue light of the television set.

Is there a cure for SAD?

Some researchers have found that light therapy—exposure to intense artificial light at a phototherapy clinic or from a commercially available personal "light-box"—has such a beneficial effect on wintertime depression that it has been dubbed a "natural Prozac." This would come as no surprise to the

ancient Greeks, who recognized the therapeutic potential of light, or to early twentieth-century physicians who advocated the use of "solariums" for the treatment of both physical and psychological ailments.

Experiments have shown that the therapeutic effect of light works through the eyes, not the skin. People who are naked but blindfolded show no antidepressant response to light therapy, while people wrapped like mummies except for their eyes respond well.

Is it necessary to expose oneself to UV light in order to cure winter depression? Maybe not. The problem with relying on typical artificial light sources for your wintertime needs may be quantity, not quality. A well-lit home or office typically has only 300 to 600 lux (a standard unit of brightness roughly equivalent to a candle flame), while a sunny summer day outdoors may provide over 100,000 lux. In any case, personal light-boxes, which typically provide about 10,000 lux, are available in both UV and UV-shielded versions.

How sleep patterns change in the winter months

When humans—of both the XX and XY persuasion—are left undisturbed to the high-latitude seasonal fluctuations of nature, this is what happens:

During long nights of winter darkness, we lie quietly for far longer than the demands of modern life would normally permit. Twelve hours seems about average, with four or five hours of deep sleep, followed by several hours of quiet, wakeful but meditative resting, followed by another four or five hours of REM (or dream) sleep.

One reason for the nonanxious, meditative character of the period of quiet wakefulness between the two sleep periods is that release of the hormone prolactin is sustained during the entire 12 hours. This is the same hormone that keeps animals from getting restless when tending the den or nest. During shorter summer nights, melatonin secretion drops dramatically, and prolactin is released in a relatively brief burst.

So if you want more natural, meditative prolactin—get lots and lots of sleep.

 EXERCISE: How not to be SAD

If you're curious about wintertime sleep the way we're "really" supposed to experience it, try the following simple experiment.

Choose a night without any conflicting obligations, hang a "do not disturb" sign on the bedroom door, cover the bedroom window so no light comes in, unplug the phone, and settle in at six or seven o'clock for a long night's slumber. Don't worry if you don't fall asleep immediately—you probably won't, but that's perfectly natural. After perhaps a couple hours of lying still and thinking, you'll probably drift off to sleep.

You probably won't sleep through the entire night, but that's OK too. If you wake up at one or two o'clock, don't feel obligated to get up and do anything—just lie still, letting your thoughts run however they like, and you'll drift back to sleep again within an hour or two. You'll probably awaken naturally at seven o'clock or so, without need of an alarm clock. Pull back the drapes and feel how wonderful, how refreshing, how calming a really good night's sleep is.

This experiment works best in the wintertime, in which case (assuming your latitude is high enough), you won't even need to shut out any unwanted natural light—just go to bed at sunset, and awaken at sunrise.

GENDER DIFFERENCES IN THE BRAIN

Many studies have shown gender differences in the brain, but the results are difficult to evaluate and easy to misinterpret. For one thing, there is almost always a huge amount of gender overlap, so that the differences only emerge in large sample sizes. Any given man's brain may fit the generalizations made about women's brains, and vice versa. In this respect, the biological differences observed in the brain mirror what is found with gender differences in cognitive abilities. Men generally perform slightly better on certain tests of spatial ability (visually rotating three-dimensional objects), while women tend to perform a bit better on certain verbal tasks—but any given woman may be a genius at visually-oriented math or physics, and any given man may be a brilliant linguist or wordsmith. Another problem is that the absolute size of a brain region, or of the brain as a whole, does not necessarily translate into a given level of intelligence. Neural density, rather than size alone, may be a more meaningful indication of mental ability.

Still, these studies can be fascinating and provocative. A recent report published in the journal *Science* indicates that, in a resting state, men have more activity in the temporal-limbic region and women have more activity in the cingulate region. The temporal-limbic region is a "primitive," action-oriented part of the limbic system, a brain structure that regulates emotions. The cingulate is also part of the limbic system but evolved more recently. It plays a role in symbolic representations of actions rather than the actions themselves.

Another study in *Science* reports that women have a greater density of neurons in the cortex of the planum temporale within the Sylvian fissure, a region involved in auditory association and part of the neural substrate of language function, especially intonation.

What is the brain so busy doing, and not doing, while we sleep?

Everyone from Plato to Freud, it seems, has had his own pet theory about why we dream. Now it's the turn of scientists with PET technology: positron-emission tomography, that is, the new high-tech method of obtaining a visual map of the brain in action.

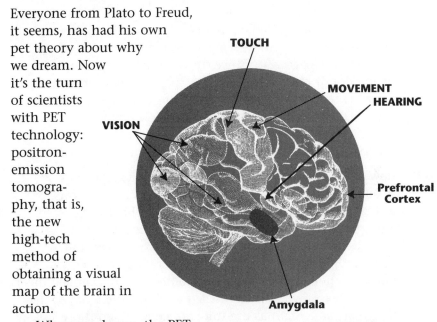

When we dream, the PET image shows that many regions of the brain are, well, asleep: dark as the arctic on a winter solstice eve. A vast section of the prefrontal cortex, for example—a part of the brain crucially involved in planning ahead and our sense of time—is completely deactivated; this may explain the curious temporal distortions we experience in our dreams. One area that lights up like a Christmas tree, though, is the amygdala—the emotional control center of the brain. (See "How the brain recognizes fear," p. 153, and diagram on pages 180–181.)

What's the connection between emotions and dreams?
Evidence is accumulating that a major function of dreaming is to reinforce lessons learned during the day. (See "The night a middle-aged man tackled his bureau in his sleep," p. 43.) When we're challenged to learn complex material, the proportion of REM sleep—the "rapid eye movement" phase, during which we dream—increases. And when REM sleep is disrupted or suppressed one or even several nights after our learning a

complex logic task, we're much more likely to forget what we've learned—even if the rest of our sleep cycle is permitted to proceed undisturbed. (It's easy to try this at home, since you can suppress your REM cycle by drinking alcohol before bed.)

Next, consider the fact that emotionally charged experiences tend strongly to be seared into permanent long-term memory (see page 180). Since the amygdala is the prime locus of emotion it must somehow be responsible for getting past the gatekeeper that prevents the details of everyday life from being remembered forever (see "Imagine a memory-enhancing drug...," p. 77.) As we dream the amygdala is performing its otherwise familiar role of mediating memory formation.

How can I trick my amygdala into helping me learn faster?

In addition to the basics—get enough sleep, don't drink too much in the evening—sleep scientists have discovered a simple but effective way to enhance memory formation. In an experiment with undergraduate psychology students, they first played a tape of a clicking sound (not too disruptive, but loud enough to be heard) while the students applied themselves to learning a difficult logic task. They then played the tape that same night as the students slept. When those students were retested on the task a week later, their performance was 23% better than that of a control group. This shows that you can use background noise as a nighttime cue to aid in the processing and memorization of learning tasks.

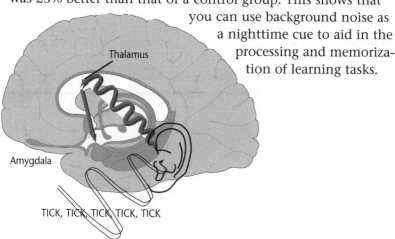

Thalamus

Amygdala

TICK, TICK, TICK, TICK, TICK

WHAT BRAIN SCANS DO

The goal of picturing brain activity without surgery is to locate damage or to identify where the brain processes different tasks, or fails to.

X-rays (1920's) showed only rough structure since they couldn't image the soft tissues such as the cortex.

The electroencephalograph, or EEG (1920's), was found to measure changes in electrical activity in the brain correlating with different kinds of mental activity.

CAT, computerized axial tomography (late 1960's), could take "snapshot" images of detailed structures, so CAT scans could be used diagnostically to locate tumors, lesions, or blood clots in the brain.

Modern PET, positron emission tomography, fMRI, magnetic resonance imaging, and MEG, magnetoencephalography, provide information about activity in different areas of the brain in response to specific stimuli— such as attempting to describe a scene, looking at a disgusting picture, reading a dull list of words or a love story, etc.

With PET scans, a volunteer is injected with a mildly radioactive solution or inhales a radioactive gas and places his head in a ring of gamma-ray detectors. The parts of the brain that are working hardest receive the most radiation-tainted oxygenated blood, and those parts show up as bright reds and yellows in a computer-generated photograph.

Magnetic resonance images of a female (left) and male (right) brain. Note that the female's corpus callosum (in the center of the brain image) is thicker towards the rear than the male's. The corpus callosum stops growing at puberty; since males reach puberty earlier, a man's corpus callosum—which connects the left and right hemispheres of the brain—is thinner than a woman's. This may account for a tendency towards more "integrative" thinking among women than men.

THE FAST TRACK:
Why the amygdala shortcuts conscious thought

When Louis Armstrong was asked once to define jazz he responded: *Man, if you gotta ask, you'll never know.* The amygdala never asks. It punches the panic button the instant the brain senses trouble. It stores the life-threatening experiences such as the heat of flame, shape of snake, or approach of an abusive parent.

Its partner, the thalamus, routes data coming in through the senses to the part of the cortex that decides how to use the information—*unless* the data appears life-threatening. Then the thalamus sends the message directly to the amygdala at the same time. In the example shown here the visual cortex can take its time considering whether this tiger is an endangered species or stuffed with kapok. Then it can override the amygdala's instantaneous reaction to the possibility that it could be lunch.

One reason adults have difficulty understanding or changing their responses to abuse experienced as children is that they have learned and stored such serious threats in this subconscious system of the primitive brain. That brain system was designed to keep us alive. It depends on emotional responses that can't afford the luxury of critical reasoning.

EXERCISE: Picking up signals

1	2	3	■	4	5	6	■	7	8	9	■	10	11	12
13			■	14			■	15			■	16		
17			■	18		19				20				
■		21	22			■	23						■	■
24	25				■	26			■	27		28	29	
30			■	31				■	32					
33			34			■	35				■			
■		36			■	37				■	■			
38	39	40			■	41					42	43	44	
45				■	46			■	47					
48			■	49			■	50						
■		51	52			■	53			■	■			
54	55				56			■		57	58	59		
60			■	61		62			■	63				
64			■	65			66			■	67			

ACROSS

1. Ship deserter
4. Boston's transit sys.
7. TV program abbr.
10. Socialite
13. — I saw Elba
14. — Lingus
15. — and a bone
16. Hematite, for one
17. After Feb.
18. Cape location
21. Pierre's state, for short
23. All — (conductor's cry)
24. Beer glass
26. Tribe
27. St. —'s fire
30. Chums
31. Cloy
32. "No man has a hope who has not had —"
33. Brain part that interprets data and signals action
35. Scans a sentence
36. Hockey great and family
37. Bullring star
38. Gazes fixedly
41. Kind of guidance
45. Trace of color
46. Part of TLC
47. Gait
48. Opposer
49. London gallery
50. Shore birds
51. Recorded
53. Paper raw material
54. Certain islander
57. Horse morsel
60. Pig's home

(cont'd on next page)

61. Movie dog's first name
62. Madrid wife
63. Presidential initials
64. The piper's son
65. Past due
66. Brain activity scanning technology
67. Defeat at bridge

DOWN

1. Kind of sleep during dreaming
2. Altar in the sky
3. Succinctly
4. Naval historian
5. Ship-building wood
6. Kennedy letters
7. Clannish
8. Breakfast food
9. Near Eastern title
10. Draws, in a way
11. Sin
12. Wager
19. Half a Washington city
20. Section of the cortex that monitors social consequences
22. Giving up, as profits
24. Watering place
25. Scottish cap
26. Coolidge and Peete
28. West of early movies
29. Hosp. units

31. Golfer's aims
32. Berne's river
34. Dreary, to a Scot
35. Skin opening
37. Weight allowance
38. RR stop
39. Wedding anniversary
40. Opposite
41. Father, to an Etonian
42. Camera supports
43. Web company initials
44. Certain linemen
46. Chicago gangster
49. Long-nosed mammal
50. Attack
52. Pielet
53. Peel
54. Kennedy visitor
55. Simpson's judge
56. Clairvoyance, for short
58. Summer cooler
59. Asian holiday

Hint: 54 Across is *Singaporean* and 18 Across is *Harwichport*.

EXERCISE: Terms test

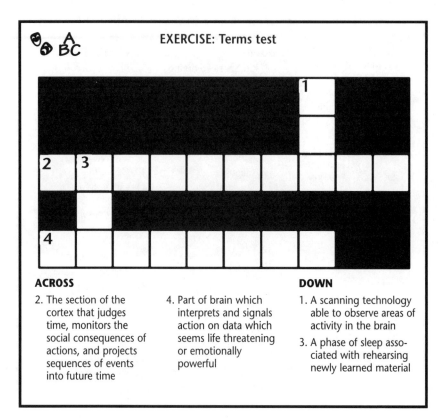

ACROSS

2. The section of the cortex that judges time, monitors the social consequences of actions, and projects sequences of events into future time

4. Part of brain which interprets and signals action on data which seems life threatening or emotionally powerful

DOWN

1. A scanning technology able to observe areas of activity in the brain

3. A phase of sleep associated with rehearsing newly learned material

Hint: 1 Down is PET.

Verbalizing unpleasant experiences helps physical health

Mounting evidence indicates that the degree to which you express negative emotions may put you at risk for a range of diseases from high blood pressure to cancer. And, contrary to what you might think, if you insist on getting your own way, and complain if you don't, you're probably better off than if you always strive to maintain a cheerful front.

Are you an internalizer or an externalizer?

When confronted with an emotion-evoking stimulus (say, an unpleasant story or picture), internalizers show little overt response, while exter-nalizers react more openly. Those who show little outward response, however, tend to react with greater internal stress, as measured by heart rate and skin conduc-tance. Also, when asked to talk into a tape recorder about their most traumatic personal experiences, those who are willing to disclose the most per-sonal and stressful details show lower skin conductance (lower stress) than those whose stories are less personal and upsetting.

These experiments suggest that when unpleasant experi-ences are suppressed, they have a more severe effect on the autonomic nervous system than if those experiences are expressed either nonverbally or verbally.

It makes a difference *why* you're inexpressive

Some infants are simply born with low expressivity. As early as the second day after birth, differences in facial animation emerge quite clearly, and these differences tend to be stable as the infant grows older. It seems, then, that emotional expressivity is at least to some extent innate.

People who are naturally inexpressive probably experience little in the way of conflict or health problems as a result. Those adults who are inexpressive because they have learned to suppress their emotions, however (a learning process that has been shown to begin as early as one to two years of age), may be at higher risk.

Forgive me, Father, for I have sinned

What are the consequences of internalizing unpleasant feelings? Research shows that many health problems are associated with inhibiting negative emotions; conversely, talking or writing about personal trauma has been shown to have a therapeutic effect and to yield improvements in health.

In one study, college students and corporate employees were asked to indicate on a questionnaire which of several categories of personal trauma (e.g., death or divorce of parents, sexual abuse) they had experienced at any time in their life. They were also asked to rate the degree to which they had talked with others about their traumas. A correlation emerged between failure to talk about a traumatic experience and diagnosis with cancer, high blood pressure, ulcers, and other health problems.

Writing may work as well as talking

Other studies have shown that writing about extremely traumatic events brings about an improvement in resistance to infection and disease, according to blood-sample measures of immune function.

But what about nonverbal communication?

Language—whether oral or written—is just one of many forms of communication we have. Other ways of giving someone else a glimpse of one's feelings are gestures made on purpose or unconsciously. Obvious examples of this are the way one composes his or her facial features or through "body language" movements and attitudes such as a leg crossed toward or away from the person one is speaking with. The moods and attitudes of artists express themselves through painting and music as powerfully, at least, as through words. Can the expression of emotion through these other symbolic systems have a beneficial effect as well? Although the evidence is less conclusive, it appears that it might.

For one thing, externalizers don't just talk about their feelings; they tend to display them on their faces. In experiments in which test subjects are shown pleasant and unpleasant pictures, judges can easily guess the nature of the pictures just by watching the facial reactions of externalizers. Judgments are less accurate with internalizers.

The inhibition of facial response has the same kind of effect on the body as the inhibition of verbal response. In a recent study, a group of normal people were given some secret "guilty knowledge" and were told to hide from the others by masking their facial expressions. They were told this "knowledge" was part of the experiment. Even so, their skin conductance levels increased just as they do when people lie or suppress their emotions in conversations or answering questions.

Art therapy—the resolution of internal psychological pain or conflict through nonverbal means such as drawing or painting—is often used with patients who have severe difficulty with verbal communication, such as autistic or abused children. It's possible that regular nonverbal artistic expression would have a beneficial effect on the nervous and immune systems of others as well.

SELF-TEST: Ink blot personality test

The Swiss psychiatrist Herman Rorschach felt that people's responses to a random image betray factors affecting their personality. Rorschach showed his test subjects ten different ink blots, some colored and some black and white, and asked the subjects to relate images and ideas evoked by each blot. With tests such as these there is no "right" or "wrong" answer, but the results may help to provide clues to a person's personality traits or temporary state of mind.

Examine the three Rorschach images below. Find a shape that reminds you of a personally unpleasant experience from your past. Describe to another person what happened and what you saw in the shape you chose that reminded you of the experience. Ask the person to whom you just opened up the window of your experience to pick a shape and do the same.

Why are you not surprised that your immune responses and brain are linked together?

The immune system has evolved as a tool for coping with threats to the body that originate both inside and outside it— much like a sixth sense. (The other five, incidentally, are sight, smell, touch, taste, and hearing.) However, the interactions of the immune system with other systems of the body (nervous/ behavioral and endocrine/hormonal) make it seem less like a single organ and more like one part of a complex system encompassing many physical sites around the body.

They even respond to each other's chemical transmitters

For example, neurotransmitters are the chemicals by which nerve cells (including neurons in the brain) communicate with one another. Cytokines are their counterpart in the cells of the immune system. While it used to be believed that the two systems worked independently, it is now known that both types of system produce and respond to *both* types of chemical. In fact, they are both parts of a single, integrated defense mechanism. The new name created for the study of the interaction between psychological states and the immune system is *psychoneuroimmunology*.

Left-handers are more susceptible to autoimmune disease

Given the acceptance of the neural basis of emotion, it shouldn't come as a shock that emotion and the immune system are linked too. The reason is that it has long been known that injury to neurons in the brain may lead to immune system problems.

Injury to the brain may increase or decrease immune system response, depending on the part of the brain injured. In mice, a lesion in the left hemisphere suppresses the activity of T-cells (the "attack troops" of the immune system), but a lesion in the right hemisphere enhances T-cell function. Perhaps this kind of asymmetry explains why left-handedness, which has been theorized to develop in response to some sort of disease or injury to the left hemisphere, has a greater-than-chance correlation with dyslexia and autoimmune disease.

How do you die from grief?

People have always known that certain stressful experiences appear to increase the risk for infection, disease, and even death. After the death of their spouse, for example, mortality among bereaved men rises. Sometimes people do, in fact, "die from grief."

This has even been known to occur in nonhuman primates. Jane Goodall observed one juvenile chimpanzee who had never fully weaned himself from an unusually intimate relationship with his mother when she died. Although fully capable of feeding and caring for himself (he was eight years old, which is well past childhood for a chimp), he never recovered psychologically from her death, and became increasingly listless and apathetic. Within a month, he died. Goodall concluded that "psychological and physiological disturbances associated with loss made him more vulnerable to disease."

How stress and depression lower your resistance to disease

On a cellular level, clinical depression is associated with a lower level of the body's natural defenses against bacterial and viral infections and disease, including T cells and so-called natural killer cells. This may mean that viruses which are always around us (including perhaps those for Parkinson's disease, various cancers, and even warts) may breach our body's defenses during periods of depression, chronic anxiety, or other kinds of stress.

Some viruses which may be present but inactive in our body may become reactivated during times of stress. This is why college students are more likely to have herpes outbreaks during exam time, for example.

Relatives of Alzheimer's patients have impaired lymphocyte reactivity (a measure of immune-system health). So did people living near Three Mile Island after the accident at the nuclear power plant there. Animals, too, are more susceptible to immune deficiencies and illness when subjected to conditions of overcrowding.

Relief from stress, on the other hand, may have the opposite effect. In one study, gay men experienced a doubling of lymphocyte reactivity (which means the white blood cells don't do their jobs of fighting infection) within a week of being told they were HIV-negative.

Pleasant experiences may have a more lasting effect than unpleasant ones

A recent study shows that pleasant experiences, such as enjoyable social activities, games, or sports, may help the immune system for two days. The immune-system-suppressing effects of routine unpleasant events, on the other hand, such as irritating or frustrating encounters with an employer or coworker, are typically gone within a day. This study had volunteers fill out daily evaluations of their ups and downs. Samples of their saliva showed how effectively their immune systems produced anitbodies to a rabbit protein pill they took each day.

The same study shows that an *absence* of pleasant events predicts susceptibility to a cold more accurately than the *presence* of mildly stressful events. In other words, it's not simply the case that stress can reduce your immunity; enjoyable experiences can actually have a *protective* effect against illness.

Psychological depression may also cause heart disease

For years, evidence has accumulated that depression and heart disease are linked, with researchers uncertain about whether the heart disease causes the depression or vice versa.

New evidence indicates that it's the depression that may be the prime culprit. How does it work? People in a state of depression secrete higher levels of potentially harmful stress hormones, including cortisol and noradrenaline. These hormones have the effect of accelerating the heart rate, disturbing sleep, raising blood pressure, increasing blood clotting, raising the blood's proportion of "bad" cholesterol, and disturbing the heart's rhythm. Cortisol can even increase the potentially life-threatening bouts of erratic heartbeats called arrhythmias. When the depression is treated, the body's biochemistry returns to normal and, often, so do erratic heart rhythms.

How can I help my mood—and my physical health?

One lesson to draw from this research is that a stressful schedule must be punctuated with fun and enjoyable activities. Obvious as this may sound, many hard-driving overachievers seem to think that recreation, adequate sleep, and a good diet are unaffordable luxuries—and pay for it, in many cases, by developing autoimmune disease or chronic fatigue syndrome.

Sometimes, feeling happier is a lot harder than following traditional commonsense wisdom—ask anybody who suffers from dysthymia (literally "ill spirit," roughly translatable as low-level depression), let alone from severe clinical depression. There is one neurotransmitter in particular—serotonin—that has been shown to have the potential to combat depression, anxiety, low self-esteem, social inhibition, and a host of other unpleasant or culturally undesirable facets of personality. Serotonin levels may be raised in many ways. Sunshine helps, as do physical exercise and adequate sleep. Since all neuro-transmitters including serotonin are manufactured from amino acids that are supplied by the food we eat, it's essential to get enough amino acids. A good source is animal protein. (One theory holds that the widespread nature of dysthymia and other depressive mood disorders stems from our undercon-sumption of lean animal protein compared to our neolithic forebears.) During the last decade, many people have found that selective serotonin reuptake inhibitors (SSRIs), such as Prozac, can have a dramatic effect on depression. This in turn reduces the chronic overproduction of stress hormones, and lowers the risk of heart disease and, possibly, immune-system-related ailments.

language function

LANGUAGE

Our acquisition of language in infancy is so instinctual and automatic that we sometimes take it for granted. Recent evidence shows us that a life-long willingness to push the envelope of our linguistic abilities helps keep our brain cell's dendritic branches from atrophying, and may even help prevent Alzheimer's.

The human language faculty is complex, mysterious, and miraculous. We are built to acquire language in infancy, and even to create linguistic structure out of relatively unstructured or chaotic raw material. Infants are not blank slates upon which caretakers write the rules of grammar, but proactive language creators. Only in rare circumstances do these little language artists fail to construct a complete mental grammar within the first few years of life. They do it by listening alone.

Spoken language is a natural faculty uniting all humans, yielding an impressively subtle and complex set of internal mental rules acquired with no formal instruction or education. Still, there are important individual differences among us.

Older people tend to have larger vocabularies than their younger counterparts. Vocabulary growth is a result of the general accumulation of experience, and is not crucially dependent on the sort of mental agility that allows 20-year-olds to beat their parents in games of rapid calculation. Why do some people have larger vocabularies than their age-mates? While vocabulary size may not depend on mental agility, it tends to correlate with other measures of intelligence, such as the ability to manipulate numbers, rotate 3-dimensional objects in the mind's eye, and perform logical operations. Reading widely, especially when young, has a significant effect lifelong.

Cause and effect runs both ways here. A large vocabulary results from an interest in reading and learning about challenging new information. Think of how much more effort and self-discipline it takes to read a work of non-fiction in the *New Yorker*, or an article in the *Wall Street Journal*, than it takes to read a supermarket tabloid.

A growing body of evidence also supports the idea that a willingness to challenge yourself linguistically helps to maintain your brain cells. In the so-called "nun study," it was found that those nuns who used a relatively complex writing style as young novitiates were much less likely to develop Alzheimer's later in life than those nuns who wrote in a style marked by simpler, shorter sentences. So a life-long willingness to challenge yourself to grapple with complex linguistic structures may have a preventive effect against Alzheimer's.

As we age, we tend to have an increasingly difficult time manipulating complex sentence structures. This probably results from an erosion of short-term working memory. So it becomes harder to analyze sentences such as *Despite having finished her pie, Henry nevertheless refused to deny Laura the opportunity to offer him a piece of cake.* It also becomes harder to "get" the acceptable reading of "garden path" sentences such as *The dog walked through the park barked.* ("Garden path" sentences are ones that "lead you down a garden path" in your linear word-by-word parsing. When you get to the end of the sentence, you're left with nonsense, prompting the realization that you must have analyzed the sentence incorrectly, and leading you to re-parse it to obtain better results. All this places a burden on your working memory.)

This ability, just like other abilities resting on working memory, is subject to the "use it or lose it" principle. Even as teenagers, we'll lose our facility with mental calculations if we rely on mechanical calculators rather than our brains. Your brain cells can grow new dendrites throughout life, so don't despair. But the longer you wait to rectify the situation, the harder it will be.

Injuries help to map the brain's language regions

Aphasia—a disturbance in the comprehension and production of language caused by disease or injury to some part of the brain—has provided over a century's worth of invaluable insight into the localization of language centers. If a specific part of the brain is damaged by a blow to the head or a stroke and a particular kind of language function is lost, then we may infer that that language function is localized in the part of the brain that was injured.

Two of the "classic" types of this syndrome are Broca's aphasia and Wernicke's aphasia, named after the pioneering 19th-century neurologists who first identified the parts of the brain associated with these two kinds of language dysfunction. Broca's area is found in the inferior left frontal gyrus (or ridge), and Wernicke's area is located in the posterior section of the left auditory-association cortex. Both are in the left hemisphere, and the identification of the role of these areas in language was an important contribution to understanding the left brain's specialization for linguistic tasks.

Misuse of Grammar

Broca's aphasics suffer from a drastic loss of fluency. Their speech is labored and delivered in a monotone, often with appropriately-selected nouns but without verbs and grammatical morphemes (such as tense and agreement suffixes)—a condition known as *agrammatism*. For example, a typical sentence might be, "Daughter...college... smart...girl." Another symptom is that, although comprehension is quite accurate, they may not be able to repeat an utterance spoken by someone else.

Damage to the Insula, hidden deep inside, causes "apraxia," the inability to organize the component sounds and rhythms to say words correctly.

Damage to Broca's area affects grammar and fluency.

Damage to Wernicke's area affects comprehension of word meaning, not fluency of speech.

Wernicke's aphasics speak rapidly and melodically, although their speech is often unintelligible because they're frequently unable to think of the right word to express the meaning they want to convey. When faced with this situation, Wernicke's patients may do any of several things. One is to omit the word altogether. Instead of saying "The lamp is on the table," they may say, "The table is under, let's assume that." A second option is to substitute another word for the desired one, a behavior known as *paraphasia*. A common strategy is to substitute a word that is related in meaning, such as "hole" for "doughnut," "dog" for "bear," "Mickey" for "mouse," or "biting" for "eating." Another option, known as *circumlocution*, is to paraphrase the desired word, as in saying "water is coming through his eyes" instead of "he's crying." Other options may be to substitute a garbled version of the intended word, as in "hipidomateous" for "hippopotamus," or a novel coinage such as "headman" for "president." Sometimes only a single specific class of words is lost, such as concrete as opposed to abstract nouns, living versus inanimate objects, fruits and vegetables, body parts, or colors.

Inability to say the right thing

While it is generally accepted that Wernicke's patients tend to have more difficulty with nouns and Broca's patients more difficulty with verbs, there is no clear-cut dichotomy: Wernicke's patients often have difficulty retrieving verbs as well. For both Broca's and Wernicke's aphasics, verb-retrieval problems are usually more disruptive than difficulties with accessing nouns, since generic nouns, such as "stuff" or "thing," or pronouns may always be used in place of a noun they can't think of.

Wernicke's patients, unlike Broca's patients, often have difficulty comprehending others' utterances, and may therefore become anxious or paranoid. Broca's patients, however, are more aware of their disability and have a stronger tendency to become frustrated and depressed.

Some language skills are right-brain—getting the point, for example

Even though all the "classic" aphasias are associated with left-hemisphere damage, there is evidence that the right hemisphere is crucially involved in language ability of a different kind. Right-hemisphere damage may lead to an impairment of discourse-related functions—getting the point of a story or joke, or organizing a narrative into a well-structured and coherent whole.

A new language area

Relatively recently, researchers have uncovered another region of the brain responsible for speech articulation. The region, called the *insula*, lies beneath the temporal and frontal lobes in the left cortex. The insula had previously been considered responsible primarily for the processing of tastes, smells, sights, and sounds in humans and monkeys.

When a specific part of the insula is damaged, the result is a problem known as *apraxia*. Apraxics have difficulty manipulating the musculature of speech in the appropriate order and with the appropriate timing. They will grope for just the right sequence of sounds, sometimes even getting it right once but then failing on a repeat effort.

Apraxia is easy to confuse with Broca's aphasia because both pathologies show themselves in slow and labored speech, articulatory errors, and a monotonous delivery. However, apraxia has none of the agrammatic (that is, non-grammatic) features of Broca's aphasia. Apraxia might be thought to resemble Wernicke's aphasia, which may also involve the garbling of the sounds of words. Unlike Wernicke's aphasia, however, apraxics have no difficulty with accessing the right word or with word perception or comprehension. Rather, apraxics' recognition of word and speech sounds remains perfectly normal and they're fully aware of their own faulty articulation— understandably a source of considerable frustration.

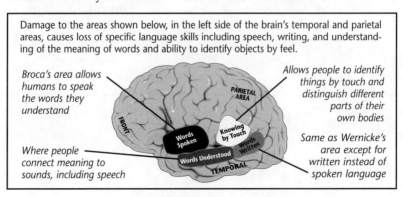

Damage to the areas shown below, in the left side of the brain's temporal and parietal areas, causes loss of specific language skills including speech, writing, and understanding of the meaning of words and ability to identify objects by feel.

Broca's area allows humans to speak the words they understand

Where people connect meaning to sounds, including speech

Allows people to identify things by touch and distinguish different parts of their own bodies

Same as Wernicke's area except for written instead of spoken language

EXERCISE: Confused speech

The 3 italic paragraphs labeled "A," "B," and "C" below contain transcriptions of recorded answers of four patients, each of whom suffered from damage to a different part of their brain. Try to match those paragraphs with the following three descriptions of the damaged areas and abilities.

"Apraxia": One of the paragraphs below is a transcript of speech by a subject who suffers from apraxia resulting from damage to the insula, an area very near the motor centers across the middle of the cortex involved in the manipulation of muscles used in speech.

"Wernicke's": Another paragraph transcribes the speech of subjects with damage to an area closer to the back of the brain. They come up with words easily and speak freely but stumble along with inappropriate words.

"Broca's": Another paragraph reconstructs recorded speech of a subject with damage to an area nearer the frontal cortex. The person understands the meaning of words but has trouble putting a meaningful idea together using verbs and grammar. Broca's aphasics speak slowly, without inflection, and in a worried, guarded way. Unlike Wernicke's aphasics, they are aware of their disability.

A *The subject was shown a drawing of a kitchen scene in which a woman didn't notice two boys stealing her cookies. Asked to describe the scene the subject said: "Mother is away here working her work to get her better, but when she's looking the two boys looking the other part. She's working another time."*

B *When the subject was asked why he returned to the hospital he said: "Yes...ah...Monday...ah...Dad and Peter Hogan, and Dad... ah... Hospital...and ah...Wednesday...Wednesday, nine o'clock and ah Thursday...ten o'clock ah doctors... two...two...an doctors and...ah...teeth...yah, And a doctor...an girl...and gums, and I."*

C *The subject, who was asked to say the word "cushion," responded: "oh, uh, uh...chookun...uh, uh, uh...dook...I know what it's called, it's c-u, uh, no, it's, it's...chook...chookun...no." When asked to repeat "catastrophe" five times, the subject said: "catastrophe, patastrophee, t, catastrophe, catasrifrobee, aw sh..., ka, kata, sh..., sh..., I don't know."*

A new approach to treating dyslexia

As you read a fairly simple sentence like this one, your brain is doing the remarkable job of processing words at a rate of about 30 to 50 letter characters a second.

Now, try reading this: *Albertyay Einsteinyay asway ayay owslay anguagelay earnerlay, adbay ellerspay, andyay oorpay eaderray. Ehay asway alsoyay obablypray yslexicday.*

How long did that take you? Longer than two or three seconds, probably. A child's game like Pig Latin requires you to make automatic sound divisions within words, and then quickly move things around in a way that makes sense. If you had to take a timed test written in Pig Latin instead of plain English, you would score much lower regardless of how large your vocabulary or how smart you are.

It's exactly this kind of rapid division into sounds or letters that cause problems for people who have dyslexia. Dyslexia, along with ADHD and depression, is a very common brain syndrome. According to current estimates, it affects one out of five English speakers, making it the most common diagnosed learning disability.

The cause is in the wiring, not the motivation

Is dyslexia a visual disorder that makes people reverse letters and written words when they're trying to read (or learn to read), or is it a problem with the sound-processing parts of the brain? In 2002 Yale University's Center for Learning and Attention scanned the brains of children as young as seven years old as they read. Each of the children had been diagnosed with reading problems. The scans showed a much lower level of activity in an area in the back of the brain that quickly converts sounds to meaning of written words. This and other patterns of brain activity, or lack thereof, matched scans of adults who had wrestled with dyslexia all their lives. These research results strongly support the evidence that dyslexia is caused by subtle differences in the wiring of the brain, not by lower general learning capacity or motivation in children.

This suggests that dyslexia is not just a visual problem of letter reversals, but a more fundamental brain difference that may express itself in language comprehension, reading, and writing. Some of the most recent research shows that dyslexia may stem from a difficulty in processing the elements of any rapidly-changing series of sounds, or perhaps even any rapid sequence in either a visual or acoustic mode. Of all our natural human skills, language places the greatest burden on the brain's ability to analyze an unfolding sequence of data with quickness and accuracy. If you're listening to someone speak, the distinctions your brain needs to notice can fly by in 10 milliseconds, or one hundredth of a second.

New evidence for a dyslexic brain difference
Some brain imaging studies have shown that the area of the brain involved in processing rapidly changing sounds is the left prefrontal cortex. When non-dyslexic readers listen to a string of rapidly changing sounds (but not a slowly changing sequence), it's the left pre-frontal cortex that becomes active. When dyslexics listen, that part of the brain remains quiet.

The prefrontal cortex is also responsible for "executive" skills, such as focusing attention on the task at hand and figuring out strategies for solving problems. One of the executive component's problem-solving tools is called the phonological loop, which lets you hold sounds in your "mind's ear" just long enough to latch onto a new word or parse a tricky sentence. In a sentence such as "Jennifer denied not having seen Joey," your mind's ear plays it back to figure out exactly what's being said ("Wait a minute—is Jennifer saying she did or didn't see Joey?"). A well-functioning phonological loop is also important for learning new words—it keeps the old word fresh in your mind while you look up the new one.

The standard view is that you can't improve the performance of your phonological loop just through practice or training. Does that mean that dyslexia is also something a person just has to learn to live with? Not necessarily. Researchers have successfully treated dyslexia in a way that seems to alter brain function and possibly brain structure as well, thereby markedly improving language function.

Rewiring the brain
Their technique involves slowing down a recorded stream of speech so that all the sounds and their transitions are particularly clear. If you hear Swahili the way it's normally spoken, it

SELF-TEST: Sound Subtractions: A simple test that predicts vocabulary, reading, and foreign-language-learning skills— and can help identify dyslexia

There are several quick and easy ways to test basic abilities that correlate with language skills, including learning new vocabulary words and reading. For most children, problems with the phonological loop component of short-term memory show up in the first few years of school, during the time they're supposed to be learning to read. If there are any underlying language difficulties that prevent them from identifying phonemes— the basic units of sound—in speech, then they'll also have a tough time matching speech sounds to letters in writing. (In older people, a dysfunctional phonological loop can also be a sign of Alzheimer's disease.)

Here is a test keyed to age. It's similar to something called an Auditory Analysis Test, designed to gauge the ability to break words down into their component sounds. Four-year-olds will usually have a hard time with it, as you can see by the expected scores for that age group. But by the time they're about 6, most children should be able to do pretty well.

Start by telling the child you're going to play a word game. For each word, say the word out loud and ask the child to repeat it. Then, tell the child to say it again without the sound indicated for each word. Always pronounce the sound, not the name of the letter. (For example, if the child is supposed to subtract the sound written with a "c" in "cloud," say "Now say it again without KUH.") If the child gets the first one or two wrong, give the correct answer to make sure he or she understands the rules.

Scoring: Stop after two errors in a row. The score is the number of the last item answered correctly. For example: 1 correct, 2 correct, 3 incorrect, 4 correct, 5 incorrect, 6 incorrect, score = 4.

1. Say: STARFISH. Then, say, NOW SAY IT AGAIN WITHOUT FISH. (Right answer "STAR")

2. SHAMPOO - SHAM ("POO")

3. CRAYON - CRAY ("ON")

4. PART - P ("ART")

5. LEG - L ("EGG")

6. MAKE - M ("ACHE")

7. FACE - F ("ACE")

8. SEAT - S ("EET")

9. CLAIM - C ("LAME")

10. TRUCK - T ("RUCK")

11. PLEASE - P ("LEES")

12. STING - S ("TING")

13. SMELL - S ("MELL")

Norms: Age 4: 1-3; age 5: 4-9; age 6; 10-13.

can be hard to follow the flow of sounds or know how to divide them up into separate words and speech sounds. So in Swahili class, the teacher pronounces the words more slowly and clearly than Swahili speakers would naturally speak. Once you start like that, you can gradually ramp up to normal speed, and from then on normally-spoken Swahili will help to reinforce what you've learned rather than just confuse you.

Never underestimate your brain
Working with recordings that slow down and stretch out speech sounds the way a language teacher does, these researchers have managed to help dyslexic children grasp the subtle differences in sounds that combine to make up words they had never before quite managed to hear. Then over a period of weeks, they gradually increase the tape to normal speed. The researchers have found that dyslexics' brains may restructure themselves permanently in response to the therapy. And even though that kind of change in brain structure tends to be easier for the younger brain, they have had success with older children well past the normal age of learning to read. Even the adult brain, it seems, can still change in fundamental ways to learn new tricks, like increased vocabulary or acquiring a wholly new language.

WHERE THE BRAIN READS WORDS

1. Sees the word TIGER. Identifies the letters T-I-G-E-R.

2. Uses Working Memory to link sounds together until able to recognizes the spoken word, ("tie-ge-er").

3. Associates word with meaning.

EXERCISE: Damaged language

Rearrange the letters of each word in the left column to create a synonym for the word opposite it in the center column. Write it in the spaces in the right. In the numbered spaces at the bottom write in the first letter of each new word to form a phrase (without word spaces) related to a preceding article.

Left		Center		Right
SCION	=	IMAGES	=	1. _ _ _ _ _
KNEAD	=	DEFOLIATED	=	2. _ _ _ _ _
JANES	=	DURABLE PANTS	=	3. _ _ _ _ _
RUSES	=	MANIPULATORS	=	4. _ _ _ _ _
LAGER	=	SUITABLE FOR A KING	=	5. _ _ _ _ _
FINER	=	DEDUCE	=	6. _ _ _ _ _
SITED	=	CUTS AND REARRANGES	=	7. _ _ _ _ _
SNAIL	=	MURDERED	=	8. _ _ _ _ _
CHARM	=	GREGORIAN 3RD MONTH	=	9. _ _ _ _ _
TACOS	=	NECK SCARF	=	10. _ _ _ _ _
GRAPE	=	BEEPER	=	11. _ _ _ _ _
BRAIL	=	ZODIAC'S SEVENTH	=	12. _ _ _ _ _
SONAR	=	BAD LIGHT	=	13. _ _ _ _ _
NERVE	=	NOT AT ALL	=	14. _ _ _ _ _
SARGE	=	TOOTHED WHEELS	=	15. _ _ _ _ _
SURGE	=	ENTREATS	=	16. _ _ _ _ _
LATER	=	TO CHANGE	=	17. _ _ _ _ _
LUGER	=	THIN PORRIDGE	=	18. _ _ _ _ _
SPICE	=	OVERSIZED NARRATIVES	=	19. _ _ _ _ _
IDEAL	=	SUFFERED	=	20. _ _ _ _ _
DIRGE	=	RAISED GROUND	=	21. _ _ _ _ _
LEASE	=	ART SUPPORT	=	22. _ _ _ _ _
WAKES	=	OUT OF LINE	=	23. _ _ _ _ _
CURBS	=	BACKUP PLAYER	=	24. _ _ _ _ _
CANOE	=	ATLANTIC OR PACIFIC	=	25. _ _ _ _ _
RIFLE	=	ADVERTISING CIRCULAR	=	26. _ _ _ _ _
GABLE	=	CEMENT DOUGHNUT	=	27. _ _ _ _ _
SPORE	=	LASSOES	=	28. _ _ _ _ _
BLAME	=	SAUNTER	=	29. _ _ _ _ _
TRINE	=	INACTIVE	=	30. _ _ _ _ _
STONE	=	MARGINALIA	=	31. _ _ _ _ _

1_	2_	3_	4_	5_	6_	7_	8_	9_	
10_	11_	12_	13_	14_	15_	16_	17_	18_	19_	20_
21_	22_	23_	24_	25_	26_	27_	28_	29_	30_	31_

Hint: The phrase reads: "Injuries map language areas of brain."

Women are more linguistically "balanced" than men

It is by now common knowledge that the "language areas" of the brain are located in the left hemisphere. A recent experiment indicates that this may be more true for men than for women. When men perform the task of breaking down words into individual distinctive sounds, they rely heavily on the left side of the inferior frontal gyrus, an area of the brain which has long been known to be specialized for language. When women perform the same linguistic task, they use both sides of the brain about equally.

In the left hemisphere of the brain two areas have long been identified as main speech processors. Broca's area in the frontal lobe turns thoughts into words. Wernicke's area in the temporal and parietal lobes turns speech into thoughts.

This important finding was enabled by the development of a new technology called functional magnetic resonance imaging, which provides a visual display of the parts of the brain being activated during the performance of a particular task.

For this experiment, 19 male and 19 female right-handers were given a rhyme-judgment task, which requires subjects to determine whether two nonsense words rhyme or not. Since the nonsense words were presented in written form, the task required visual and orthographic (letter recognition) processing as well as the mapping of the letter sequences onto phonological (sound) representations. They were also given a task of judging whether two sets of strings of letters featured the same patterns of lowercase-uppercase alternation.

Wherever the brain regions activated for the two tasks failed to overlap, these remaining regions were identified as the areas responsible for phonological processing alone. While the men showed an 11.7:5 ratio of left-right brain activation in this region, the women's ratio was a more evenly-divided 9.4:12.

Men tend to do most of their word-processing only on the left side of their brains

This supports the hypothesis that language functions are more highly lateralized in men than in women—just as they are in

ISOLATING THE "SPEECH SOUND" AREA

When you perform a rhyme judgment task of written words, both the "speech sounds" and "reading" parts of your brain are activated. With a letter recognition task, just the "reading" areas are activated. Subtract the second from the first, and you get just the "speech sound" areas.

Rhyme judgment: Do these words rhyme or not? flink/srink
Letter recognition: Do these letter sequences show the same lowercase-uppercase alternation pattern?   *dDDDdddDddDddddd/ rRRRrrrRrrRrrrr*

left-handers as opposed to in right-handers. Left-handers tend to have their language competency more equally distributed across both hemispheres than right-handers. This means that if a left-hander suffers injury to the left hemisphere, any resulting aphasia (speech loss) is less likely to be permanent than with right-handers. But left-handers tend also to be less proficient in perceptual-spatial abilities, perhaps because the distribution of language ability across both hemispheres in effect displaces some right-brain-dependent functions such as the judgment of spatial relationships and Gestalt (whole-shape) perception.

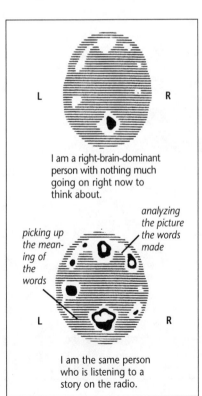

L   R

I am a right-brain-dominant person with nothing much going on right now to think about.

picking up the mean- ing of the words

analyzing the picture the words made

L   R

I am the same person who is listening to a story on the radio.

Women, and left-handed men, tend to have more difficulty working with shapes and spaces than right-handed men

The sort of left-hemisphere language specialization which is the norm for right-handed males may permit right-hemisphere spatial perception to function at a high level—to permit a simultaneous grasp of both the forest and the trees, as it were. Indeed, this is a dominant theory for the development of hemispheric lateralization in humans.

Women are less likely to suffer permanent language loss from effects of a stroke

Women's more even distribution of language across both halves of the brain may give them flexibility should something go awry. Less specialization may help women recover their linguistic abilities following a stroke or brain injury, and it may explain why girls seem to have an easier time than boys overcoming reading disabilities, including dyslexia.

EXERCISE: Circleword

Directions: Just as one word leads to another, words lead into each other, or overlap. If you start in slot #1 with the right word, you should have little trouble completing the circle with 12 additional overlapping words. Each word starts in a numbered slot that corresponds to the number of the clue.

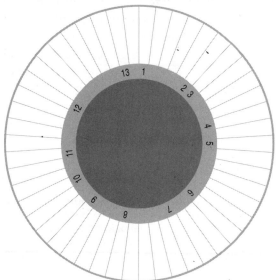

1. Lobe where Broca's area is
2. Unable to read, from brain damage
3. Wordbook or dictionary
4. Shaped like a Ben & Jerry receptacle
5. Addictive stimulant
6. Fortitude; impertinence; type of cell
7. Tediously loquacious
8. Old and feeble-minded
9. Kind of aid or age
10. Greek letter
11. With "over", delivered into custody
12. Part of a brain cell that receives messages
13. Diminutive mischief-maker

Starters: There are four major brain lobes: frontal, temporal, parietal, and occipital.

Hint: #12 is dendrite.

EXERCISE: Fancy Language

You are given one set of clues, but two grids. The correct answers to the "Fancy Language" grid below are English words rooted in Latin or French. The "Plain Speaking" grid on the next page asks for English words with Anglo Saxon roots.

ACROSS
1. Easier said than done
5. Breadbasket
6. Kindred
7. Seek information
8. Rate of motion

DOWN
2. Notion
3. Start
4. Provide with knowledge
6. Bring about

EXERCISE: Plain Speaking

The answers to these clues have simple Anglo Saxon roots. The "Fancy Language" grid on the preceding page is rooted in Latin or French words.

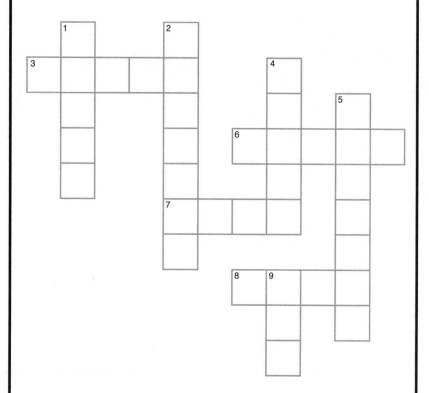

ACROSS

3. Provide with knowledge
6. Start
7. Easier said than done
8. Bring about

DOWN

1. Breadbasket
2. Notion
4. Rate of motion
5. Related
9. Seek information

EXERCISE: Unconstructible constructs

Sometimes, a perfectly reasonable question may be unaskable not because of social convention or nonsensical meaning, but simply because our mental grammar won't produce the structure underlying it. Here are examples of some such questions you'll never hear. Trying to decipher them produces a sensation similar to what you might feel when applying yourself to a very strange foreign language. This kind of exercise is excellent for challenging the kind of working memory faculty crucial for maintaining linguistic abilities into old age. Can you figure out what these questions are asking?

1. *Whom and your mother did you talk to?*
2. *Who did you know whether talked to your mother?*
3. *Whom did you talk to the woman who married?*
4. *Whom did the fact that you know bother John?*

Some sentences may be generatable in principle, but they're universally disfavored because they rely on structures that are very difficult for humans to process. With some effort, you can decipher them, but the effort required seems to be too much for everyday situations. Try your hand at translating the following examples into normal English.

5. *This is the woman whom the man whom you talked to yesterday abandoned.*
6. *This is the car that the man whom you saw talking to the woman you met yesterday parked.*
7. *This is the guy Richard sent the package that was in the room that you read the instructions through in to.*
8. *The fact that the man whom the guy you saw yesterday met told you about that I don't like you is disturbing.*

More impossibilities:
How would you ask the following question about more than one box?

9. *How big (of) a box do you need?*

How would you turn these passive sentences into their active counterparts?

10. *He was rumored to be a Mafioso.*
11. *She was reputed to be rich.*

SELF-TEST: Mental status for language ability

This can be used as a quick and simple test of verbal acuity, or of possible signs of age-related cognitive decline. Have a friend test you, or test a friend or family member who may be concerned about her mental status.

1. Explain to your friend that you're going to ask her to repeat a short phrase word for word. Then, read the following out loud:
"If you couldn't cook, I'd drop you quicker than a box of rocks."
   A. She can't repeat it correctly.
   B. She makes a mistake the first time, but gets it right the second time.
   C. She does it perfectly the first time.

2. Mention a common category, such as fruits, animals, or vegetables, and ask your friend to list as many members of that category as she can in 1 minute.
   A. She can only think of 10 or fewer.
   B. She can only think of 11 to 15.
   C. She can think of 16 or more.

3. Explain that you're going to read a sentence out loud, and that the task will be to write down the sentence word for word. Use the following sentence (or one of similar length and complexity from a newspaper article):
"New scanning methods have helped pinpoint the location of many brain functions."
   A. She can't do it at all, or makes many mistakes.
   B. She makes a couple of mistakes, but the two versions are close.
   C. She makes no mistakes.

4. Gather a collection of 6 familiar objects, such as a can opener, a corkscrew, a key, a paper clip, a thumbtack, and a shoelace. Point to each object in turn, and give your friend a couple of seconds to name each one.
   A. She can only name two or fewer correctly.
   B. She makes a few errors, such as calling a shoelace a "string."
   C. She makes no mistakes.

How a child begins to speak a complex language before it can even pull on its socks

Anyone who has raised a child from infancy knows that language acquisition is a mysterious, even miraculous, process. A 4-year-old child, who probably hasn't even learned to tie her shoes and may not be fully toilet-trained, will have mastered enough of whatever language she's been exposed to—whether English, Arabic, or Swahili—for her to be considered fluent. For an adult English speaker, achieving that level of proficiency in a language like Arabic would take years of focused, concentrated effort—and many adults would never attain fluency at all, no matter how long and hard they tried. Clearly, then, as infants we have some kind of language-acquisition faculty which we lose as we grow older. Understanding the details of this faculty—where it comes from, how long it lasts, what its stages are, and what biologically-determined expectations about "possible languages" it gives us as we enter the world— is the domain of the intersection of psychology and linguistics, called psycholinguistics.

The core question is whether humans are born with a specialized brain function dedicated only to acquiring language skills as opposed to general strategies for acquiring knowledge that may be applied to a number of tasks including language acquisition. There is no doubt that infants do bring to the task of language acquisition more than they're exposed to in their environment.

At least two kinds of evidence point to this. One is that we seem to have a biologically-given window of language acquisition (see "Critical window of opportunity..." p. 221). The other is that certain aspects of language development unfold in remarkably uniform ways for all children.

From babbling to multi-word phrases, all human infants go through predictable stages as they learn to talk

From about 4 to 6 months of age, infants produce brief, isolated consonant and vowel sounds, as well as clicks, coos, grunts, and sighs that often bear little or no resemblance to any speech sounds in any language. At about 6 months, they begin what's called the *babbling* stage—the production of a

214 BUILDING MENTAL MUSCLE

reduplicative sequence of consonant-vowel (CV), but almost
no vowel-consonant (VC), sequences—such as "KOO" but not
"OOK." (A compelling piece of evidence that this behavior is
innate is that even congenitally deaf infants will start babbling
at more or less the same age, with the same syllable-structure
preferences—although, unlike hearing children, they may
continue to babble until well beyond the babbling stage, sometimes until age 6 or 7.) Toward the end of the first year, the
infant's repertoire of syllables increases, to include not just CV,
but CVC and VC. The sequences of babbled syllables become
less repetitive and more varied.

All infants babble the same way no matter what language their parents speak

The speech sounds the infant uses in these babbling stages are
universal and independent of the speech sounds used in the
particular language to which the infant is exposed. All infants
favor oral stops (consonants we represent with the letters "p,"
"t," "k," "b," "d," "g"), nasal stops (especially "m" and "n"),
glides ("w," "y"), and "h." Of the oral stops, voiced are more
common than voiceless ones, and sounds produced toward
the front of the vocal tract (e.g., "b," "d," "m," "n") are more
common than ones produced toward the rear (e.g., "k," "ng").
(During the *pre*-babbling stage, on the other hand, back stops
are much more common.) Fricatives ("s," "th," "f," etc.),
affricates ("ch," etc.) and liquids ("r," "l") are strongly disfavored, although if the infant does produce one of these
sounds it may be one that her parents' language doesn't have
(e.g., the velar fricative found in German "Ach!" from a child
with English-speaking parents). The most common vowel in
the babbling stages is the sound in "lot"—perhaps because
that sound can be made without using tongue or face muscles
in a way that requires much practice.

The sounds that infants universally prefer in these early
stages probably explain why it is that certain sounds tend universally to appear in different languages' words (or, even more
frequently, "baby" words) for "mother" and "father"—e.g.,
papa and *mama* in English. This, combined with the babbling
preferences, also gives rise to the mother or father's gratifying
illusion that the child's "first word" is her or his own name.

THE WORLD BABBLES IN UNISON

Among all the world's languages there are more similarities in the sound of the words for *mama* and *papa* than would be expected by pure chance. They can't be explained through the inheritance of a common root because completely unrelated languages show these similarities, Chinese and English for example. To some extent, the explanation for the recurrence of certain sounds has to do with constraints on the infant's vocal apparatus during the early "babbling" period. Both oral and nasal stops ("p" and "m," for example) are strongly favored over other consonants, and front consonants ("p," "b," "t," "d," "m," "n") are favored over back consonants.

A more puzzling mystery is why nasals ("m," "n") are so strongly preferred for "mama" and orals ("p," "b," "t," "d") are so strongly favored for "papa." Again, there are exceptions—in Georgian, a Caucasian language spoken in the former Soviet Union, *mama* means "father." Somehow, there appears to be some kind of sound-symbolic association of nasals with "mother" and oral stops with "father."

Sound symbolism—the "natural" connection between a certain kind of sound and a certain kind of meaning—is a subtle but nevertheless real and fascinating motivating factor in the words used by languages to refer to things. Another universal sound-symbolic tendency is for small things to be referred to with words with high front vowels—like the vowel in *teeny*—and for large things to be referred to with low and/or back vowels—as in *large* or *huge*. By the general sound-change process known as the Great Vowel Shift, a Middle English word sounding similar to *teeny* became Modern English *tiny*—the high front vowel changed to a low vowel. Interestingly enough, while *tiny*, with its newly sound-symbolically inappropriate vowel, remains in the language as a word describing very little objects, speakers have "resurrected" the high front vowel in the word *teeny*—which simply, somehow, sounds more appropriate to many speakers, especially children, for denoting an *eentsy-weentsy* (more high front vowels!) object such as a "bikini."

EXERCISE: Mama and papa

Children use words for "mama" and "papa" that are so similar from one language to another that something more than chance is at work. (See "The world babbles in unison," p. 215.)

Among the 16 words listed here in random order, one means "mama" and one means "papa" in each of the eight languages listed.

The task in this exercise is to identify which member of the pair of words for each language means "mama" and which means "papa." To test your knowledge of linguistic geography, locate the area on the world map in which each language is spoken. These eight areas are designated by the letters A through H in the boxes on the map.

i. Welsh   *mam*
                 tad,tada,dad

ii. Hebrew   *aba*
                 ima

iii. Swahili   *mama*
                 baba

iv. Tamil   *ammaa*
                 appa

v. Chinese   *pa pa*
                 ma ma

vi. Dakota   *ena*
                 ate

vii. Turkish   *annecigim*
                 baba

viii. Greenlandic
                 anaana(q)
                 ataata(q)

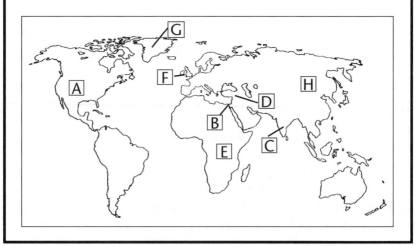

Hint: Remember that nasal consonants tend universally to be associated with "mama" words.

Educating babies

Human infants seem to be able to adapt to living conditions wherever they are born: For example, at 8,000 feet or at sea level; in third-world communities, to a daily calorie intake that is way below the starvation level of people living in industrialized countries; or to rare diseases found only in their community and nowhere else. A molecular biologist named Gerald Edelman traced the process that allows an infant's immune system to develop antibodies before it is born, which will attack and control the specific diseases it will encounter once it emerges into its outside world.

Edelman used some of those discoveries to build a theory called *neural Darwinism* to explain how a newborn infant's brain can master so much information so fast into its early childhood. Take language, for example. The rules of grammar are extremely complex and vary from one language to another, as does vocabulary. Most of us know the frustration of attempting to learn a new language as an adult. How does a newborn brain pull off that trick?

Edelman claims that the brain of a fetus is a sea of neurons grouped into areas of the brain that allow the infant to master different kinds of skills when these areas are exposed to experience. What happens is that when a newborn tries to achieve something (like moving across the floor to reach a cookie, for example) neurons that cause the specific body movements that get the infant going toward the cookie will "cluster" and remain. (The readiness of so many available neurons to devote themselves to new tasks helps explain, for example, how it is that a three-year-old can begin to be fluent in a new second language so much more quickly than an adult.) The neurons that cause whatever other random actions that do not help achieve the desired goal die off. The developing brain has so many billions of neurons that it can afford a policy of "only what works survives."

6 months

Be careful what you say; your unborn child is listening

Learning word sounds probably begins before an infant is born. A group of expectant mothers eight months into term were divided into three groups. Every day the mothers in each group read aloud, to their as-yet unborn babies, a paragraph from the same three-paragraph-long children's story, with each group reading a different paragraph from the others. This went on for about a month. Two days after each baby was born, it was given a bottle with a special nipple that allowed it to suck faster or slower without changing the amount of milk it received. The baby was fitted with earphones linked to a tape recorder that played its mother's voice reading *all three* of the paragraphs from the story—not just the one she read while the infant was in the womb, but the other two as well. The special nipple was wired to the recorder in such a way that the infant could select which of the three passages it heard by changing its rate of sucking. All the newborns changed their sucking rate so they could hear the *same* paragraph their mother read to them during the month before they were born.

8 months

Around the turn of the first year, the infant moves beyond babbling and begins to produce recognizable words in the language spoken around him

Sometimes the stage of word formation is preceded by a "silent period" (which may cause considerable anxiety or relief for the parents, as the case may be).

Within about 6 months thereafter, the average child has a vocabulary of about 50 words. From there, she moves on to the "two-word" stage. Early multi-word speech is sometimes referred to as "telegraphic," since the same sorts of words are omitted that we omit when writing a telegram—words like *the* and *is*. After that, language acquisition moves on to a bewilderingly rapid explosion of progress.

The child progresses to syntactically more complex structures by about age 3—relative clauses such as "the dog that bit me," for example. By shortly after age 4, the child has developed a grammar—*real* grammar, not artificial prescriptive rules of grammar such as "Never end a sentence with a preposition" or "Never split an infinitive"—largely the same as that of an adult speaker.

The degree to which this progression is preordained shouldn't be exaggerated. In fact, every child is different, and a girl who begins reduplicative babbling at 6 months may have a brother who waits until 12 months to enter this same stage. But within these general parameters, all children, except those with special deficits, progress on schedule, and the acquisitional stages are never out of order. In these respects, language acquisition has been claimed to be similar to other biologically-programmed behavior in humans and other species, such as learning to walk or fly.

Of course, it remains a somewhat open question to what extent these stages are determined by some language-specific part of the infant's *brain* as opposed to the infant's physiology—in particular, the structure and development of the vocal tract. The reason that infants babble for months before they show any real evidence of copying the speech of their parents may simply be that their brains haven't yet developed enough. Two critical networks of neurons are involved in auditory analysis, ability to name objects and put meaning to spoken words (Wernicke's and adjacent areas) and speech-motor output (Broca's area); this means that the 6-month-old infant may be neurologically unequipped to monitor and imitate the speech sounds produced by adults.

The critical window of opportunity to learn languages easily and fluently closes at puberty

A major argument for the biologically-determined, innate nature of a specifically linguistic "module" of the brain has to do with the concept of the critical period. There is a series of windows of opportunity lasting between six months and puberty for the acquisition of language, beyond which language learning is impaired.

While there is some disagreement about exactly how long each window remains open, it seems to be true that, up until around puberty, humans can learn whatever language or languages they're exposed to in a relatively effortless manner leading naturally to native-like fluency. After about age 12, language acquisition is much more difficult, and even if vocabulary and usage of a second language is correct and fluent, the sound of the speech always carries traces of the native language learned in infancy—as in Henry Kissinger's speech. The rare cases where children have somehow progressed through the critical period without learning any language (see "The forbidden experiment," p. 225) show that, after this period, they cannot become fluent even in their first language.

Why don't we simply keep the window open all our life?

Most of us have had the experience of wishing that we had been exposed to more languages as an infant, or that we could somehow recapture our youthful gift of language acquisition. Why do we have a critical period at all?

The reason for this frustrating course of events is probably essentially the same as why most adults have difficulty digesting dairy products: if an enzyme—or neural circuitry—is not needed beyond a certain early stage in life, then it will be shut down, or recycled to other purposes. The neural circuitry of language acquisition is an especially good candidate for dismantling or recycling since the brain is such a greedy consumer of oxygen, energy, and nutrients. A child has completed its acquisition of its native language in the first few years of its life, except for learning additional vocabulary. After that the body would be wasting valuable resources if it continued to maintain, unused into adulthood, the vast circuitry laid down to acquire structure and pronunciation. The large number of additional brain cells that a child has available to develop speech and language skills seems eventually to become unavailable except for those that have been put to work.

This means, by the way, that you should beware of any language-instruction program that promises to help you learn a foreign language with the same ease, and by the same "just-listen-and-learn" exposure, with which you acquired your native language. Adult second-language acquisition by necessity relies on much more conscious, effortful strategies than child language acquisition.

"HYPERLEXIA": When children are linguistically retarded, but precociously literate

Most children pick up spoken language effortlessly and with no deliberate instruction in their preschool years, and pick up reading and writing skills later, after the expenditure of considerable time and conscious effort. There are, however, a few children who seem to do it backwards, or do the latter without ever attaining normal ability in the former. Known as "hyperlexics," these children may be almost entirely mute, may show linguistic and other development in the moderately to severely retarded range, and yet have reading and writing skills well beyond those of their agemates. In most cases, their reading ability seems to emerge abruptly and spontaneously, with no conscious instruction on the part of the parents.

One case reported in the literature is that of "V," a 5-and-a-half-year-old child who was admitted to the UCLA Neuropsychiatric Institute because of severe behavioral and developmental problems. She had no expressive speech, but had advanced reading skills. (Indeed, almost the only way she could respond to cognitive-evaluation test questions was to point to the answer in a written text.) She responded perfectly to written commands (in contrast to most 5-year-olds, who can respond to oral commands but not written commands at all), and was just as avid a reader of hospital charts as children's books. She had also taught herself to use a typewriter, and occasionally used this skill to answer questions.

EXERCISE: Child speak

It takes a surprisingly long time for a child to learn to use some simple "concept" words in an "adult" way.

The following five pairs of sentences use the simple words *really*, *have to*, *still*, *since* and *while* in two different senses. A young child would have no hesitation identifying one member of each pair as something he or she might say, and the other not. This isn't because of the content of the utterance as a whole. Rather, it's because of the sense in which the words are used. A child may learn these words at a young age, but they are only used with a certain meaning. Other senses are acquired only later, and give the older child the more sophisticated sound of a grown-up.

Which of the two usages, A or B, would be less natural to a young child?

1. A. *Daddy is* really *Santa Claus.*

   B. Really, *I don't think you should say that.*

2. A. *He* has to *be Santa Claus—I saw him wearing a red hat.*

   B. *He* has to *go now.*

3. A. Still, *I think you're wrong.*

   B. *Are you* still *up?*

4. A. *He's been here* since *Friday.*

   B. Since *you're eating all the cookies, I'll drink all the milk.*

5. A. *I'll fetch the cookies* while *you fetch the milk.*

   B. While *I like cookies, she likes milk.*

Hint: The later-acquired senses tend to be, for want of a better word, more abstract.

EXERCISE: Stages of language acquisition

Match the following 11 sounds, words and sentences (1–11) with the four stages (A, B, C, D) of a child's development of language ability

Stages: *A: Babbling (6 months); B: First words (end of first year); C: Early multi-word speech (second year); D: More complex sentences (age 3 on).*

Sounds and Words:

1. *Will you help me?*

2. *hi mama, pants off*

3. *Why you smiling?*

4. *bababa*

5. *wawa*

6. *He was stuck and I got him out.*

7. *more cookie*

8. *mama*

9. *What cowboy doing?*

10. *nana*

11. *I want the ones that Mommy got.*

EXERCISE: Letters into words

The letters stacked up in each column below go into the boxes directly under them, but not necessarily in the order in which they are shown in their stack. When all the boxes have been filled in, a sentence or phrase from the preceding article will appear.

H	C	L	L	S	P	S	L	A	T	G	P	U	B	E	S	T	Y
A	L	I	O	O	I	P	O	C	A	U	L	A	I	N	R	O	E
	O	F	C	R	N	A	I	A	N	L	U	W	G	Y	D	L	O
	S	E	A	R	E	T	N	R	T	F	N	I	E	E	T	T	W
T		E		Y			D					U	T	N			Y

The forbidden experiment: What happens when a child is deprived of any linguistic stimulation?

Since the dawn of history, people have wondered what kind of language, if any, would be developed by a child completely isolated from environmental linguistic influence. Writing in the 5th century B.C., the Greek historian Herodotus relates the story of the 7th-century B.C. Egyptian king Psamtik I, who decided to conduct an experiment to settle the matter once and for all. According to Herodotus's account, Psamtik took two infants from their mother at birth and left them in an isolated hut in the care of a shepherd. The shepherd was instructed never to utter a word to the infants, and to pay particular attention to the first sound that came out of their mouths. One day when the infants were about two years old, upon returning to the hut from his daily chores, the shepherd was greeted with what sounded to him like *"bekos."* Since *bekos* was the word for "bread" in Phrygian, an Indo-European language spoken in Asia Minor before the arrival of Turkic invaders, Psamtik concluded that Phrygian must have been the world's first language.

How much of what an infant does in the process of learning her first language is instinctive and how much determined by her surroundings?

While the methods of this experiment and Psamtik's conclusion from it obviously leave much to be desired, the basic question remains a compelling one: How much of language acquisition is "nature" and how much is "nurture"? If the genetic linguistic blueprint were permitted to express itself without any outside influence, what would it look like?

For obvious reasons of ethics, nobody nowadays can actually run an experiment on a human child that would answer this question. However, some sadly natural events do provide some insight. Congenitally deaf children who—because of ignorance about the "proper" parental response—are denied the opportunity to learn sign language (of which, by the way, there are many varieties around the world with just as complete and legitimate a linguistic status as spoken languages like

English and Cantonese), or even manacled to prevent them from using manual gestures, may pass through the window of first-language acquisition without really learning language at all, and may remain this way for the rest of their lives.

A "feral" child is an infant abandoned after birth and raised by social wild animals, such as wolves

When a "wild child" emerges from the wilderness after having been socialized by whatever animal raised him, any expressive noises—such as grunts, howls, and barks—will be those of the child's adoptive "parents." Even such biologically preordained behaviors as walking erect, grasping objects between the fingers and opposable thumb, and displaying sensitivity to extremes of heat or cold may be absent. Instead a feral child may walk or scamper on all fours, paw or scratch, pull hot potatoes bare-handed out of the fire or cavort naked in the snow. This shows that whatever genetic blueprint we have for many natural human abilities, including language, is either so general that it won't express itself as anything resembling human language in the absence of an appropriate environmental model, or that this blueprint will fail to express itself at all lacking relevant environmental input. If the latter conclusion is true, then language development is much like vision: if a newborn cat has a patch applied to one eye, then the eye will never develop as a visual organ; when the patch is later removed, the cat is blind in that eye, and will remain so for the rest of its life.

For the development of any of the body's "organs"—whether literal or metaphorical—exposure to appropriate stimuli *at the right age* is crucially important. This doesn't mean that the eye's capacity for vision derives from nothing but external stimuli rather than its innate biological structure, but rather that the division between "nature" and "nurture," or "empiricism" and "rationalism," is not as clear-cut nor even as real as we are sometimes led to believe.

Language, too, has its own critical period, beyond which the task of acquisition becomes at the very least considerably harder, and less likely to succeed, than it is for infants (see "How a child begins to speak a complex language...," p. 213). Most of our understanding about this window of opportunity—closing, at different times for different specific abilities, by the age of about 12—comes from evidence of the increased difficulty of acquiring a *second* (non-native) language as an adult. But what about *first* language acquisition? What would happen if a child were somehow denied the chance to learn any language at all until after the critical period had ended?

The Wild Boy of Aveyron

While any evidence that we could use to answer this question is, fortunately, rarely available, once in a while something of relevance does fall into our laps. Victor, the Wild Boy of Aveyron depicted in François Truffaut's film *The Wild Child*, was discovered in rural southern France in 1800. Nobody was sure exactly how old he was, but he seemed to be about 12. Nothing was known about his personal history beyond the fact that his throat had been cut in infancy, presumably when he had been left to die in the woods. The fact that he had survived probably meant that he had been raised by wild animals. He spoke not a word of language.

The best efforts of Jean-Marc-Gaspard Itard, a young physician at Paris's National Institute of Deaf-Mutes, resulted in an initial, promising flurry of language acquisition—the learning of names for individual objects, and even the ability to understand and formulate rudimentary multiword utterances—but nothing beyond this. Eventually, once the initial enthusiasm had faded over the opportunity Victor provided for testing certain Enlightenment ideas about human perfectibility, Victor was abandoned to obscurity in an inconspicuous home on the Impasse de Feuillantines, supported by a caretaker and a modest pension. He died there at age 40.

EXERCISE: The forbidden hidden

As if you were doing an acrostic puzzle, think of a synonym for each word in the left column that fits in the numbered spaces opposite that word in the right column. Write the correspondingly numbered letters into the numbered squares in the grid below. (If you are not an *experienced* genius, write in pencil.) The letters you write correctly into the grid below will reveal a phrase from the preceding article on feral children and language.

CONTAMINATED	9	17	32	48	54	21	3	11
LARGE NUMBER	50	12	6	67	64	53	15	13
RABBIT FOOD			68	1	10	45	26	
UNDISCIPLINED			58	62	20	39	27	63
JEWELED CROWN			33	59	5	4	66	
LACKING HEARING				61	34	19	2	
LIVING KINGDOM			56	28	16	65	41	60
MARK INDELIBLY			23	35	14	42	30	
EXTENDED GRASP			38	29	22	7	8	
POST-THURSDAY			18	44	37	43	24	51
FEDORA & BOWLER				57	46	49	52	
TO FORCE EXILE			36	31	25	55	47	40

1		2	3	4	5	6		7	8	9	10
11		12	13		14	15		16	17	18	19
20	21		22	23	24	25	26	27	28	29	30
	31	32	33	34	35		36	37	38	39	40
	41	42	43		44	45	46	47	48	49	
50	51		52	53	54	55	56	57		58	59
60	61		62	63	64	65	66	67	68		

The tragic case of "Genie" from L.A., whose "language-learning" window was sealed shut from the age of 20 months to 13½ years

A recent case of a child who passed through her critical acquisition period without learning language is that of "Genie," a severely abused and neglected child discovered in 1970 in, of all places, Los Angeles. After a relatively normal early infancy, from about the age of 20 months until she was brought to the light of day at 13 and a half years of age, Genie had been confined to a small bedroom in the back of her parents' house, and often harnessed to an infant's potty seat or in a straightjacket, with very little human contact or stimulation of any kind. From infancy on, almost the only exposure she had to human vocalization was when her father or brother barked or growled at her like a dog. The father forbade anyone in the family, including Genie's mother, to talk to her.

When she was discovered, Genie was malnourished, animal-like, and neither spoke nor understood language beyond a few words. (She was also near-sighted to precisely the distance— 10 feet—from one edge of her room to the opposite wall.) The only words she uttered, or seemed capable of uttering, were "stopit" and "nomore"; she appeared to understand about a dozen isolated words, including her own name, "door," "walk," "go," and "no." Presumably, despite the father's prohibition, Genie's mother had managed to teach her a tiny, rudimentary vocabulary—although it's possible that these few words were nothing more than a memory from a distant, relatively normal infancy.

Genie passed through what is generally considered the "critical period" with no language acquisition

From infancy until about 12 years of age Genie did not learn to speak. She could understand about as many words as a typical family dog. It was very much an open question whether she would ever be able to become a linguistically full-fledged adult. Perhaps unfortunately for Genie, she became the object of competing academic, scientific, and personal interests to the point where her needs as a human being were—despite good intentions all around—only questionably served.

While she was being studied by UCLA linguists (in particu- lar Susan Curtiss, who turned her study into a doctoral disser- tation), Genie did make some progress in her comprehension and production of language, albeit sometimes with a puzzling waxing and waning of specific abilities. To some degree, her progress followed that of a normal child in the early stages of language learning, although much more slowly. For the first two or three years, she spoke very little, and she always remained much more reticent, and less linguistically playful and exploratory, than a normal child in the first few years of language acquisition. And while normal children experience an explosion of learning after the two-word stage at around age three (see "Around the turn of the first year...," p. 219), Genie remained stuck in a "telegraphic" stage. For her, the normal developmental explosion simply never occurred.

Genie never learned simple grammatical structures the rest of us take for granted

Some of the seemingly unremarkable structures Genie never learned to use properly or, in test situations, to understand, were

- tense/aspect markers (e.g., walked)
- possessive markers (e.g., John's)
- some prepositions (especially under)
- modal verbs (may, can, must, etc.)
- quantifiers (many, most, few, fewest)
- the conjunction or
- possessive pronouns (my, your, etc.)
- first- and second-person object pronouns (me, you)
- all third-person pronouns (he, she, him, her, etc.)
- relative pronouns ("the man whom I saw," "the cat that bit me")

She had ongoing difficulties matching the "actor" and "patient" with the subject and object of both active and passive sentences ("The cat is biting the dog" vs. "The dog is biting the cat"). While she understood "wh"-questions (e.g., "Whom did you see today?"), she never learned to produce them spontaneously.

Genie often seemed to understand language better than she could demonstrate in test situations

Genie could understand better than one would guess from her speech, but it wasn't clear to what extent this comprehension was due to contextual clues that don't depend on linguistic knowledge as such. Curtiss speculated that Genie, having missed language acquisition during her critical period, may have failed to develop the left-brain specialization for linguistic knowledge typical of humans. We all rely on contextual information and pragmatic expectations in our linguistic interactions with others, but perhaps Genie was more dependent on these right-brain faculties than most of us.

After being bounced from caretaker to caretaker, Genie moved into a home for mentally retarded adults, withdrew into a state of unresponsiveness and depression, and disappeared from the world of scientists and health-care providers who had studied her and argued over her for years. The only person from her past she continues to have contact with is her own mother, whom Genie visits once a week.

EXAMPLES OF GENIE'S SPEECH, WITH GLOSSES:

"At school scratch face": *Someone/I scratched my face at school/ I scratched someone's face at school* (after $2^1/_2$ years of language exposure)

"Not spit bus": *I didn't spit on the bus* (after $3^1/_2$ years)

"Mama is feed you": *Mama is feeding you/me* (after $3^1/_2$ years)

"I supermarket surprise Roy": *I surprised/will surprise/want to surprise Roy in the supermarket* (after $4^1/_2$ years)

Genie: "Genie have yellow material at school"

(M: "What are you using it for?")

Genie: "Paint. Paint picture. Take home. Ask teacher yellow material. Blue paint. Yellow green paint. Genie have blue material, teacher said no. Genie use material paint. I want use material at home." (after $4^1/_2$ years)

"I want you open my mouth": *I want you to open your mouth* (after $4^1/_2$ years)

"Mama not have baby grow up": *(meaning uncertain)* (after $4^1/_2$ years)

HOW PIDGINS BECOME CREOLES

In many ways, Genie's telegraphic, structurally impoverished speech resembles what are known as *pidgins*. Pidgins are rudimentary semi-languages jerry-built in situations where different speakers share no common language and quick communication is required—in situations of trade or slavery, for example. A pidgin, in other words, is nobody's native language, and is hastily assembled by adults well past the critical language-acquisition period who simply need to communicate with one another on a basic level. Such structures as tense and agreement markers, relative clause markers, morphological plural markers, and many "function" words are simply omitted from a communication system consisting largely of nouns and verbs strung together in a fairly unstructured manner.

One of the fascinating things about pidgins is that, when they are passed on to the subsequent generation, they change. Infants exposed to the parents' pidgin as their first language actually add complexity and structure, rather than simply learning or imitating what they hear. Of course, infants don't create the material for this increased complexity de novo, like Athena from the head of Zeus. Rather, they recruit "function" words and markers from other more "concrete" words they're exposed to. This process is recapitulated continuously in "normal" languages—consider the recruitment of English tense-aspect markers out of verbs like *finish* and *go* (as in, "He's *going* to leave" to express future), or the development of prepositions out of body-part nouns (e.g., *ahead [of]*).

A pidgin that has become more complex by developing into a subsequent generation's primary language is known as a *creole*. The creativity infants display in turning their parents' pidgin into a creole has inspired University of Hawaii linguist Derek Bickerton to look to creoles, or to the difference between creoles and pidgins, for evidence of our innate "bio-program"—the genetic language-acquisition blueprint we bring as infants to the task of learning language.

EXERCISE: Translating from the pidgin

The following are examples of pidgins transcribed from the speech of Asian immigrants to Hawaii around the turn of the last century. The first is from a native Japanese speaker, the second a native Korean speaker, and the third a native speaker of Filipino. See if you can decipher them. Any Hawaiian-language words are underlined and translated in the lower line to help you out. The other words are English-based.

> 1. *Ifu laik <u>meiki</u>, mo beta make time, mani no kaen <u>hapai</u>.*
>   "die"   "carry"

> 2. *Aena tu macha churen, samawl churen, haus mani pei.*

> 3. *<u>Luna</u>, hu <u>hapai</u>? Hapai awl, <u>hemo</u> awl.*
>   "foreman" "carry"   "cut"

Tok Pisin (literally "pidgin-talk"), spoken in Papua New Guinea, is an English-based creole undergoing a gradual process of development. In this process, "grammatical" or "function" words and markers evolve their new uses out of pre-existing words. Take a look at the following examples of Tok Pisin speech, together with their translations:

> *Mi no stap long ples ol paitim em long-en*
> I no stop at   place they beat up him at it
> "I wasn't there where they beat him up"

> *Husat i kukim dispela haus?*
> who   burn this   house
> "Who burned down this house?"

In the following examples, long "at," longen "at it," and husat "who?" show evidence of having evolved into words with a different function. Can you decipher these and figure out the new function of long, longen, and husat?

> 4. *Mi paitim em long diwai mi holim longen.*

> 5. *Bai mi toktok long ol asua husat bai i kamap sapos Tok Pisin i*
>   *kamap nambawan tokples bilong Papua Niugini.*

Hint: Diwai means "stick"; bai is a future marker; asua means "problem"; tokples means "language."

New technology for testing theories about language processing

A new kind of tool is now available for testing the validity of different theories about how we organize our mental grammar. In an experiment presented recently in the premier journal in the field of linguistics, Jaeger et al. (1996) report the results of PET scans (see "What is the brain so busy doing," p. 177) of the brains of volunteers performing past-tense-inflection tasks on three different kinds of verbs: regularly-inflected verbs, such as *ask*, irregularly-inflected verbs, such as *fall*, and made-up "nonce" verbs, such as *baff*. (The nonce words were carefully chosen so as not to resemble real irregular verbs; therefore, the past-tense forms supplied for them by the volunteers featured the regular inflection.) The PET images reveal that many of the parts of the brain activated in irregular past-tense formation are distinct from those activated in regular past-tense formation. Overall, irregular past-tense formation is not simply a more taxing task in requiring more time and resulting in more errors—irregular past tenses also require the involvement of much more of the brain, at a higher level of activation, than regular verbs.

The simplest conclusion from this is that we may indeed be relying on fundamentally different strategies for producing and processing irregular patterns, such as irregular past-tense forms, than we do for regular patterns. The evidence seems at least to suggest that the most efficient way for us to deal with irregular patterns is to store the various forms as listed entries in our mental lexicon, while the most efficient way for us to deal with regular, productive patterns is to store them as rules that may be applied to lexical stems (uninflected forms) in on-line fashion.

The PET scans do, admittedly, show overlapping activation for all three past-tense tasks centering on and around Broca's area—a traditionally-conceived locus of grammatical processing. In addition, however, an area at the extreme front of the left frontal lobe is activated only with the irregular and nonce past-tense tasks. Also activated only in irregular past-tense ormation is an area in the left temporal lobe, and two areas

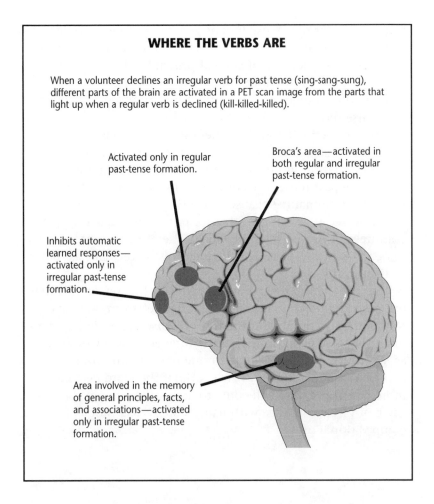

WHERE THE VERBS ARE

When a volunteer declines an irregular verb for past tense (sing-sang-sung), different parts of the brain are activated in a PET scan image from the parts that light up when a regular verb is declined (kill-killed-killed).

Activated only in regular past-tense formation.

Broca's area—activated in both regular and irregular past-tense formation.

Inhibits automatic learned responses—activated only in irregular past-tense formation.

Area involved in the memory of general principles, facts, and associations—activated only in irregular past-tense formation.

in the parietal lobe. Two areas activated in just the regular and nonce inflection tasks are in the prefrontal cortex and cingulate cortex.

One of the areas involved in just the irregular and nonce past-tense tasks has been independently found to have a function of inhibiting automatic learned responses to stimuli. It is activated in novel learning tasks, but the activation disappears with practice and familiarity. Therefore, this region is probably responsible for suppressing activation of the regular past-tense formation rule—at least until it can be determined whether the regular rule should apply. Another area, activated only in the irregular past-tense task, is generally thought to be associated with auditory memory, especially long-term "semantic" memory—the memory of general principles, facts, and associations. It seems, then, that irregular past-tense retrieval is supported by a memory component not involved in regular past-tense retrieval.

An area activated in the generation of just regular and nonce past-tense forms is independently involved in the willful manipulation of items in long-term memory storage. The reason the past-tense inflection of nonce forms activated this region is presumably because, since the nonce verbs were carefully selected to avoid resemblance to real irregular verbs, the volunteers inflected them regularly. Therefore, this area seems to be the best candidate for the locus of the regular past-tense suffixation process.

One of the interesting implications of this research is that our rules of mental grammar will "migrate" from one region of the brain to another as the rules themselves undergo a natural process of evolution. The first time you use a word such as *re-shellack*, you'll process it in one part of your brain as a complex item composed of two parts. If the word becomes more familiar, its use will come to activate a different part of the brain in accordance with its new status as a single, noncompositional unit.

SELF-TEST: Regular and irregular past-tense formation under time pressure

Even though irregular verbs comprise a large portion of our most common, everyday vocabulary, there are many different patterns represented by irregular past-tense forms. When supplying past-tense forms for a list of irregular verbs, getting the right form for each verb is a relatively slow and difficult process.

Below are two lists of common verbs—regular and irregular. For the regular list, give the past-tense forms as quickly as you can, and time how long it takes. Next, try the same thing with the irregular list. You'll need more time for the second list, and you'll probably make more errors.

Note: For an especially difficult exercise, try supplying not just the "simple" past-tense form (as in, "Yesterday I drank the wine") but the compound past form as well (as in, "I have drunk the wine," yielding drink-drank-drunk).

Regular list:	Irregular list:	Regular list:	Irregular list:
pass	think	love	flow
ask	draw	count	blow
rub	fall	name	feed
drop	dig	look	hear
load	catch	watch	bring
dress	sell	blow	keep
push	fight	pay	drink
plan	teach	kill	ride
burn	reach	tie	sing
jump	sleep	start	grow
walk	stand	add	bite
form	hold	laugh	sweep
list	fly	work	send
place	flee	visit	wear

We mixed one irregular verb in with the regulars, and two regulars with the irregulars. Did you spot them and inflect them properly?

EXERCISE: Word storage

The letters stacked up in each column below go into the boxes directly under them, but not necessarily in the order in which they are shown in their stack. When all the boxes have been filled in, a sentence or phrase from the preceding article will appear.

	T	U	M	T	R	G	G	T	L	D	L	S	P	F	C	F	S	S	R	S
	U	N	I	I	M	A	N	E	A	A	E	L	R	O	I	R	E	P	N	O
F	G	D	A	N	E	B	A	N	R	E	Y	Y	D	T	E	F	O	I	N
W	E	S	R	R	E	T	U	G	I	R	P			I	O	T		R	R	E
N	D	C	A	Y		E			L					A	N	G		E	N

Hint: The fourth word is "relying." The letters in the second column will be rearranged in the column below them in this vertical order: e, u, t, d, g.

EXERCISE: PET (Positron Emission Tomography) brain scans

The photos (**A, B, C, D**) here are retouched brain scans that show what areas primarily become active while the brain is processing different language tasks. Their captions have been switched. Can you place them correctly?

A

While reading silently

B

While reciting words

C

While hearing words spoken

D

While thinking and speaking

math function

MATH

Almost all of us fall within the same range of basic mathematical ability. Why, then, do so many of us avoid mental arithmetic calculations and math-games with the excuse that we're just "not good at math"?

We tend to think of math as something we're "good at" or "not good at." In fact, almost all of us are united by a common basic level of ability. For example, if you have a friend read aloud to you the sequence of numbers in the box in the center of this page, chances are great you'll be able to repeat back only about six of them. Very few people are able to recall only three or four, and even fewer—a vanishingly small number—can repeat over 10.

7, 12, 3, 5, 9, 11, 5, 1, 6, 2, 8, 7, 4, 15

Have a friend read aloud to you the first four numbers, then repeat them back. Repeat for five numbers, and so on, until you make a mistake. What's your limit? For almost all people, it's around six or seven.

But those of us who think of math as something we're simply not good at tend to leave the mental calculations to others. When we go out to eat, we let someone else perform the reckoning of the tip, or let someone else verify that the change returned is correct. By allowing ourselves to settle into this kind of pattern, we allow our mathematical acuity, and general mental alertness, to slip. This is, in fact, exactly why most of us who really are "not good at math" have become this way—because we've become comfortable *thinking* of ourselves this way.

That's why you should take a look at this chapter even if you're not one of those who are "good at math"—perhaps especially so. The more math games you play, the better you become, and the more your self-perception shifts from one who isn't good at math to one who is.

Beyond keeping your mathematical ability from falling fallow, there's a lot you can do with your lifestyle to keep mathematically nimble. That's because math skills, more than perhaps any other facet of general intelligence, tend to fluctuate with your mood and momentary mental alertness. So good sleep and the right kind of nutrition are particularly important for mathematical performance. And the kind of lunch you should eat if you want to perform well on math tasks during the afternoon is not the same as what you should have in the evening if you want to ensure a good night's sleep. This chapter will tell you about those things too.

Some of the most revealing research into how the human mind manipulates numbers to achieve goals in the real world comes from studying how infants learn number concepts and how individuals with extraordinary mathematical skills solve problems. For example, even newborns are able to perceive a difference between three and four dots flashed onto a screen in front of them. Idiot savants who are able to perform complex calculations involving multi-digit numbers have developed different strategies to accomplish these feats. Some even involve visualizing numbers in terms of color, sound or shape; some break a calculation into component parts, solve those serially and retain the components in memory by visualizing them. In somewhat the same way people learn to remember names by linking some meaning of the name with a visual picture related to the way the person looks.

Why are musicians often also accomplished in mathematics? Could it have something to do with perceiving and manipulating intervals by seeing them with the mind's eye?

Are human infants born with number skills?

As with most domains of human cognitive ability, there's considerable debate about whether our arithmetic skills are simply learned through instruction and interaction with the environment, or whether we're born with specific mathematical skills on which we may build as we mature.

There is evidence that humans are indeed innately endowed with a rudimentary sense of numerical quantity. If a newborn infant is shown a picture of three dots, he will be initially attentive. After repeated showings, he becomes "habituated," and loses any interest in the picture. If the *number* of dots is changed, however—even after he's become bored with the first picture—he'll perk up again and treat the picture with a dot added or subtracted as if it were completely new.

This may show that human infants have an innate understanding of the difference between, say, 3 and 4—years before they learn to "count" in the usual sense, or even to talk. It's interesting that the experiment only works for classes of items up to 3 or 4. Newborns don't seem to have the ability to distinguish, say, 6 from 7. Even at age 3, after learning to recite the names for numbers 1 through 10, children can correctly label a set of items as "three," but normally can't correctly assign the word "eight" to a set of eight items.

Are children of all cultures equally good in arithmetic?

At a basic level, there seems to be little cross-cultural variation in the mathematical abilities of children. Differences do emerge, however, due to the influence of school systems and even due to differences in the kinds of names different languages give to numbers.

In English, the learning of numbers higher than 10 is particularly difficult for children, since many number names are arbitrary and "opaque," rather than transparently and iconically motivated. To see how this works, consider the difference between "sixteen" and "eleven." Once a child has learned "six" and "ten," the new number-name "sixteen" would be relatively easy to learn because it's transparently composed of the smaller number-words. Perhaps even more importantly, this compositionality helps in the acquisition and reinforcement of the understanding of 16 as 6 plus 10. Thus, it's not only the case that sixteen is easy to learn as a new number-word, the very structure of the word helps to teach the child about the concept of addition.

On the other hand, "eleven" is quite arbitrary: it bears no relevant discernible resemblance to smaller number-words (such as "one" or "ten"), and must simply be learned as a completely new label with no compositionality or internal motivation. (The origin of "eleven," by the way, is "one-left," and "twelve" originally meant "two-left"; that is, after counting up to ten on your fingers, there is one item left.)

To imagine how difficult a *completely* arbitrary number-naming system would be, imagine that instead of "two hundred" we had a word "flart." Imagine further that, instead of "two hundred and one," we had "sneel," and that instead of "two hundred and two," we had "lentel," and so on. Obviously, such a system would require much more time and effort to learn, and it would fail completely to express an understanding of these larger numbers as composed of smaller numbers added or multiplied together.

In some languages, number-words are much more transparently compositional than in English. In Japanese, number-words below 100 are transparently composed of the words for 10 and for 1–9 (see p. 245). And even though the English number-word "ninety-seven" is fairly transparent and internally motivated by other names for smaller numbers, the French word for the same number is much more so: *quatre-vingt-dix-sept*, literally meaning "four (times) twenty (plus) ten (plus) seven." (At the same time, this difference points out a *disadvantage* of maximally transparent naming-systems: they tend to get quite cumbersome.)

Children learning languages with more transparent number-naming systems than English, then, tend to have an easier time learning the number-names and grasping the concept of larger numbers as being composed of smaller numbers. Inconsistencies in even the relatively transparent English number-names give rise to typical errors among young learners. While the number we write as "51" is logically enough identified by the name "fifty-one," with the "five" before the "one," the opposite is true for "15." So young English-speaking children often write the spoken word "fifteen" as "51."

> The transparent compositionality of the Japanese language's number-names helps a Japanese child understand the concepts of addition and multiplication. The word for 12 is "ten-two," the word for 20 is "two-ten," and so on.
>
> | | | |
> |---|---|---|
> | iti "one" | zyuuiti "eleven" | |
> | ni "two" | zyuuni "twelve" | nizyuu "twenty" |
> | san "three" | zyuusan "thirteen" | sanzyuu "thirty" |
> | si or yon "four" | zyuusi "fourteen" | yonzyuu "forty" |
> | go "five" | zyuugo "fifteen" | gozyuu "fifty" |
> | roku "six" | zyuuroku "sixteen" | rokuzyuu "sixty" |
> | siti or nana "seven" | zyuusiti "seventeen" | nanazyuu "seventy" |
> | hati "eight" | zyuuhati "eighteen" | hatizyuu "eighty" |
> | ku or kyuu "nine" | zyuuku "nineteen" | kyuuzyu "ninety" |
> | zyuu "ten" | | |

How do you know if your child *really* understands what the number-names mean?

Although it's second nature to adults, young children do not automatically understand that the number-word used to count the last item in a set of items may also be used to identify the *quantity* of the set as a whole. How can you tell if your child has successfully made this conceptual jump? Just ask her to count the number of fingers on your hands. Then, ask her how many fingers you have. If she has to re-count, then she doesn't really understand the significance of the last number-word mentioned in a counting sequence.

To make absolutely sure that your child truly understands this concept rather than simply having learned that repeating the last-counted item's number-name will evoke a favorable reaction from an adult, try this next simple test. Ask her to hand you a certain fairly small number of items—say, seven peanuts. If she counts out seven peanuts and then hands them to you, she's reached an understanding of *cardinality* attained by most 4- or 5-year-olds, but by only a minority of 3-year-olds. If she simply hands you a bunch of peanuts without counting, she's still at the typical 3-year-old stage.

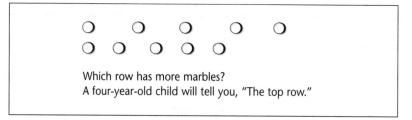

Which row has more marbles?
A four-year-old child will tell you, "The top row."

Even for 4- and 5-year-olds, this understanding of cardinality is rather tentative. Piaget showed that 5-year-olds are easily deceived into thinking that a more spread-out, longer row of a given number of objects has *more* items than a row of the same number of objects more tightly spaced. It usually isn't until 7 or 8 years of age that a child will consistently rely on cardinality alone in making these judgments, as opposed to relying on other, non-numerical perceptual cues.

+ ÷
− *

EXERCISE: An algebraic dispute

A little girl and her brother are hunting Easter eggs.

The boy says to his sister:

> Give me seven of your eggs and I'll have twice as many as you!

To which the little girl replies:

> Not fair! Give me seven of yours and we'll have the same amount.

How many eggs does each have?

Hint: Since the girl's quantity plus seven equals the boy's total minus seven, they are fourteen apart: He must have fourteen more eggs than she.

"Idiot" savants

Idiot savants (such as the character played by Dustin Hoffman in the movie *Rain Man*) have long intrigued psychiatrists because of their combination of low I.Q. (although not usually so low that they would be "idiots" according to the technical definition of the term) with impressive, sometimes phenomenal, feats of memory, artistic ability, or calculation. Some of the most famous savants have been calendar calculators, able to rapidly figure the day of the week for any date going back several decades; one celebrated pair of identical twin savants could reputedly perform such calculations over a span of 8,000 years. Another savant is reported to have had the ability to repeat a discourse of any length in any language without the omission of so much as a syllable.

Strangely, such skills may appear or disappear quite suddenly and unexpectedly
When savantism develops or disappears, it may do so in tandem with the loss or development of a seemingly unrelated and sometimes quite commonplace ability. Sometimes, impaired mental functioning may occur together with the appearance of a hitherto unglimpsed prodigious talent after a head trauma or illness.

Their loss of left-brain function may explain why so many savants show extremes of both ability and disability
One theory about the coexistence of such extreme ability and disability in many savants is that they suffer from left-brain deficit, which causes the right hemisphere to take over. This is a particularly plausible hypothesis in the case of one autistic child whose linguistic development (primarily associated with the left brain hemisphere) displaced a phenomenal artistic skill (right hemisphere). Another intriguing perspective on the savantism puzzle is that the impressive concrete memory together with poor powers of abstract reasoning that savants typically display may actually be caused by an inability to sort through and selectively *forget* sensory input, rather than any increased ability to remember per se. (Also see "If you want to remember complex data," p. 91.)

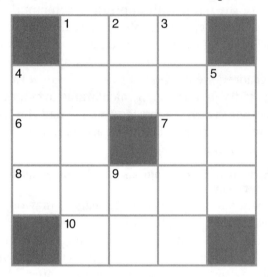

+÷
−*

EXERCISE: Numberlocker

Directions: Use only the digits 1 through 9. There are no zeros. Only one digit may be placed in each box, and a digit may be used more than once in a combination. Where it appears that more than one combination of digits is possible, look for additional clues in interlocking numbers.

Starters: A good "entry" for this puzzle is 1 Across. Given the information that 1 Across starts with a one-digit cube, and that the second and third are that first digit's square, there's only one possible answer; then, it's easy to get 1, 2, and 3 Down. Remember, a prime number is divisible only by itself and 1.

ACROSS

1. The second and third digits are the square of the first, which is itself a cube (even number)
4. The first digit is the same as the last (even number)
6. Prime number
7. The sum of the digits is 11 (even number)
8. The sum of the digits is 24 (odd number)
10. Odd number whose digits increase by threes

DOWN

1. The first two digits are the square and the last three are the cube of a number which is itself a square (odd number)
2. Even number which is both a square and a cube
3. The first two digits are the square of a prime number, the last three the cube of the same prime number
4. The cube of an even number; the sum of its digits is 9
5. The square of 6 Across; the sum of its digits is 19
9. Square of the number found in 4 Down; the sum of its digits is 9

Brain-changing nutrition and the "post-lunch dip"

Given the phenomenon of the "post-lunch dip" (a fall-off in alertness and performance after lunch, due at least in part to internal circadian body rhythm), much research has been devoted to the question of the optimal type of lunch to increase performance, or at least minimize the dip.

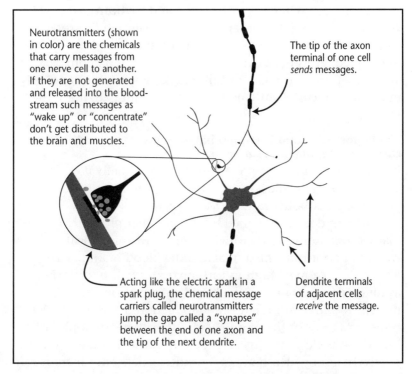

Neurotransmitters (shown in color) are the chemicals that carry messages from one nerve cell to another. If they are not generated and released into the bloodstream such messages as "wake up" or "concentrate" don't get distributed to the brain and muscles.

The tip of the axon terminal of one cell *sends* messages.

Acting like the electric spark in a spark plug, the chemical message carriers called neurotransmitters jump the gap called a "synapse" between the end of one axon and the tip of the next dendrite.

Dendrite terminals of adjacent cells *receive* the message.

Since the 1970's, some interesting studies have focused on the effects of certain "brain-modifying" nutrients, including the amino acids tryptophan and tyrosine, and a component of lecithin called choline. It makes sense that these substances would interact with mental function, since they are all *precursors of neurotransmitters:* they are converted into substances that convey messages across the synapse between one neuron and another.

Different neurotransmitters, and therefore their precursors, have different effects. Tryptophan is converted into the neurotransmitter serotonin, which, among other things, is conducive to calmness or mental alertness (depending on factors such as time of day, personality type, etc.). Tyrosine is used in the synthesis of dopamine, norepinephrine, and epinephrine, which help you remain mentally alert, energetic, and motivated. Choline is converted into acetylcholine, crucial to memory function. (See p. 110).

Tryptophan and tyrosine are especially plentiful in foods rich in protein, while egg yolks, liver and soybeans are especially rich in choline. Perhaps, then, a meal high in protein (since protein is rich in tryptophan and tyrosine) would result in elevated levels of serotonin, dopamine, norepinephrine, and epinephrine, thereby (ideally) making you simultaneously more calm, focused, and alert. However, things are not quite so simple.

The important thing is a good balance of protein and carbohydrate, not protein alone

It turns out that a high-protein meal may actually *decrease* serotonin levels while a meal with moderate amounts of protein and carbohydrates *increases* them.

The paradox is explained by the fact that protein contains many other amino acids which compete with and beat out tryptophan for transmission across the blood-brain barrier. Even though a meal high in carbohydrates fails to introduce as much tryptophan into the blood-stream as one high in protein would, it stimulates the production of insulin, which transports most of the amino acids other than tryptophan into the muscle cells. Any tryptophan in the blood is therefore relatively unimpeded for access to the carrier cells for transport into the brain.

The best lunch for minimizing the post-lunch dip, then, seems to be one that features lean protein, little fat, moderate carbohydrate, and, overall, moderate calories

Protein is important for the synthesis of the "alertness" neurotransmitters which your brain would otherwise be running low on. Low fat and moderate calories are important because a heavy meal that's hard to digest diverts blood from your brain to your stomach and is conducive to grogginess. If the carbohydrate-to-protein ratio is moderate, little enough serotonin will be synthesized to avoid the sleepiness which might otherwise occur when that "calming" neurotransmitter interacts with your early-afternoon circadian dip.

How NOT to meet your protein requirements

The amino acid tryptophan is the chemical from which the body makes the neurotransmitter serotonin. Amino acids are also the building blocks of protein, and tryptophan is one of the "essential" amino acids, meaning that it can't be manufactured by the body and must be obtained from foods. Some foods, such as gelatin, contain many of the amino acids required for complete protein but lack tryptophan. If you try to satisfy your protein requirements with such foods, your body will use any available tryptophan for protein synthesis, leaving little or nothing for the production of serotonin. In an experiment on the effects of a gelatin-protein diet, subjects had a tendency to become tired, irritable, and depressed.

A good way to calm down is to go for the sweets

When tense or unfocused, or if you are trying to fall asleep when overly anxious, have a meal or snack consisting of nothing but glucose-containing carbohydrates, including most "sugars" (including table sugar, corn sweetener, and honey, but not fructose or purely fructose-containing foods, i.e., fruits) and "starch," which is composed of long chains of glucose molecules. Such foods will release insulin into your bloodstream, and hence tryptophan from your blood plasma into your brain, resulting in serotonin production and a sensation of calm. This is one reason why we think of pasta as a "comfort" food, and may be part of the explanation for why women often reach for sweets during their premenstrual period.

You can set up your own experiment by trying the concentration exercises on the following pages during, and again after, lunches with and without protein.

SELF-TEST: Sleepy brains find this more difficult

Here are examples of the kind of task that becomes harder if you're sleep-deprived, or if you're older:

Frontal-lobe thinking test #1

For each noun in the list, supply as many appropriate verbs as you can think of. Example: APPLE: bite, eat, chew, munch, polish. Limit yourself to one minute for each word.

KNIFE

SHOE

CUP

GAME

MOVIE THEATER

Norms
Young adult (19–27): 30 verbs.
Middle-aged adult (55–64): 22 verbs.
Older adult (66–85): 16 verbs.
Young sleep-deprived adult: 22 verbs.

(Based on Harrison, Horne, and Rothwell 2000)

Frontal-lobe thinking test #2

For each incomplete sentence, there's an obvious word you can use to finish it. For example, if you're given the incomplete sentence, "The letter was mailed without a(n)—," the obvious word to complete it is stamp. So you'd have to complete it with a different word—for example, care, or envelope.

Captain Bligh wanted to stay with the sinking —. (ship)

They went as far as they —. (could)

The old house will be torn —. (down)

Most cats see very well at —. (night)

It's hard to admit when you're —. (wrong)

Marilyn was glad the affair was —. (over)

Her job was easy most of the —. (time)

When you go to bed turn off the —. (light(s))

The game was called off when it started to —. (rain)

The dispute was settled by a third —. (party)

(Based on Bloom and Fischler 1980)

Lack of sleep, especially the phase when you are dreaming, reduces problem-solving ability

The fact that sleep plays a critical role in effective cognitive functioning is obvious. Beyond the common-sense knowledge that a bad night's sleep is detrimental to optimal performance the next day, there have been experiments showing that the learning of conditioned-avoidance tasks in rats is followed by an increase in REM sleep (rapid eye movement, associated with dreaming in humans). Their learning is impaired by lack of REM sleep, as well. A human study of mathematics graduate students shows that they are unable to perform even the simplest calculations if awakened from recovery sleep following a 48-hour period of sleep deprivation.

That part of your brain that regulates sleeping and alertness patterns is very similar in all mammals

As shown in the diagram below, the primary alertness and sleep-control centers are located in a peg-shaped area at the top front of the brainstem, the most most primitive part of the brain. At the top of this area a cluster of cells called the *locus coeruleus,* controls secretions which put the brain into deep sleep, including REM. Other clusters of cells control the secretion of *norepinephrine* ("norepi," for short) alerting the brain, especially to the unexpected, even in sleep.

Controls secretion of hormone that brings on the dreaming phase in the sleep cycle

Secretes a chemical that brings on light sleep—the phase in which a disrupted sleeper is easily awakened

It is a flood of norepinephrine, released into the brain during moments of acute stress, that gives rise to the "slow motion" effect we experience during an automobile accident, for example. It makes our brain *so* alert that it's as if we were taking in several times the normal amount of information that we normally would in the same span of time.

When sleep starts, production of norepinephrine falls to half its normal levels. At about 100 minutes into each sleep cycle it shuts down completely during the phase of deep sleep when dreaming and REM sleep take over. In the diagram on p. 253 the row of smaller dark-colored cells below the locus coeruleus represents the *raphe nuclei*, which secrete a substance causing a state of light sleep.

The body's internal "clock" is hidden deep inside the brain at the top of its most primitive parts

This diagram below represents the brain sliced in half to show the location of the *pineal gland*. (Note that both the *thalami* have been removed from this diagram for clarity.) It is located at the very top of the brainstem. It sets the *circadian rhythm* "clock," which controls timing of sleep and wakefulness by secreting the hormone *melatonin* in response to a number of factors including daylight and darkness. (See p. 173.) Melatonin is produced from serotonin, and appears to counter-act the production of the "alertness" hormone norepinephrine (a.k.a. noradrenaline). Some research suggests that a so-called "S" chemical builds up gradually when humans are awake until it reaches a saturation level which starts the sleep cycle.

When the "S" chemical is drawn from humans and injected into laboratory rats they become drowsy.

Pineal gland that controls the body's internal "clock"

+ ÷
− ✳
EXERCISE: Addlock

Directions: Write a single digit in each box so the sum of the digits equals the total given in the clue for that row or column. No number is used more than once in any answer, and zero is not used.

In this Addlock, all answers end in an even number, and the number 9 is not used.

1	2	3		4	5	
	6		7			
8			9			10
11	12		**5**			**8**
13		14			15	
	16			17		
18				19		**4**

ACROSS

1.	7	13.	26
4.	8	15.	11
6.	20	16.	28
9.	25	18.	17
11.	15	19.	18

DOWN

2.	6	10.	18
3.	12	12.	24
4.	14	14.	19
5.	11	15.	19
7.	23	17.	15
8.	21		

Starters: The top left corner is a good place to start. Then, you can deduce the three numbers you need to complete 6 Across, with the only question being the order of the first two of those three. (Remember that all answers must end in an even digit.) 4 Down plus answers intersecting with that will help determine the order.

Hint: One possible answer for 7 Down is 17564.

EXERCISE: Faces and hands

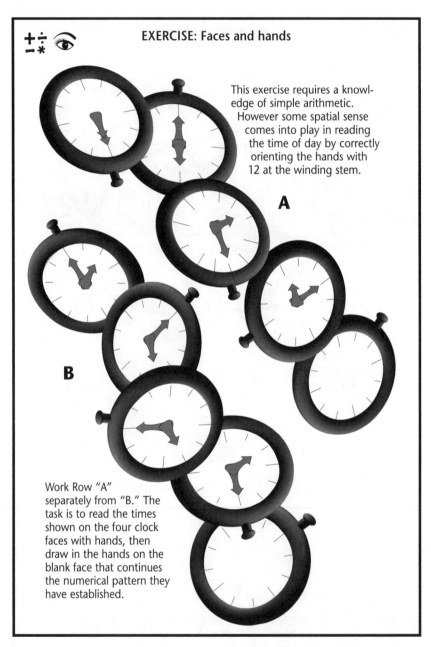

This exercise requires a knowledge of simple arithmetic. However some spatial sense comes into play in reading the time of day by correctly orienting the hands with 12 at the winding stem.

A

B

Work Row "A" separately from "B." The task is to read the times shown on the four clock faces with hands, then draw in the hands on the blank face that continues the numerical pattern they have established.

Hint for Row A: Try multiplying the second time by the first. Don't forget that the hands go completely around every 12. **Hint for Row B:** Try working the problem from right to left so that each time to the left is double the number of hours of the time to its right. Don't forget that the hands go completely around every 12 hours.

The genius who thought in pictures but expressed his ideas in math

Since the publication of an article some 25 years ago, it has been popular to refer to the young Albert Einstein as "learning disabled," possibly dyslexic or even aphasic. ("Aphasia" is a language impairment resulting from damage to some part of the brain's language areas—see p. 197.) Others have more recently pointed out that such diagnoses are difficult enough for living people, let alone dead ones, and that the evidence for them in the cases of Einstein, Edison, Rodin and others is often flimsy at best.

Be that as it may, the evidence does show that Einstein was relatively weak in certain left-brain abilities, opening the door to speculation that his phenomenal genius may be partly attributed to right-brain compensation for a poorly developed left hemisphere. Most notable are his early difficulties with language—a largely left-brain skill—some aspects of which continued throughout his life. By the report of his sister, as well as his own recollection, he only began to speak at age three, and by all accounts had difficult, labored speech until about age ten. Throughout his adult life, Einstein admitted to being a poor speller, reader and writer: "When I read I hear the words. Writing is difficult, and I communicate this way very badly."

Words and math were both difficult for Einstein

It may come as a shock to learn that Einstein was also no genius at left-brain-dependent mathematical calculations. As a schoolboy, arithmetic was almost as much a struggle for him as foreign languages, and even during his residency at Princeton, after winning the Nobel Prize for physics, he had difficulty helping high-school students with their calculus homework.

Einstein did, on the other hand, have an unusual gift for visual conceptualization, and for kinds of math involving—or which he could translate into—spatial configurations (a right-brain-dependent ability). When his uncle Jakob Einstein, an engineer, introduced him to geometry's Pythagorean Theorem, Einstein thought the theorem so obvious from simple visual inspection that it failed to require proof. He did, however, devise a formal proof quite different from the standard one which would have been taught in school—and he did this before the age of ten. It was only after leaving the authoritarian German school system and enrolling in the Kanton School at Aarau, Switzerland, that his unique gifts began to blossom. The school at Aarau was founded by the Swiss education reformer Pestalozzi, who believed that a flexible, radically visually-oriented curriculum was the way to let young minds develop freely.

Einstein always maintained that, for him, thought was essentially imagistic and non-verbal, and that words or language entered his mind only during the late stage of translating his insights into a communicable form. "For me," he claimed, "it is not dubious that our thinking goes on for the most part without use of words."

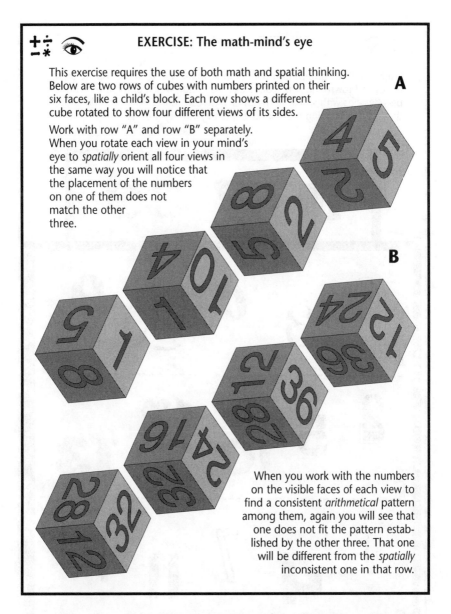

EXERCISE: The math-mind's eye

This exercise requires the use of both math and spatial thinking. Below are two rows of cubes with numbers printed on their six faces, like a child's block. Each row shows a different cube rotated to show four different views of its sides.

A

Work with row "A" and row "B" separately. When you rotate each view in your mind's eye to *spatially* orient all four views in the same way you will notice that the placement of the numbers on one of them does not match the other three.

B

When you work with the numbers on the visible faces of each view to find a consistent *arithmetical* pattern among them, again you will see that one does not fit the pattern established by the other three. That one will be different from the *spatially* inconsistent one in that row.

Hint for Row A: Multiply the numbers on the visible faces of each cube. One produces a product that differs from the other three. Notice the orientation of the 5 and 8 on the other cubes compared to the one which is mathematically inconsistent. **Hint for Row B:** Add the numbers on the visible faces of each cube. One produces a sum that differs from the other three. Notice the orientation of the 12 and 36 on the other cubes compared to the mathematically inconsistent one.

EXERCISE: Now don't get mad!

Study the three groups of black numbers marked A, B, and C. Above them are three brown numbers. Your task is to decide which of the brown numbers belongs with which of the three lettered groups. When you do figure this out in a blinding flash of rage and anguish, try it on your local Einstein.

Hint: Note that there are two symbols next to the title of this Exercise. One indicates that the subject is math and the other indicates a spatial subject. In this puzzle the numerical values are irrelevant.

The magical number 7: How it limits us, and how we can overcome it

Have you ever wondered what it is about the number 7 that makes it recur so frequently in lists of important things? There are seven days of the week, seven wonders of the world, seven ages of man, seven notes on the musical scale. Telephone numbers have seven digits, and psychological tests frequently employ a 7-point rating scale.

There may be something more than just coincidence lying behind the ubiquity of the number 7. Our brain seems to have a built-in limitation organized around this number in its span of judgment, attention, and memory. The limitation isn't hard and fast, but again and again our discriminatory abilities seem to hover around seven categories or points on a scale, give or take a few.

Let's say you hear two musical tones, one after the other. You're told that the lower-pitched tone is "tone number 1," and the higher-pitched one is "tone number 2." If you then hear one of the tones played again, you'll have no problem assigning the correct number to it. You can try this with a larger range of tones, and you'll soon reach the point where you make a lot of mistakes. That point, for almost all people, seems to be around six.

This doesn't just have to do with the larger number of tones being closer to each other in pitch, and therefore inherently easier to confuse. If you try the experiment with five high-pitched tones, it's easy to avoid errors. Confusion is equally unlikely with five low-pitched tones. But combine the five high-pitched tones with the five low-pitched ones in a single sequence, and you'll have to resort to guesswork, resulting in frequent mistakes. So there's something about the absolute number of categories we have to discriminate that represents a limit to our abilities.

Below 7, you count—above 7, you guess

The same numerical limit shows itself in experiments requiring people to perform quick estimates of the number of dots flashed on a computer screen. Below six or seven dots, people make no errors. At seven or above, errors become routine, as *estimations* of the number of dots replace accurate instantaneous counts.

If there's really this numerical limit to our discriminatory abilities, then how is it that we're able to differentiate so many words, so many faces, and so on? The answer seems to be that, with faces and words, we're increasing the number of dimensions we're relying on for our categorical judgments, or stringing several units along in succession and thereby dramatically increasing our discriminatory capacity. If the distinctive characteristic of faces were simply one single variable such as darkness or color, then we would indeed have difficulty distinguishing the faces of over seven people. But every face consists of many more than one variable: different noses, eyes, mouths, ears, and two-dimensional spatial relationships among all these features. And words consist of not just a single distinctive sound, but of many such sounds strung together. Each single sound is typically, in any given language, definable in terms of about seven binary distinctive features (plus or minus consonantal, plus or minus voiced, and so on), and arranging such sounds in sequence results in our ability to distinguish thousands of different words.

"Chunking" helps you memorize more data

Another way around the limit imposed by the number 7 on our memory capacity is by what is sometimes called "chunking." A telephone number including the area code consists of 10 digits. We can make the task of memorizing such a long string of numbers easier by memorizing the area code separately from the rest, or by rearranging the numbers into a shorter sequence of two-digit numbers—as when we memorize an area-code sequence of 5, 1 and 0 as "five-ten."

The same motivation may underlie the rhythmic breath-groups into which we arrange the letters of the alphabet. If you recite the alphabet, you'll find you pause after "g" (the seventh letter), after "p" (the ninth letter after that), and finally "v" (the sixth letter after that), before finishing the sequence. On the one hand, these pauses may simply be viewed as a holdover from the rhythmic groupings in the alphabet song we learn as children. On the other hand, one reason the song makes the alphabet easier to learn is that it breaks down an unmanageably long sequence of items into groups consisting of an easily-managed sequence of 7 letters, give or take a couple.

±÷ 👁 EXERCISE: Opposing digits

Each of the three geometric figures, below, demonstrates a different arithmetical pattern. When you find it you can figure out what number should be substituted for the question mark in each case.

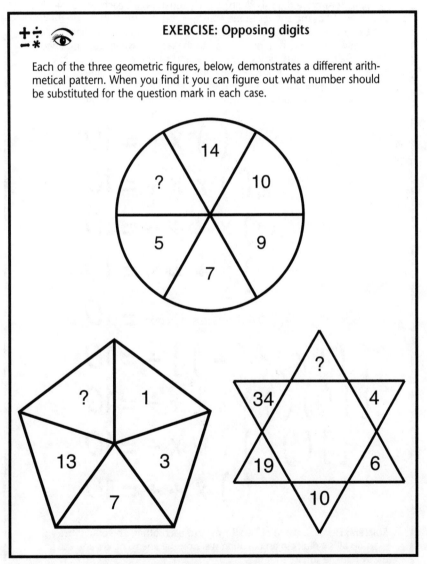

Hint: Most people find the six-pointed star the most difficult until they realize that it is made up of two, overlapping, geometric figures.

+÷
−* 　　　　　　**EXERCISE: Algebra Game**

In this puzzle, you're given both the numbers and the mathematical signs you'll need to get a correct answer. Combine arithmetical signs and identical digits (not more than six digits in each equation) on each line as needed to express 10 as the answer to the equation you construct. Begin on the first line using only 1's. Continue on the second line using only 2's (hint: you'll need only four 2's) and so on through to the last line where you use only 9's. All the plus, minus, times, divided by, and square root signs are in an order you can use in the answer we figured out—except for line 8. (You'll still have to figure out where to put the parentheses and brackets; square brackets go around curved parentheses, as we've shown you in line 6.)

$$( )\ \text{x} - = 10$$

$$( )\ \text{x x} + = 10$$

$$( )\ \text{x x} + \div = 10$$

$$( )\ \text{x} + \div \sqrt{} = 10$$

$$+ = 10$$

$$[\ (+\text{x}) - (+)]\ \div = 10$$

$$[\ ]\ ( )\ ( )\ \text{x} + + + \div = 10$$

$$[\ ]\ ( )\ ( )\ + + \text{x} \div = 10$$

$$( )\ \text{x} + \div = 10$$

Starters: Eleven is made of two 1's next to each other. The only times we used up all six digits in an equation were on the line using 6's and the line using 7's. The square root of 4 is 2.

Hint: One possible answer for line 3 is "(3 × 3 × 3 + 3) ÷ 3 = 10."

spatial function

SPATIAL

Your visuo-spatial ability is in fact many different kinds of ability, ranging from picking out details, to perceiving the arrangement of those details into patterns, to fitting those patterns into a knowledge base so you know what to do with them.

The study of vision has yielded some of the most fascinating insights (no pun intended) into the nature of human consciousness. Even though we rely most heavily on our visual sense in our interpretation of the world around us, psychologists have been telling us for decades that what we think we see out there may not really be out there at all. Take a look, for example, at the white blob in the box in the middle of this page. White blob? In reality, all there is is a circular arrangement of irregular black blobs. Our brain constructs the white blob, complete with an imaginary border separating that imaginary blob from the white space outside it, out of nothing but negative space. If your brain is playing this kind of trick on you, what else might it be doing behind your back?

Focus on the top dot. Are you aware of a white shape defined by the black images? Now focus on the bottom dot. Are you more aware of the white shape, or less? Most people see it more clearly.

It's easy to miss the fact that there are different kinds of ability underlying what we think of as a unified visual awareness. We have a largely left-brain-dependent awareness of visual details—the trees in the forest—and a right-brain perception of the pattern into which the details fit—the overall shape of the forest. The illusion of the white blob is your right brain playing tricks on you, creating a shape out of hints provided by bits and pieces of detail. Usually, we rely on both atomistic and configurational awareness in our processing of the world of visual stimuli around us. The communication lines between different parts of our brain are so rapid that we don't even notice that these various facets of awareness are separate things. But if you meet someone whose vision is just as good as yours, but who somehow cannot fit visually-perceived objects into any kind of knowledge base that would allow her to recognize what those objects are and what to do with them, then you begin to realize what a complex and multifaceted faculty visual awareness is.

Like your other faculties, your visuo-spatial intelligence can be maintained or left to deteriorate. Visual close-ups can challenge you to project those details onto a larger pattern, thus exercising your right-brain-dependent holistic-imaging skills. Familiar patterns with a subtle detail or two out of place can test your attention to objective minutiae. And tasks demanding mental rotation of three-dimensional visual objects can be a real brain-buster, until you learn to get the hang of it.

Seeing both the forest and the trees: Different parts of the brain are specialized for different visual tasks

When you look at a person's face, or a mosaic design, or the stars in the night sky, there are at least two levels of visual awareness you can have. You can focus on the individual tiles, or facial features, or stars, as discrete items of detail, or you can perceive the parts as forming a more inclusive, patterned whole. Usually, you have to switch from one mode of seeing to the other, rather than doing both simultaneously. But both options are available to us.

Not so for people who have suffered damage to either the left or the right visual cortex. The right hemisphere, in vision as in other aspects of our interpretation of the world around us, is the creative department of the brain, best at getting the big picture and grasping global patterns. The left hemisphere is the brain's accounting department, nit-pickingly focused on details. So when the left visual cortex is damaged, the ability to perceive and focus on detail suffers, while right-hemisphere damage impairs the integration of those details into a global whole.

The right hemisphere corresponds to your left visual field (that is, everything to the left of whatever point you're focusing your eyes on), and the left hemisphere to the right visual field. So in theory, you should be better at seeing the details of objects in your right field, and at perceiving patterns in your left field. But you rarely ever notice any difference, mainly because, simply put, you look at what you're looking at—things you're focusing on cross the center of your visual field and spread into both the left and the right fields. Also, communication across both halves of the brain is so automatic and instantaneous that the bias in specialization is pretty much neutralized.

Things are different, however, for those who have a severed corpus callosum—the bundle of fibers connecting the right hemisphere to the left. (Sometimes, epilepsy patients have their corpus callosum deliberately severed in an operation designed to control their seizures.) These individuals can perceive *only* details in their right field of vision, and only global patterns in their left field. So if, say, a picture of a mosaic design is moved from the left side of their visual field to the right, a dramatic switch occurs halfway across: what began as a pattern becomes an unpatterned assortment of random individual tiles.

V or L? Your right brain shows you the large letters, your left brain the small ones—but not both at the same time.

Your upper and lower visual fields are specialized too

Psychologists have long been interested in a phenomenon referred to as *illusory contours*, whereby the human mind projects a boundary onto an image where no boundary actually exists. This kind of projection illustrates dramatically that what we see in the world around us is not so much an objective image of the world "out there" as an automatic subconscious organization of visual stimuli into actively created images.

For some reason, the *lower* visual field is better at perceiving illusory contours than the upper visual field—despite the fact that neither the upper nor the lower field is better at perceiving images *in general*. One can only speculate about the reasons for lower visual-field specialization for such a narrow skill. Perhaps it has to do with the kinds of visual perception that, in our evolutionary past, was especially useful for objects on the ground as opposed to objects at or above eye level.

SELF-TEST: Something's fishy

Giuseppi Arcimboldo (Italian, 1537–93) painted portraits using combinations of objects from nature such as the one shown below composed of marine life. If the nerve cells connecting the right and left halves of your brain were destroyed, you would see only fish, not the image of a man, if this picture were held to your right as you looked straight ahead. The left lobe processes what's seen in the right field of vision and vice versa. The left lobe handles details but the right lobe perceives the big picture.

EXERCISE: Shapes in space

What we see is partly governed by what we expect to see related to past experience. Research on monkeys isolated specific areas in different parts of the brain that respond only to food (a yellow banana but not a yellow flower, for example), another area that responds to objects seen before, but not new ones (a large red balloon but not a small blue one), and a still different area that recognizes different faces.

The brain can perceive only one interpretation of a shape at one time. Our experience may lead us to expect that the "background" is less significant than what we see as a "shape" in the "foreground." We try to identify shapes with familiar objects ("If it looks a lot like a wrench, it's a wrench") and we can be wildly mistaken. The images on this page demonstrate some of those tricks of the mind.

How good are your right-brain compositional skills? Did you already identify these three familiar objects from the two sets of broken drawings on the two preceding pages?

Facial recognition depends on visual-spatial processing by the right side of your brain—but that's not all

We've all had the experience of remembering a face without recalling the name attached to that face. When we find ourselves in the mildly embarrassing situation of forgetting the name of someone who greets us by name, we may fall back on the excuse that we're good at memorizing faces, but not names. In fact, virtually all people are better at memorizing faces than names. Facial recognition relies on a right-brain-based visual-spatial ability which develops during the first ten years of life, but which somehow also lets us memorize faces even better than we can memorize other, otherwise comparable, visual images. It's an impressive gift that we sometimes take for granted.

We humans have a prodigious ability to store other human faces in our long-term memory, and to access those stored images years later. In one study, subjects were asked to identify a high-school classmate from among five photographs taken from yearbooks from the same period. Recognition rates were 90%—regardless of the time elapsed since graduation (from three months to 35 years) and class size (90 to 800). Over the three or four years of high school, in other words, it is just as easy to memorize 800 faces as 90—and it is just as easy to remember them for 35 years as for three months. All this is done largely unconsciously, with no deliberate effort or mnemonic tricks.

Face recognition must be fluid enough that we can identify a face from different angles, and through changes of hairstyle, expression, aging, and weight loss or gain. Damage to the right brain may result in a complete or partial loss of facial recognition abilities under changing conditions of lighting, paraphernalia such as eyeglasses or earrings, or angle of view. Since faces may be thought of as visual patterns, and since the right hemisphere is the general locus of visual-spatial abilities, it makes sense that facial recognition may be right-hemisphere-dependent. But there's more to it.

Some kinds of changes make it harder to recognize a face

If you turn a photograph of a familiar face upside-down, it's much harder to recognize. You might think this is just because the inverted representation is so different from the way you would have stored the visual image in your mind. But other visual images—stick figures, costumes, various inanimate objects— are almost as easy to recognize upside-down as rightside-up. And that's not all. If you try to memorize novel faces presented upside-down, your performance will be, on average, 30% worse than if the faces are presented rightside-up. In other words, even though you'll later be shown the same upside-down face among other upside-down faces, you won't have anything near your usual ability to recognize which one is the same as the one presented earlier. So whatever ability we're using to encode,

In memorizing and recognizing upside-down faces, adults are forced to fall back on the piecemeal processing strategy children rely on in analyzing rightside-up faces. That means that we focus on the specific components only, not on their spatial configuration, and our performance on facial recognition tests is poor.

memorize, and retrieve facial images, it's more specific than, or somehow different from, the equivalent ability when applied to other kinds of objects.

Children rely on different strategies to memorize and recognize faces

Faces are complex visual images, and in theory we might rely

Do you notice anything unusual about this face? Take a look at it for a few seconds, then turn the book upside-down.

For upside-down faces, we process the individual component parts, but we're not very good at noticing distortions in the orientation of these specific features.

on either (or both) of two different kinds of information in memorizing them: piecemeal information about individual components or features (eyebrows, a mole, etc.), or configurational information about the spatial relations among the component parts of the overall facial pattern. In general, we may rely on either strategy in processing visual forms. Adults seem to rely on both strategies when memorizing faces, but the relational-configurational strategy seems to be particularly important. Children under the age of 10, on the other hand, seem to rely primarily on the componential strategy. Evidence for this comes from experiments that show that 6-year-old children are no better at memorizing rightside-up faces than they are at processing inverted faces, with 8-year-olds falling halfway between the 6-year-olds and adults.

In both tasks, children are relying primarily on information about specific facial features rather than the overall configurational gestalt. For adults, performance is much better on upright faces. We can immediately recognize, for example, the difference between two otherwise identical upright faces with some kind of facial distortion among the individual features. Spatial distortions are difficult to perceive for upside-down faces, so we fall back on a reliance on examination of individual features only.

Do you notice anything unusual about this face? Take a look at it for a few seconds, then turn the book upside-down.

We're *much* better and quicker at recognizing spatial distortions of upright faces than of inverted faces. What looks grotesque rightside-up looks relatively normal upside-down.

The difference between 6-year-olds and adults, then, is not that children are better at processing upside-down faces, but that they're worse at processing rightside-up faces. (Children are also much more easily thrown off by facial expressions—two faces might be identified as the same if they're both smiling, for example—and extraneous paraphernalia such as eyeglasses and earrings.) By the age of 10, children have developed the spatial-configurational ability to discriminate, identify, and memorize faces at the adult level.

EXERCISE: About faces

Do you recognize these famous faces?

Hint: Four of the five were pivotal figures in monumental political events of the 20th century related to senseless deaths.

EXERCISE: Eyeball busters

The brain draws on experience to recognize objects. When a closeup detail of an object is all that is visible, and the shape of the entire object cannot be seen, even familiar objects are difficult to identify. The hints may help.

Mouse alert	Classic case	Brit's breakfast
Tender foliage	Smooth closeup	Grabbers galore
Amber waves	This removes...	...these
Point taken	Bonded servitude	Hit the road

SELF-TEST: Facing nature

A stained glass artist from Milan, Giuseppi Arcimboldo, became court painter to a long line of 16th-century Hapsburg kings. He sometimes made surrealistic-looking pictures using combinations of familiar objects.

The brain finds the overall pattern of a face easier to recognize when the face is right side up. What do you think you will see when you turn this photo upside down?

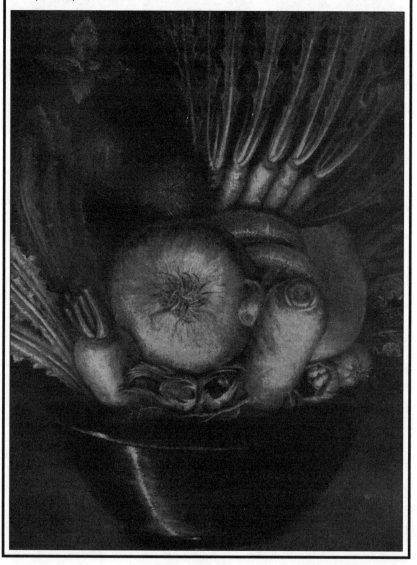

A gene for visual-spatial ability

Advances in chromosomal mapping techniques have led to the identification of a single gene responsible for pattern-construction tasks—building a model, for example, or assembling different-colored blocks into a design. This discovery represents what is reported to be the first identification of a gene involved in cognition.

Depending on how much of the "pattern" gene—LIM-kinase1 (LIMK1)—and an adjacent gene—Elastin—are missing or defective, an affected person may have anything from limited physical and cognitive abnormalities to full-blown Williams syndrome, a disorder featuring vascular disease, elfin facial features, and mental retardation, but (for some as-yet unknown reason) curiously strong rote memory and language abilities.

People with a limited deletion of LIMK1 may have a more-or-less normal overall IQ, and will be able to cope adequately with the routine demands of everyday life. However, even they will have great difficulty with the simplest exercises requiring visual and spatial representations, so they cope with their problem by going through life avoiding any tasks involving such reasoning or images. Sketching a map of the neighborhood, then, would be as arduous a chore for them as dismantling and re-assembling a VCR would be for those of us with full expression of the gene.

Williams syndrome child's
rendition of an elephant.

Can complex human behavior really derive from a single gene?
The media are speculating that the discovery of other genes
responsible for higher cognitive functions, such as spatial, may
be just around the corner. A "spatial gene" represents something of a holy grail for some neurolinguists and evolutionary
anthropologists, who have gone so far as to venture that the
development of such a gene may have been responsible for
the meteoric rise in dominance of our species during our
recent evolution. Is it in fact likely that such a gene will
soon be found?

Probably not. While the human spatial faculty does indeed
have a genetic basis, it involves many different kinds of ability
distributed over a sizeable region of the left hemisphere. Many
different genes, then, must be responsible for different facets
of this ability. Consider, too, that while there is admittedly
(as far as we can tell, at least) a clear qualitative difference
between human spatial function and the communication
systems of other animals, it is not possible to draw as decisive
a line as we might like between what we do and what some
other animals do. As is well known, chimpanzees and gorillas
can readily learn to recognize and manipulate arbitrary symbols to receive and send information. While people may argue
about whether what they do is "really" spatial, the point may
be moot: regardless of what label you give to such behavior, it
is clearly a prerequisite for what we do call spatial in humans.

**A single genetic defect may disrupt a complex ability, but a
single gene alone doesn't account for it**
Imagine if there were a gene crucially responsible for such
symbol manipulation—say, a gene responsible for the ability
to associate a given form (either visual or auditory) with a
given meaning to which it has no necessary or inherent connection. This gene, then, would be responsible for precisely the
sorts of arbitrary associations—the association between the
concept "tree" with the word *tree* in one spatial function, and
with the word *arbre* or *baum* in another—that we consider to
lie at the core of spatial function. If this gene were damaged
or ill-formed, then spatial function as we know it would be
impossible. Would such a gene, then, be the "spatial gene"?
No. As neurolinguist Steven Pinker has written, "A single gene

[may] disrupt grammar, but that does not mean a single gene controls grammar."

The same objection applies to the identification of the "spatial" gene discussed above. When the gene is defective or missing, spatial ability is indeed severely impaired. Does this mean that a single gene is responsible for spatial reasoning? No. For one thing, although those with the defective LIMK1 gene will never become engineers, many spatially-oriented abilities are intact—otherwise, they couldn't so much as walk or eat with a fork. Also, the fact that a defective LIMK1 gene will disrupt spatial ability to some degree doesn't mean that it alone is responsible even for those specific abilities it affects. Pinker's analogy with reference to the possibility of a "spatial gene" is apropos here: "Removing the distributor wire prevents a car from moving, but that does not mean a car is controlled by its distributor wire."

Williams syndrome child's attempts (bottom) at copying a simple line-drawing image (top).

Williams syndrome child's attempts (bottom) at arranging blocks in the configuration shown at top.

Nicotine improves spatial memory, learning, and information processing. Some research also suggests that it lessens memory deficits associated with aging and Alzheimer's

Shakespeare wrote that "there is some soul of goodness in things evil, would men observingly distill it out." The bard's pithy wisdom seems particularly relevant to recent studies showing that the psychoactive compound in tobacco, nicotine, has a wide range of potential benefits for learning and memory,

 EXERCISE: The Embedded Figures Test

In this multiple-choice test, only one of the designs in the right-hand columns contains the figure in the left. Which one? On a task like this, caffeine can worsen performance initially, but improve performance after the task becomes more familiar.

and may even help forestall Alzheimer's and Parkinson's diseases. This has prompted efforts to synthesize nicotine-like compounds that have all the advantages of nicotine for the brain without any of its unwanted side effects.

Cigarette smoking is, despite what the tobacco companies would have you believe, immensely destructive, responsible for millions of deaths each year through cancer, heart disease, stroke, and other diseases. At the same time, it has long been known that tobacco has at least two valued effects on the mind: one, it induces a sense of well-being, and two, it at least seems to enhance memory and alertness. These effects and their neurological bases have now been confirmed in a series of experiments on animals and humans.

Nicotine—a new "smart" drug?
Nicotine affects the brain by binding to receptors that stimulate the release of a host of neurotransmitters, including dopamine and acetylcholine, thereby facilitating transmission of signals between brain cells. Recent evidence indicates that a locus with a particularly high density for nicotinic receptors is the hippocampus, a part of the brain which plays a central role in learning and memory.

In experiments with rats, nicotine has been shown to steepen the learning curve in maze-mastering exercises and to improve memory—in some cases, up to four weeks after the nicotine is administered. In tests on humans, nicotine improves rapid information processing. It also improves short-term recall, spatial memory, and reaction times in Alzheimer's patients.

The cortical nicotinic receptors that appear to be involved in these cognitive tasks are precisely the ones that decline in concentration in patients with Alzheimer's, and experimental drug-induced blockade of neurons that produce or respond to acetylcholine has been shown to mimic the effects of the disease in healthy young test subjects. There's even some indication that nicotine may not only enhance transmission across nerve cells involved in memory-formation, but may counteract the formation of toxic plaques responsible for the development of Alzheimer's.

The source of a cigarette's hedonistic allure

Nicotine also interacts with dopamine—the "hedonistic" neuro-transmitter—and dopamine receptors. In fact, there appears to be a precise region of the forebrain that is activated by nicotine, cocaine, amphetamine, and morphine alike. Lest this lead to bewilderment at the perversity of nature, let it be understood that it is not the case that we have evolved these receptors specifically to make us a drug-addicted species; rather, the compounds in these drugs simply mimic the chemical structure of compounds that are naturally produced in the brain itself. Anything that stimulates dopamine transmission is associated by the brain with a powerful, pleasurable reward, and the brain will want to return to that stimulus again and again—hence the strongly psychologically addictive nature of these drugs.

Why smokers are 50% less likely to develop Parkinson's

By stimulating the release of dopamine, nicotine appears to have the potential to lower the risk of developing Parkinson's disease, and to lessen the severity of the disease in those who already have it. Parkinson's is a degenerative brain disease which kills the brain cells that manufacture dopamine. This results not only in a dour, stoic demeanor, but loss of body control—tremors and, ultimately, complete immobilization.

Many of the advances in the burgeoning field of neuro-transmitter research result from improving the specificity of drugs that interact with the neurotransmitters or the receptors to which they bind. Drugs that have a broad, imprecise effect are called "dirty," while more specific versions are relatively "clean." Now that the potential benefits of nicotine have been proven, a lot of research money will be devoted to synthesizing nicotine-like compounds that affect just the receptors affected by a particular ailment. Among other things, this will mean fine-tuning the chemical structure of the nicotine look-alike so as to interact with just the relevant brain cells, rather than also acting in undesired ways on the central nervous system.

Which way do we go? A story of two different strategies

One of the most notorious stereotypes about men is their reluctance to ask for directions. Put a man in a boat in the middle of the ocean, or on a busy street in any city of the world—he will generally feel confident that he can find his way by himself. Surprisingly, the reason for this single-minded focus may be that men are simply obeying a deep-seated instinct—their brains may have been optimized for navigating in unfamiliar territory.

Scientists reveal clues about why men use very different strategies for pathfinding

A German study published in the April 2000 issue of Nature Neuroscience revealed that men and women use different parts of their brains to navigate through space. The test subjects were instructed to find their way out of a three-dimensional, virtual-reality maze displayed on a computer (see below). While these subjects were doing this task the researchers were able to map their brain activity using functional magnetic resonance imaging (fMRI)—a tool that provides electronic pictures of how and where brain activity occurs—while the test subjects performed their navigation.

The maze protocol: (A) typical view from inside the virtual maze. (B) arial view showing possible paths (not shown to subjects).

286 BUILDING MENTAL MUSCLE

The results
The men navigated their way out of the maze in an average of
2 minutes and 22 seconds, which was nearly one minute faster
than the women's average score of 3 minutes and 16 seconds.
But the researchers noted some distinctive differences in the
way men and women used their brains to steer their way to
the exit.

FMRI results showed that both men and women used the
right side of the hippocampus—a part of the brain associated
with spatial learning—to help find their way out of the maze.
(In fact, the more accurate the route, the higher the rate of
activity in the right hippocampus.) But there were also some
unique differences: *only* the women employed their right
parietal and prefrontal cortex; *only* the men used their left
hippocampus. See photos of the brain scans that revealed
the different tools used by men and women to find their way
(see illustration, opposite).

These results, which support similar research studies on sex
differences in the brain, suggest that men and women may use
different cognitive strategies for navigation and spatial perception. The parietal and prefrontal cortex areas used by women
in this study are associated with recalling a series of landmarks.
(As in, "Go three blocks past the school, and look for the stop
sign.") The left hippocampus used by men indicates that they
visualized the spaces traveled through and their shapes, the
same way they would process geometry. ("Go southeast to the
end and make a left at 11 o'clock.") And while the geometric
cues used by men may get them to their destination more
quickly, other studies have shown that women tend to remember landmark cues better than men.

The idea that sex may be the common variable in behavior
differences is also borne out by a study done on rats at Duke
University, which found virtually identical results to the Nature
Neuroscience study: females used landmark cues in spatial
learning tasks, while males used geometric clues.

**Why would men and women use different strategies for
navigation?**
Some researchers believe the reason is rooted in the evolutionary history of humanoid brain development over the last 50

HOW DIFFERENT STRATEGIES SHOW UP IN THE BRAIN

Women minus Men

Men minus Women

These illustrations show composites of the brain-scans of all the women tested and all the men tested. The illustrations on the left are side views showing the right sides of their brains. The illustrations on the right are top views that show both sides with the front of the head facing right. The white spots show where only women's brains were active (top photos, "Women Minus Men") or the places where only men's brains lighted up (bottom photos, "Men Minus Women"). The big difference is that men used only an area called the "hippo-campus" specialized for remembering directions. It is located in the center of the brain with a more primitive group of "limbic" brain systems. The women used many other tools near the top of their brains in the parietal (top central) and frontal (in the forehead over the eyes) areas of the cortex which helps them compare and organize specific locations they have seen before.

Adapted from Grön, G. et al, University of Ulm, Germany, "Brain activation during human navication" Nature *Neuroscience* vol.3, no.4, April 2000 million years. They speculate that women were in charge of gathering food, provisioning and securing the home, and teaching and caring for helpless infants who were born much less mature than other animals. To ensure their own and their community's survival, females developed language and social skills, fierce nurturing skills to protect their children, and strong landmark discrimination memory to find food near the protection of their dwellings. Men traveled far to hunt game and protect territories. Those who survived had to have developed, target-directed motor skills, complex spatial perception, and navigational ability for tracking game and finding their way back to their home cave. Over time, the conditions under which they lived may have selected for the specialized skill-sets that male and female brains demonstrate today.

Whatever the reason, it does seem that males and females consistently exhibit some neural differences in the way they perceive space and navigate unfamiliar places. However, there may be times when innate navigational ability is overshadowed by practicality. The next time you get lost, you may want to consider who is most likely to arrive at their destination faster: the person who has asked for good directions, or the person with "a good sense" of direction?

WHY LONDON CABBIES GROW BIGGER BRAINS

London cabbies have larger hippocampi than most other people because driving around London is very confusing. The city has no natural order so they have to keep track of where they are all the time they are driving through it. Cabbies must constantly rely on the right hemisphere to visualize areas in which they must find their way. That is why the hippocampus on the right side of a cab driver's brain is enlarged by experience.

"Blindsight," a suprising finding, and other curiosities: The riddle of consciousness

No one would deny that the collective cognitive sciences have made tremendous strides in understanding the material underpinnings of many aspects of our experience of life and the world around us: vision, memory, spatial, fear, even love. But the biggest questions remain elusive: What ties it all together? What accounts for our ability to ask these questions at all? What, in other words, is the locus of consciousness?

In a person with normal sight, the occipital lobes in the brain convert all the patterns, forms and colors from the outside world into meaningful objects.

Many kinds of brain injury may disrupt some aspect of consciousness, but no single locus serves as the seat of consciousness per se. In patients with something called "blindsight," there is a clear separation of vision (and response to visual stimuli) and awareness. True, even though we can say that their injury has affected their awareness, it is only one *aspect* of their awareness that's affected. But curiosities such as blindsight might still help us get our foot in the door of the question of the neurological nature of consciousness.

Blindsight: vision without awareness

What is blindsight? People who have lost their primary visual cortex have no awareness of visual objects, and no ability to identify visual objects, while they nevertheless follow such objects with their eyes. In some sense, they "see" the objects despite being absolutely unaware of that fact.

Different animals suffer different degrees or types of visual impairment from loss of the primary visual cortex. Tree shrews and cats seem to retain most of their visual ability, and remain able to avoid obstacles and discriminate between visual patterns. New World monkeys suffer more extensive impairment, but can still visually follow and even reach out for visually presented objects—even though they indicate that "no object was present" in a learning task. Old World monkeys and humans experience the most profound loss of the ability to be aware of and use the vision which still in some sense remains at least partly intact. An indirect visual pathway still remains from the retina through the midbrain and thalamus, but without the mediation of the primary visual cortex, there is no visual awareness.

Where do "gut feelings" come from?
This kind of evidence makes us wonder how many of our "gut feelings" and "instincts" derive from parts of the brain that partly or wholly lack connection to structures, such as the primary visual cortex, that mediate in fully conscious awareness. This is similar to the possibility that iron particles in our brain cells may still play some vestigial role in helping us to orient ourselves with respect to the earth's magnetic field.

A brain divided against itself
Consider, too, people whose epilepsy is so severe that doctors sever their corpus callosum, the bundle of fibers connecting the two halves of the brain. If you place their left hand in a bowl of ice water and ask them if their hand feels cold, they answer both "yes" and "no" in turn. Give them a piece of paper with the words "yes" and "no" written on it, and their left hand will point to one answer while their right hand points to the other. They have, in effect, two centers of consciousness.

But having two centers of consciousness of a stimulus presented to one or the other side of the body is different from having no consciousness at all—from being an unreflecting automaton. Of course, you can make someone unconscious in the sense of shutting down the activity of everything but the brain stem. But this shuts down most or all of the "higher" brain functions, so it's not the case that they are acting in ways that they're not conscious of. Also, this is different from saying that consciousness derives from the integration of the brain's functions in some single defined area.

The "blindsight" evidence shows that even something as apparently unified as visual perception in fact involves many facets that we distinguish only when they become dissociated by injury. In forming a perception—visual, olfactory, or what have you—there's no single site where everything is integrated. Different neurons fire in different regions of the brain, and the mystery is how they're experienced subjectively in a unified way. This is what's known as the "binding problem."

Why aren't we unreflecting automatons?

Many tentative solutions have been proposed to the binding problem, none of them very satisfactory. One is that widely scattered neurons might be subjectively associated if they oscillate at the same frequency. Another is that this sort of association may happen when neurons fire at the same time. Neither of these approaches appears to handle the facts very well, though, since the activated neurons corresponding to a subjectively unified experience usually fire at neither the same frequency nor the same time. Others speculate that the apparently chaotic firing of neurons at various sites may in fact contain a hidden pattern which might somehow explain their integration—if only their code could be cracked.

There are also those, of course, who remain deeply skeptical that a material explanation will ever be found for the problem of consciousness. From one common-sense perspective, we should simply accept that our brain, having evolved to meet the demands of our material environment, has inherent limitations just as does the brain of any other biological organism. Some questions may by their nature—or ours—be inherently unanswerable. The fact remains, though, that we do feel satisfied to have developed an understanding of other points, which presumably have little survival value to understand and which a dog or geranium would presumably be incapable of understanding—the structure of DNA, for example, or the essential features of the reconstructed ancestor of all the Indo-European languages.

What's the survival advantage of self-awareness?

Even if the material underpinnings of consciousness are eventually identified, however, this will not necessarily answer what may be the ultimate, and hardest, question the study of consciousness faces: *Why* do we have a subjective integration of experience? Why, in other words, are we self-aware? This seems to be as hard, and perhaps as intractable, a question as the other chestnuts that have thus far resisted being cracked by Western science: How can life emerge out of inert matter? Will the universe ever cease to exist? And, while we're at it—What is the key to true wisdom?

EXERCISE: Spatial intelligence?

Here is an exercise set for the right hemisphere of the brain (assuming you are right handed).

Pictured below are five groups of similar figures labeled A, B, C, D and E. They are a component of a classic test called the "Stanford-Binet," after its original compilers. Your task is to spot the similarities and differences among these five figures in each column. In each case one figure breaks the "correct" pattern—that is, the most consistent and predictable pattern. It is not wrong, of course, just different—much like the only boy in the schoolyard with his shoelaces neatly tied.

Most people find that the challenge becomes progressively more difficult as they move from A toward E.

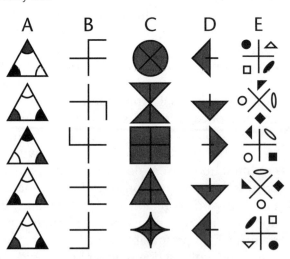

Hint: On A and D try rotating the figures and see how they line up. On E look at how the figures relate to one another when the lines are diagonal vs. horizontal and vertical.

Seeing without understanding: Visual object agnosia

One of the most frequent complaints among the middle-aged and elderly is an inability to remember the name of an object. In a momentary lapse, a mailbox may be called "the thing you put letters in," or a corkscrew may be referred to as "the little metal coil for the wine."

This kind of mental lapse, which is by no means necessarily a sign of the onset of dreaded Alzheimer's, is sometimes referred to as "benign senescent forgetfulness"—which sounds much nicer than the old-fashioned term "senility." Although it may be mildly disconcerting, normal age-related forgetfulness is *nothing* compared with the considerably rarer phenomenon known as *visual object agnosia*—a disorder affecting not just the *naming* of objects but the very recognition of their identity or function.

There are two basic kinds of visual object agnosia: apperceptive and associative. Apperceptive agnosics have, according to the standard tests, relatively good visual capabilities, such as color vision and brightness discrimination. But they not only cannot name or recognize a visually perceived object; they cannot even reproduce it in a simple sketch.

Apperceptive agnosic's attempt to copy a simple line drawing of a house. An apperceptive agnosic has good visual perception, but can neither recognize nor reproduce an object such as the house on the left.

Associative agnosics, on the other hand, can muster reasonably faithful line-drawing copies of pictures. And yet, they are no better than apperceptive agnosics at naming or recognizing what they've drawn. Their perception of objects is all detail, and no pattern. They are much like illiterate counterfeiters who painstakingly reproduce every line and curve of a document or signature without having any idea what it says.

Other characteristics of associative agnosia are equally bizarre. An associative agnosic will be utterly unable to name or identify an object by sight alone, but will immediately recognize it upon feeling it. He will have no idea what the foods on his dinner plate are, or even whether they are edible, until putting them in his mouth.

You might think that agnosia simply involves some kind of dissociation between the visual and spatial centers of the brain. This theory would be disproved, however, by the fact that it isn't just *naming* that's affected, but the very recognition of the object at the most basic level.

A better theory implicates the role of internally-stored visual images used in the task of object recognition. If these stored images were somehow to become destroyed or inaccessible, then an external visual image would have nothing to match up to. In effect, it would be as if the most commonplace objects were being seen for the very first time.

An even better theory might rest on an understanding of recognition and memory as stored in connections between neurons forming a network: the stronger the connections, the stronger the memory. When an associative agnosic makes a line-drawing copy of a picture, he does so slowly, painstakingly, and with no recognition of the pattern the individual features of the picture represent. If associative agnosia derives from a destruction of a neural network, without any damage to the neurons themselves, this would explain why it is the overall patterns of the images, not the details, that are inaccessible.

SELF-TEST: Right brain inattention

Damage to the right hemisphere may result in a problem called *visual inattention* or *neglect*, involving a loss of awareness of visual stimuli in one half of the visual field. For example, someone with a right-brain stroke may eat only the food on the right half of his plate, and then complain about having been served an inadequate helping.

In 10 seconds, count as many of the dots as you can. As you count a dot, check it off with a pencil.

Results:

Under-counting the dots in the left or right half of the square may indicate damage to the hemisphere opposite to the neglected side.

A circadian rhythm and sunlight tell us when to sleep

Humans have a built-in "neural pacemaker" which regulates our daily cycle of sleeping and waking. If uninfluenced by the solar cycle or an externally-imposed schedule, we naturally fall into a cycle of rest and activity slightly in excess of 24 hours—in other words, we go to sleep and wake up a little later each day. There has been serious speculation that all of human civilization, from the creative stimulus to destructive acts, is a response to the tension created by this disharmony!

Normally, however, our internal pacemaker is "entrained" by the sun: our internal clock adjusts itself on an ongoing basis to the length of the day. The exact manner in which this happens is only just coming to be understood. It turns out that we probably have a special set of retinal photoreceptors specifically involved in governing circadian rhythms. These receptors project through the optic nerve to the hypothalamus of the brain, which appears to be the physical locus of our neural pacemaker.

Melatonin levels, supposedly affected by sunlight, change as normally in some blind people as they do in the sighted

Compelling evidence that the photoreceptors involved in this process are distinct from those normally used in vision comes from a recent study of blind people with no conscious perception of light. It has long been known that, while some blind people suffer from bouts of insomnia due to a presumed inability to adjust their internal clocks to the shifting cycles of the sun, others never have such problems. A number of such subjects were shown to display increased melatonin levels—which is independently associated with exposure to light—precisely when exposed to bright light, and only when their eyes were uncovered. Thus, their eyes, while otherwise quite useless, seemed to have retained a special type of photoreceptor in perfect working order.

We hope you've enjoyed this book. Best regards to your brains.
The Editors

EXERCISE: Time intervals

Examine the sequence of times shown in the first four of these five clock faces. Reading upper left to lower right, can you identify the logic behind the time intervals shown by their hands?

When you think you have uncovered it, draw the hands into the fifth clock face that correctly continue the pattern.

Hint: Don't be fooled by the fact that the third clock has been rotated. It reads 6:00, not 2:45. It might help to work backwards from the fourth clock.

EXERCISE: False faces

The white pattern shown above the pile of seven numbered blocks shows the location and orientation of the letters on their six sides—but not for *all* seven blocks. Which of the numbered blocks could *not* have been formed from the pattern?

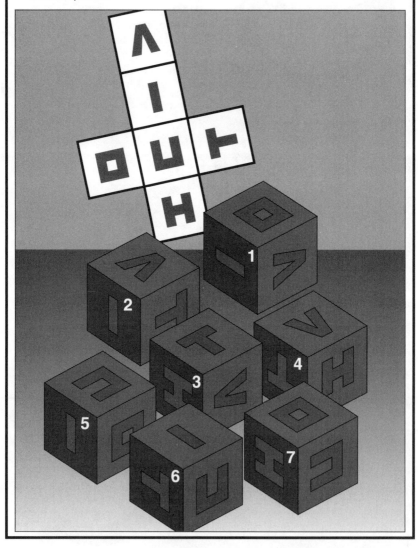

Hint: If you can't fold the sample cube with your mind's eye, try unfolding the others. Notice which end of a letter faces which side of another letter—the open side of the C and the H for example.

SOLUTIONS

Abandon hope all ye who enter here. —Dante Alighieri

EXECUTIVE & SOCIAL

p. 18–21 **Mixed-up toons**

Panels are shown below in correct order. Numbers correspond to mixed-up order.

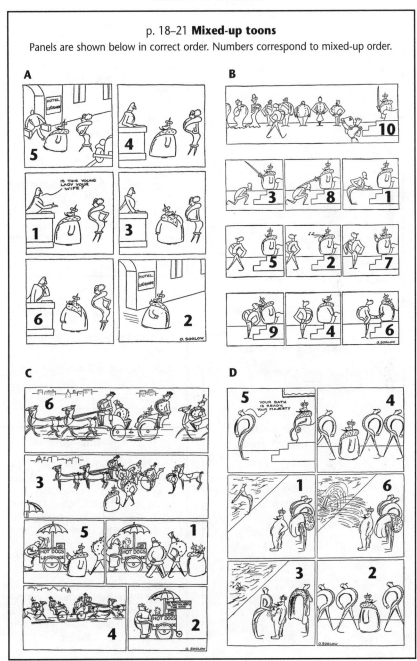

p. 22 **Mixed-up toons**

Panels are shown below in correct order. Numbers correspond to mixed-up order.

p. 26 **"Right" side of a person**

Neither positive nor negative, hence neutral emotion. The right side of a person's face is more likely to display positive emotions. The left side displays negative attitudes. When you see the stranger face-to-face the right hemisphere of your brain (which is the dominant hemisphere for the perception of emotion) picks up the expression on the half of his face to the left of his nose as you face him. For him, that is the right half of his own face, which, normally, is controlled by the left (positive feelings) hemisphere of his brain, not his right hemisphere (negative feelings). So, you are more likely to miss any signs of the negative "side" of his personality.

p. 24 **Judgment of emotion**

The right-hand image is reversed.

p. 31–32 **The eyes have it**

1. Condescending eyes with smiling mouth

2. Neutral eyes with smiling mouth

3. Angry eyes with smiling mouth

p. 28 **Right-brain pattern abstraction/abstract reading**

1) 9	11) smart
2) I	12) bill
3) check	13) 9
4) ray	14) G
5) to	15) cud
6) on	16) 352897
7) stop	17) nip
8) do	18) F
9) 1324	19) 9
10) lit	20) sure

p. 37 **A familial dilemma**

First, he drives his mother over to the restaurant. Next, he drives back and picks up his mother-in-law, and drives her to the restaurant. When he drops off his mother-in-law, he tells his mother to get back in the car with him and takes her back home. When he and his mother get home, he lets his mother out, picks up his wife, drives back to the restaurant, and leaves his wife at the restaurant with his mother-in-law. Finally, he drives back home to pick up his mother again, and returns to the restaurant with her.

p. 36 **Case of confused identity**

Part 1 No—at least, not if one of the twins really is the murderer. Either both will answer "Yes," or both will answer "No," and it will be impossible to tell who is telling the truth and who isn't. There are two variables here—one brother is a liar and the other is a truth-teller, and one brother is a murderer and the other is not. If the first is a liar and answers "Yes," then he, not his brother, is definitely the murderer. This means that his brother is an innocent truth-teller, in which case he will also answer "Yes" in response to the question of whether his brother is a murderer. If the first brother is a liar and answers "No," then the other brother is the murderer—but that means the second brother is a murdering truth-teller, and will likewise answer "No" in response to the question of whether his brother is the murderer. Either way, both brothers will give the same answer, and it will be impossible to know who is telling the truth—and who is the murderer.

Part 2 Assuming the truth of the premise that one brother is a consistent liar and the other always tells the truth, then there are only two possibilities. The first is that the eye-witness must be mistaken—neither brother can have committed the murder. Here's the logic: If the first brother is a liar and answers "Yes," then the second brother cannot be the murderer. Also, if the first brother is a liar, the second must be telling

the truth. But then, if the second brother answers that his brother did not commit the murders, the first brother must be innocent. Hence, both are innocent.

The second possibility is that both brothers committed the murders. Let's assume that it's the first brother who is the truth-teller. Then, the second brother must be guilty. That means the second brother is a lying murderer. But the second brother answers "No" to the prosecutor's question whether the first brother committed the murders, meaning (since the second brother is a liar) that the first brother must be guilty. Hence, both brothers must be guilty.

Part 3 The first trick is to find out which twin is the liar. This may be done by asking the first twin any question to which you both already know the answer. "Do you have a twin brother?" will do. If the first twin answers "Yes," then you know the second twin is a liar. Then you can ask the second twin, "Did you commit the murders?" If he says "Yes," then you know (since he's a liar, and assuming that one of the twins is indeed the murderer) that the first twin is the murderer.

If, on the other hand, the first twin answers "No" to the first question, you know the second twin is a truth-teller, and will truthfully answer a direct question about his guilt.

p. 38 **Fox, goose and grain**

Take the goose over first, then return to pick up the fox. Take the fox over, put the goose back in the boat and return with the goose to the first bank. Leave the goose there, put the grain in the boat, and take the grain to the other bank and leave it there with the fox. Finally, return to pick up the goose.

It doesn't matter whether Antonio picks up the wife or the mother-in-law second, or whether the farmer picks up the fox or the grain second; the only crucial thing is that the first one over is the one which is least compatible with the others, i.e. the mother in the first story or the goose in the second.

p. 39 **Anders' dilemma**

It would take three travellers. One assistant carries four days' supplies, and after the first day's trek, he gives one day's supplies to the other assistant and one to Anders. This gives them each four full days' supplies again. The first assistant, with his day's supply remaining, then returns home. The other two complete another day's trip, at the end of which the other assistant gives one day's supplies to Anders, who again has four days' supplies, sufficient to reach the outpost. His assistant still has enough to reach home in two days.

p. 68 **The fastest track**

1-F; 2-B; 3-D; 4-A; 5-E; 6-C
Assuming the rate of improvement between the years of 1906-1960 but starting from the under-10-sec. time in 1984, the under-9-sec. time will happen around the year 2038.

p. 40 **Menu, please**

JENKINS   JENNINGS

JORDAN   JACKSON

JONES

1. Joe Jackson had a martini, roast beef and cake. 2. Jerry Jones had scotch, pheasant and cheese pie. 3. John Jordan had a martini, steak and cake. 4. Jack Jenkins had a cola, roast beef and pie. 5. Jamie Jennings had scotch, steak and ice cream.

p. 58 **If-then thinking**

The fourth statement is the only one that could be true because it correctly identifies all the others as false.

p. 54–58 **Frontal lobe logic**

Part1 If it is true that only one envelope has correct instructions, then that envelope has to be B, meaning that A is wrong—therefore, A does not have a contract renewal inside. Imagine A were right. Then, B would have to be wrong. But, assuming the correctness of the premise that one of the envelopes has a pink slip, B must be right. **Part 2** The right envelope. Let's imagine the left envelope contains a contract renewal. Then its instructions must be correct, and we may conclude (since the instructions say it makes no difference which envelope is picked) that the right envelope must also contain a contract renewal. But if that were true, then what's written on the right-hand envelope must be false, since we're told that the statement on the right envelope is false if a contract renewal is inside. Therefore, it's false that the left envelope has a contract renewal, which contradicts the first assumption, so that first assumption must be false: the left envelope cannot contain a contract renewal. **Part 3** Envelope A. Let's say envelope A is true, and it really does contain a pink slip. Then, the others must be false. If envelope B is false, it contains a pink slip too. So far, so good. If envelope C is false, then envelope B contains a contract renewal, not a pink slip—a contradiction, so envelope A must be false. Therefore, envelope A contains a contract renewal, not a pink slip.

MEMORY

p. 76 **Card senses**

p. 79 **Word Overlapping**

1. Plume	6. Neuron
2. Measles	7. Onset
3. Lesion	8. Tempest
4. Ontario	9. Stigma
5. Own	10. map

p. 86 **Memory terms**

```
    B       M
    L   A M N E S I A
    I       E
E   N I     M     P
X   D M     O     R
P R O S O P A G N O S I A
L   I   L   I     M
I   G   I   C     I
C   H   C         N
I   T   I         G
T       T
```

p. 90 **Memory Test**

1. Popeye (94%)
2. Wright (92%) Arson (88%)
4. Toto (84%)
5. Paul Revere (82%)
6. Houdini (80%)
7. Blubber (77%)
8. Polo (75%)
9. Sahara (70%)
10. Venice (68%)
11. Atlantis (65%)
12. Hibachi (62%)
13. Cyclops (60%)
14. Custer (58%)
15. Sistine (55%)
16. Fathom (52%)
17. Florence Nightingale (47%)
18. Mongoose (41%)
19. Trigger (37%)
20. Orwell (33%)
21. Nero (31%)
22. Hemlock (25%)
23. Watson (22%)
24. Martin Luther (20%)
25. Excalibur (19%)
26. Beagle (14%)
27. Helsinki (12%)
28. Ural (9%)
29. Bannister (7%)
30. Batista (4%)
31. Wood (3%)
32. Coventry (1%)
33. Aconcagua (0%)

p. 116 **Geographics**

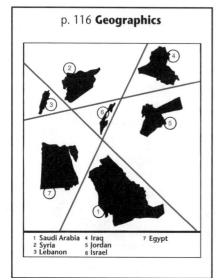

1 Saudi Arabia   4 Iraq   7 Egypt
2 Syria   5 Jordan
3 Lebanon   6 Israel

p. 120 **Neuron and off**

A	X	O	N		E	T	U	I		O	B	I
R	E	V	E		T	E	N	S		R	O	T
E	D	E	R		A	N	D	S		E	R	E
		R	O	M		N	E	U	R	O	N	S
T	E	A	S	E	D		L	E	A			
E	R	G		D	E	T	E	R	M	I	N	E
A	S	E	S		N	A	T		S	N	I	T
R	E	S	T	U	D	I	E	D		S	N	O
		A	P	R		D	E	M	E	A	N	
C	H	A	B	L	I	S		S	E	C		
L	A	B		I	T	E	M		C	U	B	A
A	C	E		F	E	T	A		C	R	A	M
D	E	L		T	S	A	R		A	E	R	O

p. 122 **Personal pairs**

(One Possibility)
flower — bee
carved bust — chisel
bell buoy — ship
milk — glass
cow— butter
watering can — saltshaker
marine signal flags — music
hatchet — tree
oak leaf — acorn
knife — bread

(Another Possibility)
carved bust — music
bell buoy — marine signal flags
ship — glass
milk — cow
butter — saltshaker
knife — bread
acorn — tree
leaf — watering can
hatchet — chisel
bee — flower

p. 130–131 **Strategies**

The optimal strategy is to break the grid down into ever-smaller halves, in any order. A sample sequence: "Is it in the top half of the grid?" ("No"—you know it's in the bottom half.) "Is it in the right half of the bottom half?" ("Yes.") "Is it in the top half of that section?" And so on. Using this strategy, you'll still need two questions with a small 2 X 2 grid, but with larger grids the advantage over the row-by-row method is dramatic. For an 8 X 8 grid, you'll never need more than six questions, and for a 100 X 100 grid— with 10,000 squares—you'll always get the answer in 12 questions!

p. 132 **Eliminating possibilities**

Select the box with the cover marked "six and six." If you blind-picked a banana, a dozen bananas must be in that box (because the covers were switched). The box with the "twelve bananas" cover must contain twelve lemons. The lemons box, therefore, contains the six lemons and six bananas. If on the other hand, you blind-picked a lemon from the box marked "six and six," a dozen lemons must be in that box, the dozen bananas in the "twelve lemons" box, and the lemons and bananas in the bananas box.

p. 136 **Singles only**

 Sheep

 Lion

Jockey and horse

 Artist's palette

 Box of tea   Bull

EMOTIONAL

p. 155 **Facial expressions and emotions**

Happiness   Sadness   Anger

Disgust   Surprise   Fear

p. 159 **Pick the punch line**

The original punch line to the story was #3. The point is that loss of memory is associated with aging. If the residents of the retirement house forget their own name they know they can go to the caregiver at the front desk who will remind them.

p. 164 **Emotions**

A	M	Y	G	D	A	L	A	
					N			
	D	I	S	G	U	S	T	
					E		A	
	F	E	A	R			D	
							N	
S	U	R	P	R	I	S	E	
							S	
H	A	P	P	I	N	E	S	S

p. 164 **Melencolia I**

The central figure of the angel symbolizes the frustration and despair of the inquiring, creative mind. Her wing, trapped behind the hourglass, suggests that time imposes its strict limits on the efforts of artist and artisan.

All the measuring devices are tools of design and construction: hourglass, dividers in her hand, scales and a straight-edged board with holes in either end for drawing a circle.

Other tools and materials of construction visible include the saw and plane at her feet, nails, a pattern for cutting decorative moldings, a hammer, a fire with a crucible for melting metal, a stone wheel and cube with two opposing corners lopped off (which looks, at first glance, like a prism).

Many of these objects are also icons of geometry and mathematics as is the sphere at her feet, the magic square above her head and the arc of the rainbow.

The keys and purse attached to her belt symbolize power and wealth; perhaps as rewards from the pursuit of knowledge and skill or, perhaps, to symbolize their irrelevance before the "melancholy" caused by creative effort and pursuit of knowledge.

p. 165 **Humors**

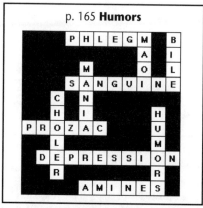

p. 182–183 **Picking up signals**

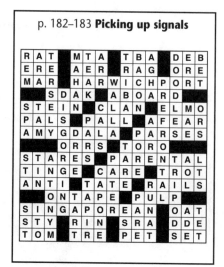

p. 184 **Terms test**

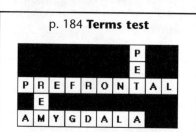

LANGUAGE

p. 205 **Damaged language**

1. scion = icons
2. knead = naked
3. janes = jeans
4. ruses = users
5. lager = regal
6. finer = infer
7. sited = edits
8. snail = slain
9. charm = march
10. tacos = ascot
11. grape = pager
12. brail = libra
13. sonar = arson
14. nerve = never
15. sarge = gears
16. surge = urges
17. later = alter
18. luger = gruel
19. spice = epics
20. ideal = ailed
21. dirge = ridge
22. lease = easel
23. wakes = askew
24. curbs = scrub
25. canoe = ocean
26. rifle = flier
27. gable = bagel
28. spore = ropes
29. blame = amble
30. trine = inert
31. stone = notes

"injuries map language areas of brain"

p. 208 **Circleword**

1. Frontal
2. Alexic
3. Lexicon
4. Conic
5. Nicotine
6. Nerve
7. Verbose
8. Senile
9. Legal
10. Alpha
11. Handed
12. Dendrite
13. Elf

p. 209 **Fancy Language**

ACROSS	DOWN
1. Difficult	2. Idea
5. Adomen	3. Commence
6. Cognate	4. Instruct
7. Inquire	6. Cause
8. Velocity	

p. 210 **Plain Speaking**

ACROSS	DOWN
3. Teach	1. Belly
6. Begin	2. Thought
7. Hard	4. Speed
8. Make	5. Kindred
	9. Ask

p. 211 **Unconstructible constructs**

1. You talked to your mother and some-one else; who is that someone else?

2. You know whether a given person talked to your mother; who is that person?

3. You talked to the woman who married someone; who is that someone?

4. It bothered John that you know a cer-tain person; who is that person?

5. This is the woman who was abandoned by the guy whom you talked to yesterday.

6. This is the car that was parked by the man whom you saw talking to the woman you met yesterday.

7. This is the guy to whom Richard sent the package that was in the room in which you read through the instructions.

8. The fact that I don't like you—which was told to you by the man who was met by the guy you saw yesterday—is disturb-ing.

9. You just can't do it using the same con-struction. Instead, you have to switch to a different construction altogether: What size boxes do you need?

10 & 11. You just can't do it. Rumored and reputed are passive "orphans"—their active-voice transitive counterparts no longer exist.

p. 223 **Child speak**

1. B; 2. A; 3. A; 4. B; 5. B

p. 212 **Mental status for language**

For each "A," give 1 point, for each "B," give 2 points, and for each "C," give 3 points.

Totals:

7 points or fewer: You may want to get a professional evaluation.

8–10 points: You have some signs of mild cognitive decline. You should work a lit-tle harder to keep yourself mentally fit.

11–12 points: You're in good shape. Keep it that way!

p. 216 **Mama and papa**

Word pairs:

i. Welsh mam "mama" tad "papa"

ii. Hebrew aba "papa" ima "mama"

iii. Swahili mama "mama" baba "papa"

iv. Tamil ammaa "mama" appa "papa"

v. Chinese pa pa "papa" ma ma "mama"

vi. Dakota ena "mama" ate "papa"

vii. Turkish annecigim "mama" baba "papa"

viii. Greenlandic anaana(q) "mama" ataata(q) "papa"

Linguistic geography:

A. Dakota; B. Hebrew; C. Tamil; D. Turkish; E. Swahili; F. Welsh; G. Greenlandic; H. Chinese

p. 224 **Stages of language acquisition**

1. D, 2. C, 3. D, 4. A, 5. B, 6. D, 7. C, 8. A, 9. D, 10. B, 11. D

p. 224 **Letters into words**

"The critical window of opportunity to learn languages easily and fluently closes at puberty."

p. 238 **Word storage**

"We may be relying on fundamentally different strategies for producing and processing irregular patterns."

p. 238 **PET brain scans**

A: Thinking and speaking. B: Hearing words spoken. C: Reciting words. D: Reading silently.

p. 228 **The forbidden hidden**

contaminated = infected

large number = billions

rabbit food = salad

undisciplined = wanton

jeweled crown = tiara

lacks hearing = deaf

living kingdom = animal

mark indelibly = brand

extend grasp = reach

post-Thursday = Friday

fedora & bowler = lids

to force exile = banish

"A feral child is an infant abandoned after birth and raised by social wild animals."

p. 233 **Translating from the pidgin**

1. Ifu laik meiki, mo beta make time, mani no kaen hapai.

   if like make more better die time money no can carry

   "If you want to build (something), you should do it just before you die, you can't take it with you!"

2. Aena tu macha churen, samawl churen, haus mani pei.

   and too much children small children house money pay

   "And I had many children, small children, and I had to pay the rent."

3. Luna, hu hapai? Hapai awl, hemo awl.

   foreman, who carry? carry all, cut all

   "Who'll carry it, boss? Everyone will cut

it and everyone will carry it."

4. Mi paitim em long diwai me holim longen.

   I beat him with stick I hold at it/that.

   "I beat him with the stick that I was holding."

5. Bai me toktok long ol asua husat bai i kamap…

   I future talk-talk about problems who/that come up

   …sapos Tok Pisin i kamap nambawan tokples bilong Papua Niugini.

   suppose Tok Pisin come up number-one language belong Papua New Guinea.

   "I will discuss the problem that would arise if Tok Pisin (Pidgin Talk) became the national language of New Guinea."

MATH

p. 246 **Algebraic dispute**

The girl has 35; the boy 49. Since there are 14 eggs (lots of chickens) between them, when the girl says, "Give me seven of yours and we will be even" she is not only accurate, she is responding at a level of social accommodation that may save all our bacon. Francis Bacon might agree.

p. 255 **Addlock**

1 2	4		1	3	4
4	8	1	5	2	
6		7	8	6	4
7	8	5			8
8	7 5	6		5	6
	3	6	4	7	8
3	6	8		8 6	4

p. 248 **Numberlocker**

	8	6	4	
2	1	4	9	2
1	7		3	8
6	2	3	4	9
	9	6	3	

p. 259 **The math-mind's eye**

Row A

Multiply the numbers visible on the face of each view of the cube. They all total 40 except the third from the left, which totals 80: the math culprit.

Notice the orientation of the 5 and 8 on the faces of that cube and on the first cube on the left. Since a different cube is spatially inconsistent from the one that is mathematically inconsistent, the first cube is the spatial culprit.

Row B

Add the numbers visible on the face of each view of the cube. They all total 72 except the third from the left, which totals 76: the math culprit.

Notice the orientation of the 36 and 12 on the faces of that cube and on the last cube in the row. The cube that is spatially inconsistent is a different cube from the one that is mathematically inconsistent. Therefore the last cube in the row is the spatial culprit.

p. 256 **Faces and hands**

Row A

The blank face should show 2:15. That is half the number of hours shown on the face to its left, and so on. 2:15 is half of 4:30, which is half of 9:00, which is half of 18 hours (during which the hands rotated 12 hours plus 6 more to 6:00), which is half of 12:00.

Row B

The blank face should show 4:00. Multiply the time shown on the second face by the time shown on the first. (2 x 4 = 8) and that number will show on the third face. The prior two faces multiplied together equal 64. The remainder, after the hands have gone around five times, is 4.

p. 263 **Opposing digits**

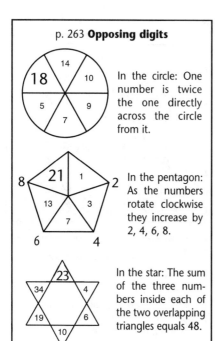

In the circle: One number is twice the one directly across the circle from it.

In the pentagon: As the numbers rotate clockwise they increase by 2, 4, 6, 8.

In the star: The sum of the three numbers inside each of the two overlapping triangles equals 48.

p. 260 **Now don't get mad!**

The numbers in group A are all shapes with only *curves*. Group C has only *straight lines*. Group B contains *both* curved and straight lines. So 38 belongs in group A; 16 in group B; and 17 in group C. Now calm down! You *promised* you wouldn't get mad.

p. 264 **Algebra Game**

$$(11 \times 1) - 1 = 10$$
$$(2 \times 2 \times 2) + 2 = 10$$
$$(3 \times 3 \times 3 + 3) \div 3 = 10$$
$$(4 \times 4 + 4) \div \sqrt{4} = 10$$
$$5 + 5 = 10$$
$$[(6+6) \times 6 - (6+6)] \div 6 = 10$$
$$[(7 \times 7) + (7 + 7 + 7)] \div 7 = 10$$
$$[(8 \times 8) + (8 + 8)] \div 8 = 10$$
$$(9 \times 9 + 9) \div 9 = 10$$

SPATIAL

p. 272 **Shapes in space**

A. We *want* it to be a 3-pronged fork, but the artist, Escher, makes that middle prong appear and disappear.

B. Do you see a row of abstract puzzle pieces or the letters of a word? How do you FEEL now?

C. Do you see a vase of grasses or profiles of two human faces looking at each other? Most people see the vase first because their experience tells them that the "foreground" object is black.

p. 276 **About faces**

Joseph Stalin

Lyndon Johnson

Jackie Onassis

Winston Churchill

Franklin D. Roosevelt

p. 277 **Eyeball busters**

Row 1: Cat's ear
Row 2: $10, $1, $20 bills
Row 3: Shredded wheat
Row 4: Fingernail

Coke logo
Razor blade cartridges
Staple remover
Book spine

English muffin
Safety pins
Staples
Tire tread

p. 282 **Embedded figures**

Figures A, C and E are in Column 1; Figures B and D are in Column 2

p. 292 **Spatial intelligence?**

A. The fourth figure's brown and black corners have been reversed; B. The fourth figure's tail has been reversed. C. The fourth figure's areas are not symmetrical. D. The fourth figure is not rotated in the proper direction. E. The third figure's circle and oval should be black and the square and triangle should be white.

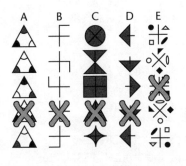

p. 297 **Time intervals**

1:30. Each clock registers half the number of hours shown on the clock face to its left. Reading the intervals of time from left to right in hours: 24, 12, 6, 3, 1.5.

p. 299 **False faces**

Three of the cubes could not have been made from the pattern. In number 2, the T should be rotated 90 degrees as shown. In number 6, the T should be an O. In number 7, the C is backwards.

INDEX

Creating newly valid information excites the spirit.
Finding it feeds the mind. —Anonymous, c. 2003

Dyslexia; causes of, 201–202;
incidence of, 201; prediction
of, 203; treatments for, 202,
204
Dysthymia, 192

Eberstark, Hans, 92–93, 94
Edelman, Gerald, 217
Edison, Thomas, 257
Einstein, Albert, 257–258
Ekman, Paul, 141–142, 156
Elastin, 279
Electroencephalograph (EEG),
179
Emotions, 139–140; brain and,
23, 161–163; color and, 143–
146; control of, 141–143; and
dreams, 177–178; exercises
on, 164–165, 175, 182–184;
facial expression and, 142;
feedback and, 41, 141–142;
health consequences of, 189–
192; historical view of, 160–
161; illusions and, 147–152;
internalization of, 185, 186;
management of, 191–192;
and memory, 111–114;
relation to consciousness, 13;
relation to reason, 23; self-
tests on, 24, 166–172, 188;
verbalization and, 185–188
Epinephrine; diet and, 250; and
memory, 108, 110
Executive function; brain basis of,
13–17; emotion and, 52–53;
exercises of, 18–22; logic,
36–40, 54–58; perception,
29–32; physical condition
and, 65–68

Exercise; brain benefits of, 65–67;
longevity benefits of, 68
Expressivity; health benefits of,
185; infantile, 186
Externalization, 185; modalities
of, 187
Extraversion, self-inventory for,
166, 170
Faces; emotions reflected on,
155, 156; exercises regarding,
276; image processing of, 27;
perceiving deceit on, 29–32;
recall of, 126, 128; recognition of, 126, 128, 273–275;
strategies for recognizing,
274–275
FACS (Facial Action Coding
System), 156
False memory, 119
Feynman, Richard, 46
Forgetting; causes of, 87; types
of, 87–89
Freud, Sigmund, 33, 35
Friesen, Wallace, 156
Frontal lobes; and depression, 23;
and emotions, 23–25;
exercises for, 54–58, 252;
functions of, 13; and identity,
15

Gage, Fred, 119
Gage, Phineas, 15–16, 17
Garbo, Greta, 146
Genie, case study, 229–231
Glucocorticoids; and memory,
108; receptors for, 111
Goodall, Jane, 190
Gould, Elizabeth, 119
Grief, adverse effects of, 190